WHITNEY HOUSTON

All The Top 40 Hits

Craig Halstead

Copyright © Craig Halstead 2020

All rights reserved. No part of this publication may be reproduced, stored in a retrieval system, or transmitted in any form or by any means, electronic, mechanical, photocopy, recording or otherwise, without prior written permission of the copyright owner. Nor can it be circulated in any form of binding or cover other than that in which it is published and without similar condition including this condition being imposed on a subsequent purchaser.

First Edition

for Aaron

BY THE SAME AUTHOR

Christmas Number Ones

This book details the Christmas No.1 singles in the UK from 1940 to date, and also reveals the Christmas No.2 single and Christmas No.1 album. The book also features the Christmas No.1s in five other countries, namely Australia, Germany, Ireland, the Netherlands and the USA, and is up-dated annually in January.

The 'All The Top 40 Hits' Series

This series documents, in chronological order, all the Top 40 Hit Singles and Albums by the featured artist:

ABBA
Annie Lennox
Blondie
Boney M.
Carpenters
Chi-Lites & Stylistics
Donna Summer
Janet Jackson
Michael Jackson
The Jacksons
(Jackson 5 / Jacksons / Jermaine / La Toya / Rebbie / 3T)
Olivia Newton-John
Tina Turner

Top 40 Music Videos are also detailed in the three Jackson books.

The 'For The Record' Series

The books in this series are more comprehensive than the 'All The Top 40 Hits' volumes, and typically include: The Songs (released & unreleased), The Albums, The Home Videos, The TV Shows/Films, The Concerts, Chartography & USA/UK Chart Runs, USA Discography & UK Discography.

Donna Summer
Janet Jackson
Michael Jackson
Whitney Houston

ACKNOWLEDGEMENTS

I would like to thank Chris Cadman, my former writing partner, for helping to make my writing dreams come true. It's incredible to think how far we have come, since we got together to compile 'The Complete Michael Jackson Discography 1972-1990', for Adrian Grant's *Off the Wall* fan magazine in 1990. Good luck with your future projects, Chris!

Chris Kimberley, it's hard to believe we have been corresponding and exchanging chart action for 30+ years! A big thank you, I will always value your friendship.

I would like to thank the online music community, who so readily share and exchange information at: Chartbusters (chartbusters.forumfree.it), ukmix (ukmix.org/forums), Haven (fatherandy2.proboards.com) & Buzzjack (buzzjack.com/forums). In particular, I would like to thank:

- 'BrainDamagell' & 'Wayne' for posting current Canadian charts on ukmix;
- 'flatdeejay' & 'ChartFreaky' for posting German chart action, and 'Indi' for answering my queries regarding Germany, on ukmix;
- 'mario' for posting Japanese chart action, and 'danavon' for answering my queries regarding Japan, on ukmix;
- 'Davidalic' for posting Spanish chart action on ukmix;
- 'Shakyfan', 'CZB', 'beatlened', 'trebor' & 'smiffj' for posting Irish charts on ukmix & buzzjack;
- 'janjensen' for posting Danish singles charts from 1979 onwards on ukmix;
- 'Hanboo' for posting and up-dating on request full UK & USA chart runs on ukmix. R.I.P., Hanboo ~ like everyone on ukmix, I was shocked and deeply saddened to learn of your passing.

If you can fill any of the gaps in the chart information in this book, or have chart runs from a country not already featured in the book, I would love to hear from you. You can contact me by email: **craig.halstead2@ntlworld.com** ~ thank you!

CONTENTS

INTRODUCTION	7
ALL THE TOP 40 SINGLES	19
THE ALMOST TOP 40 SINGLES	147
WHITNEY'S TOP 30 SINGLES	148
SINGLES TRIVIA	152
ALL THE TOP 40 ALBUMS	167
THE ALMOST TOP 40 ALBUMS	249
WHITNEY'S TOP 15 ALBUMS	250
ALBUMS TRIVIA	252

INTRODUCTION

Whitney Elizabeth Houston was born on 9th August 1963 in Newark, New Jersey, the daughter of Emily 'Cissy' Drinkard and John Houston. She was named after Whitney Blake, an actress who co-starred in one her mother Cissy's favourite US sitcoms, *Hazel*.

Throughout most of the 1960s, Cissy Houston earned her living as an in-demand backing singing, working with a multitude of famous names, including her niece Dionne Warwick, Aretha Franklin (Whitney's god-mother), Solomon Burke, Donny Hathaway, Wilson Pickett and Elvis Presley. Then, in 1968, Cissy formed her own R&B/gospel group, The Sweet Inspirations. The group were very popular live, and scored several hits in the States, most notably *Sweet Inspiration*, which achieved no.5 on the R&B chart and no.18 on the Hot 100.

Whitney made her public singing debut when she was aged eight, when she sang *Guide Me, O Thou Great Jehovah* in the New Hope Baptist Church Choir, a choir her mother Cissy was a founder member of. She grew up surrounded by music.

'I remember when I was about twelve,' she said, 'I would go into our basement, where my mother has her recording equipment, and I'd take the mike and put on Aretha (Franklin), and we'd go at it for hours. I'd just close my eyes and imagine I was on stage singing to a packed house.'

Whitney made her commercial recording debut when she was fifteen, when she and her mother sang backing for The Michael Zager Band on *Life's A Party*. Michael Zager was keen to sign Whitney to his record label, but her parents felt she was too young and turned Zager down.

'They were adamant I have a childhood,' said Whitney. 'They wanted me to move into adulthood in a natural progression. But I really wanted to sing. I was anxious to get on with my career, especially after that first record.'

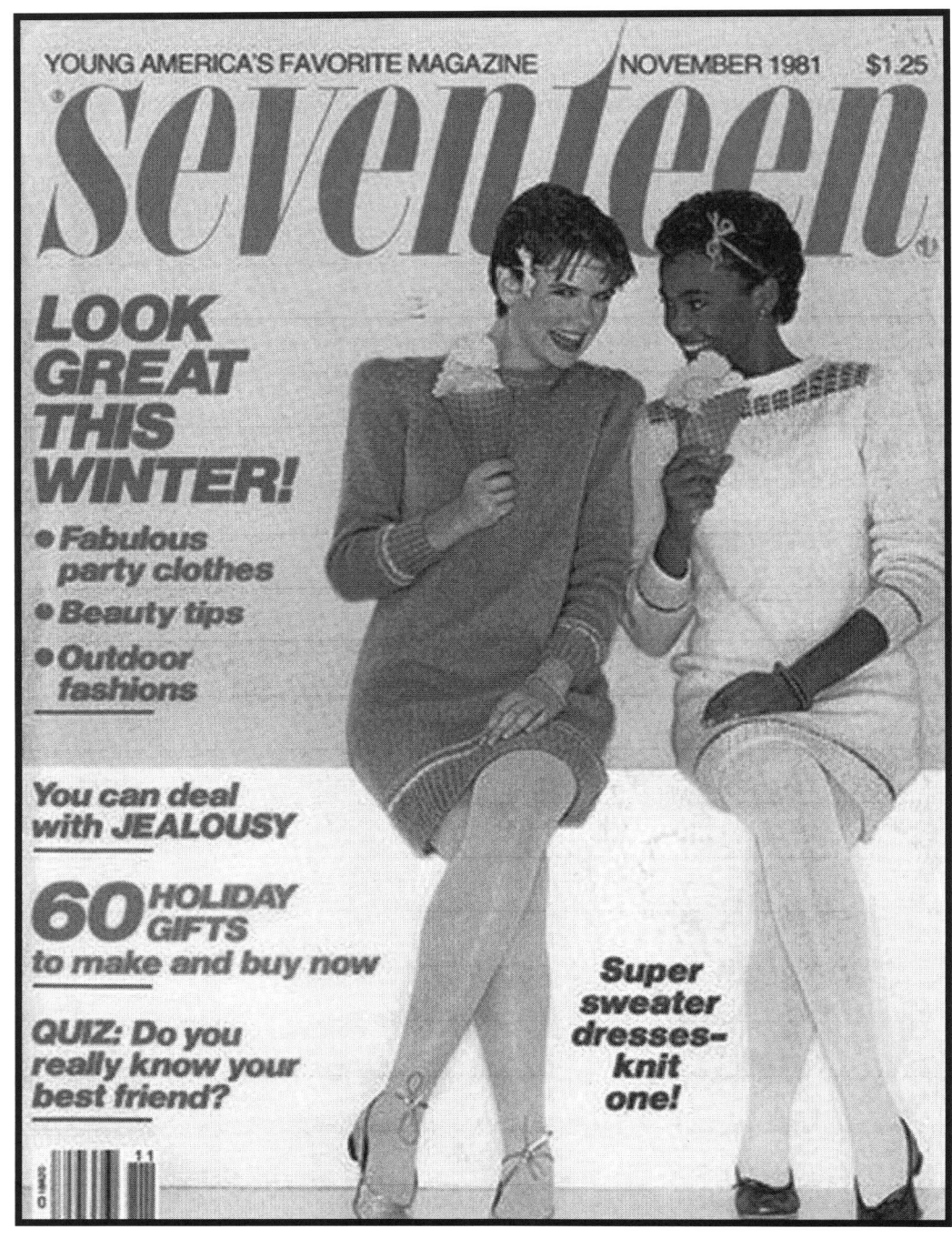

By the following year, Whitney was modelling professionally. She went on to sign with the prestigious New York Agency, Wilhelmina, and appeared in numerous magazines including *Cosmopolitan, Young Miss, Mademoiselle, Glamour & Seventeen*. But, although the money was good, Whitney quickly realised modelling wasn't for her. 'I found it degrading,' she later admitted. 'It wasn't a life that I wanted to live.'

In 1977, to promote herself and her new self-titled album, Cissy Houston created a nightclub act, and appeared at numerous Manhattan clubs, including *Reno Sweeney's* and *Les Mouches*. Whitney travelled with her mother, appearing on stage with her as a backing vocalist, and she did so well her mother eventually offered her a solo spot. Her first solo, at *Town Hall* on Manhattan's West Forty-Third Street, took place on 18th February 1978. Whitney performed *Tomorrow*, from the musical *Annie*, but her mother had to step in, to help her out at the start of the song.

'I was pretty nervous,' confessed Whitney. 'I was scared to death, in fact. I just fell in love with my mom that night. She was so wonderful, but I was very, very scared ... I found out that there was something inside me that made me feel incredible when I am singing ~ it really is like magic.'

In June 1980, Cissy Houston and her family ~ including Whitney ~ opened for Dave Valentin, at the *Bottom Line Nightclub* in New York City. Valentin was signed to Arista Records and, as it was his opening night, Gerry Griffith was in attendance, to represent Arista. But Whitney had an off-night and failed to impress Griffith. 'I'd never seen or heard of Whitney,' he said. 'She did the song, *Home* (from the musical, *The Wiz)*. I thought it was good, but that was about it. I didn't think any more about it.'

Two years on, Griffith took a phone call, and he learned Elektra Records were planning to sign Whitney. He arranged to see her again, and caught her at the 7th Avenue South Club in Greenwich Village. This time Griffith was impressed. 'She had grown so much,' he observed. 'She did *Home* again, and *Tomorrow* ~ and wiped me out!'

Griffith immediately arranged a 30 minute showcase for Whitney, staged at Manhattan's *Top Hat Rehearsal Hall,* designed to impress Arista's founder and president, Clive Davis. But Davis, initially, was indifferent, and he was only willing to offer Whitney a 'singles' deal, to record one single and its flip-side. However, the industry buzz surrounding Whitney was such, he reconsidered, and he upped his offer to a one album deal. With Elektra's offer already on the table, this left young Whitney with a difficult decision to make.

'Everyone put their bids in,' said Whitney. 'So I sat down with my managers and my parents, and I remember this long, drawn out meeting. What are you gonna do? Who are you gonna do it with? It was all very tense. I remember stopping the meeting, and saying, "I have to take a break!".'

Cissy advised her daughter 'you should go where you're going to get the best guidance … don't go with the company that offers you the most freedom, because freedom is not what you need at this point.'

Wise words, but Whitney was adamant no-one was going to tell her what to do, or which songs she was going to record, either.

'Clive Davis said, we'll give you this amount of money,' said Whitney, 'and we'll sit down and discuss everything that happens. And as far as songs that you want to do, I will help you. I will say "Whitney, this song has potential, this song doesn't". He assured me that he wouldn't dictate anything to me, but that he would help me to make rational decisions about songs.'

Whitney signed with Arista Records in April 1983, however, it was the best part of two years before her debut album finally appeared.

Known as 'Nippy' by her friends, Whitney was often referred to as 'The Voice' by her legion of fans. As Mariah Carey stated: 'Whitney has a really rich, strong mid-belt that very few people have. She sounds really good, really strong.'

'The first Whitney Houston CD was genius,' said Brandy, 'That CD introduced the world to her angelic yet powerful voice. Without Whitney, half of this generation of singers wouldn't be singing.'

During the 1980s, Whitney was one of the first black artists to enjoy heavy rotation on MTV, and in her homeland she became the first act to take seven consecutive singles to no.1 on Billboard's Hot 100.

Throughout the 1980s and 1990s, she won numerous awards, including six Grammys and 21 American Music Awards, placing her third in the latter category to only Alabama and Michael Jackson.

Whitney made her film debut in November 1992 in *The Bodyguard*, which went on to gross over $410 million globally, and gave Whitney the biggest hit of her career: *I Will Always Love You*. Just a few months earlier, on 18th July, she married Bobby Brown, a former member of New Edition who had a 'bad' boy' image. The couple's only child, Bobbi Kristina, was born on 4th March 1993.

It was around this time that Whitney first became seriously involved with taking illegal substances, something she managed to keep hidden for many years. However, after being arrested at an airport in Hawaii for being in possession of an illegal substance, Whitney made her troubles public in 2002, when she was interviewed by Diane Sawyer. Whitney spoke in some details about her drugs of choice, but insisted she drew the line at crack cocaine, famously stating 'Crack is wack'.

Whitney's divorce from Bobby Brown was finalised in April 2007 and, when she released a new album *I LOOK TO YOU* two years later, she appeared to be making a determined effort to conquer her addictions. However, her *Nothing But Love World Tour* ~ her first for over a decade ~ wasn't the success she might have hoped it would be, with her voice attracting much negative criticism.

Toward the end of 2011, playing Jordin Sparks's mother, Whitney filmed a remake of the 1976 film, *Sparkle*, and there was talk of her appearing in the sequel to *Waiting To Exhale* as well but, sadly, it wasn't to be.

On 9th February 2012, Whitney and her mentor Clive Davis paid a visit to Brandy and Monica, who were rehearsing for Davis's pre-Grammy Awards party at the Beverly Hilton Hotel in Beverly Hills. The same day, in what would be her last public performance, she briefly joined Kelly Price on stage at a party to sing *Jesus Loves Me*.

Two days later, Whitney was found dead in her suite at the Beverly Hilton Hotel. She was found submerged in her bath, and although paramedics arrived within minutes, Whitney couldn't be resuscitated and she was proclaimed dead at 3.55pm local time.

Whitney's funeral took place on Saturday 18th February 2012 at the New Hope Baptist Church in her home town, Newark, New Jersey.

Tragically, Whitney's daughter Bobbi Kristina was found face down in a bathtub at her Georgia home on 31st January 2015. After spending six months in a coma, she died of pneumonia on 26th July 2015, aged just 22 years. Bobbi Kristina was buried next to her mother, Whitney.

Whitney was posthumously inducted into the Rock 'N' Roll Hall of Fame in 2020.

All The Top 40 Hits

For the purposes of this book, to qualify as a Top 40 hit, a single or album must have entered the Top 40 singles/albums chart in at least one of the featured countries: Australia, Austria, Belgium, Canada, Denmark (singles only), Finland, France, Germany, Ireland (singles only), Italy, Japan, the Netherlands, New Zealand, Norway, Spain, Sweden, Switzerland, the United Kingdom, the United States of America and Zimbabwe.

The Top 40 singles and albums are detailed chronologically, according to the date they first entered the chart in one or more of the featured countries. Each Top 40 single and album is illustrated and the catalogue numbers and release dates are detailed, for both the USA and the UK, followed by the chart runs in each featured country, including any chart re-entries. Where full chart runs are unavailable, peak position and weeks on the chart are given. Soundtrack albums featuring Whitney, although strictly speaking not credited as Whitney Houston albums, are included with her Top 40 albums.

For both singles and albums, the main listing is followed by 'The Almost Top 40 Singles/Albums', which gives an honorable mention to Whitney's singles/albums that peaked between no.41 and no.50 in one or more countries. There is also a points-based list of Whitney's Top 30 Singles and Top 15 Albums, plus a fascinating 'Trivia' section at the end of each section which looks at Whitney's most successful singles and albums in each of the featured countries.

The Charts

The charts from an increasing number of countries are now freely available online, and for many countries it is possible to research weekly chart runs. Although this book focuses on Top 40 hits, longer charts runs are included where available, up to the Top 100 for countries where a Top 100 or longer is published.

Nowadays, charts are compiled and published on a weekly basis – in the past, however, some countries published charts on a bi-weekly or monthly basis, and most charts listed far fewer titles than they do today. There follows a summary of the current charts from each country featured in this book, together with relevant online resources and chart books.

Australia
Current charts: Top 100 Singles & Top 100 Albums.
Online resources: current weekly Top 50 Singles & Albums, but no archive, at **ariacharts.com.au**; archive of complete weekly charts dating back to 2001 at **pandora.nla.gov.au/tep/23790**; searchable archive of Top 50 Singles & Albums dating back to 1988 at **australian-charts.com**.
Books: 'Australian Chart Book 1970-1992' & 'Australian Chart Book 1993-2009' by David Kent.
Note: the information in this book relates to the Kent Music Report (i.e. David Kent's books) up to 2000, and to the ARIA charts from 2001 onwards. The Pandora archive hasn't been up-dated since September 2019.

Austria
Current charts: Top 75 Singles & Top 75 Albums.
Online resources: current weekly charts and a searchable archive dating back to 1965 for singles and 1973 for albums at **austriancharts.at**.

Belgium
Current charts: Top 50 Singles & Top 200 Albums for two different regions, Flanders (the Dutch speaking north of the country) and Wallonia (the French speaking south).
Online resources: current weekly charts and a searchable archive dating back to 1956 for singles and 1995 for albums at **ultratop.be**.
Book: '*Het Belgisch Hitboek – 40 Jaar Hits In Vlaanderen*' by Robert Collin.
Note: the information in this book for Belgium relates to the Flanders region.

Canada
Current charts: Hot 100 Singles & Top 100 Albums.
Online resources: weekly charts and a searchable archive of weekly charts from the Nielsen SoundScan era at **billboard.com/biz** (subscription only); incomplete archive of weekly RPM charts dating back to 1964 for singles and 1967 for albums at **bac-lac.gc.ca/eng/discover/films-videos-sound-recordings/rpm/Pages/rpm.aspx** (RPM folded in 2000).
Book: 'The Canadian Singles Chart Book 1975-1996' by Nanda Lwin.
Note: the information in this book relates to the RPM chart up to 1999, but there are gaps; post-1999, the information is even more patchy and incomplete.

Denmark
Current Charts: Top 40 Singles & Top 40 Albums.
Online resources: weekly charts at **hitlisten.nu**, and formally an archive dating back to 2001 at **danishcharts.com**. No archive currently exists for charts before 2001. 'CZB' has posted weekly Top 20s from September 1994 to December 1999 on **ukmix.org**, and 'janjensen' has posted singles charts from January 1977 onwards on the same forum.

Finland
Current charts: Top 20 Singles & Top 50 Albums.
Online resources: current weekly charts and a searchable archive dating back to 1995 at **finnishcharts.com**.
Book: '*Sisältää Hitin*' by Timo Pennanen.

France
Current charts: Top 200 Singles & Top 200 Albums.
Online resources: current weekly charts at **snepmusique.com**, plus weekly charts and a searchable archive dating back to 1984 for singles and 1997 for albums at **lescharts.com**; searchable archive for earlier/other charts at **infodisc.fr**.
Book: '*Hit Parades 1950-1998*' by Daniel Lesueur.

Note: Compilation albums were excluded from the main chart until 2008, when a Top 200 Comprehensive chart was launched.

Germany
Current charts: Top 100 Singles & Top 100 Albums.
Online resources: current weekly charts, plus charts dating back to 1977 (but no searchable archive) at **offiziellecharts.de**; Top 10s and a searchable archive dating back to 2007 at **germancharts.com**.
Books: '*Deutsche Chart Singles 1956-1980*', '*Deutsche Chart Singles 1981-90*', '*Deutsche Chart Singles 1991-1995*' & '*Deutsche Chart LP's 1962-1986*' published by Taurus Press.

Ireland
Current charts: Top 100 Singles & Top 100 Albums.
Online resources: current weekly charts are published at IRMA (**irma.ie**); there is a searchable archive for Top 30 singles (entry date, peak position and week on chart only) at **irishcharts.ie**; an annual Irish Chart Thread has been published annually from 2007 to date, plus singles charts from pre-2007 and incomplete album charts have been published at ukmix (**ukmix.org**).
Note: the information presented in this book is for singles only.

Italy
Current charts: Top 100 Singles & Top 100 Albums.
Online resources: weekly charts and a weekly chart archive dating back to 2005 at **fimi.it**; a searchable archive of Top 20 charts dating back to 2000 at **italiancharts.com**; pre-2000 information has been posted at ukmix (**ukmix.org**).
Note: as the FIMI-Neilsen charts didn't start until 1995, the information detailed in this book before then is from the Musica & Dischi chart.

Japan
Current charts: Top 200 Singles & Top 300 Albums.
Online resources: current weekly charts (in Japanese) at **oricon.co.jp/rank**; selected information is available on the Japanese Chart/The Newest Charts and Japanese Chart/The Archives threads at **ukmix.org**.

Netherlands
Current charts: Top 100 Singles & Top 100 Albums.
Online resources: current weekly charts and a searchable archive dating back to 1956 for singles and 1969 for albums at **dutchcharts.nl**.

New Zealand
Current charts: Top 40 Singles & Top 40 Albums.
Online resources: current weekly charts and archive singles and albums dating back to 1975 at **nztop40.co.nz**.

Book: 'The Complete New Zealand Music Charts 1966-2006' by Dean Scapolo.

Norway
Current charts: Top 20 Singles & Top 40 Albums.
Online resources: current weekly charts and a searchable archive dating back to 1958 for singles and 1967 for albums at **norwegiancharts.com**.

Spain
Current charts: Top 50 Singles & Top 100 Albums.
Online resources: current weekly charts and a searchable archive dating back to 2005 at **spanishcharts.com**.
Book: *'Sólo éxitos 1959-2002 Año a Año'* by Fernando Salaverri.

Sweden
Current charts: Top 60 Singles & Top 100 Albums.
Online resources: current weekly charts and a searchable archive dating back to 1975 at **swedishcharts.com**.
Note: before 1975, a weekly Top 20 *Kvällstoppen* charts was published, which was a sales-based, mixed singles/albums chart.

Switzerland
Current charts: Top 75 Singles & Top 100 Albums.
Online resources: current weekly charts and a searchable archive dating back to 1968 for singles and 1983 for albums at **hitparade.ch**.

UK
Current Charts: Top 100 Singles & Top 200 Albums.
Online resources: current weekly Top 100 charts and a searchable archive dating back to 1960 at **officialcharts.com**; weekly charts are posted on a number of music forums, including ukmix (**ukmix.org**), Haven (**fatherandy2.proboards.com**) and Buzzjack (**buzzjack.com**).
Note: weekly Top 200 album chart is only available via subscription from UK ChartsPlus (**ukchartsplus.co.uk**).

USA
Current charts: Hot 100 Singles & Billboard 200 Albums.
Online resources: current weekly charts are available at **billboard.com**, however, to access Billboard's searchable archive at **billboard.com/biz** you must be a subscriber; weekly charts are posted on a number of music forums, including ukmix (**ukmix.org**), Haven (**fatherandy2.proboards.com**) and Buzzjack (**buzzjack.com**).
Note: older 'catalog' albums (i.e. albums older than two years) were excluded from the Billboard 200 before December 2009, so the chart didn't accurately reflect the country's best-selling albums. Therefore, in this book Billboard's Top Comprehensive Albums chart has been used from December 2003 to December 2009, as this did include all albums. In

December 2009 the Top Comprehensive Albums chart became the Billboard 200, and Billboard launched a new Top Current Albums chart – effectively, the old Billboard 200.

Zimbabwe
Current charts: no official charts.
Online resources: none known.
Books: 'Zimbabwe Singles Chart Book' by Christopher Kimberley.
Note: Zimbabwe was, of course, known as Rhodesia before 1980, but the country is referred to by its present name throughout this book.

Note: In the past, there was often one or more weeks over Christmas and New Year when no new album chart was published in some countries. In such cases, the previous week's chart has been used to complete a chart run. Similarly, where a bi-weekly or monthly chart was in place, for chart runs these are counted at two and four weeks, respectively.

All The Top 40 Singles

Sweetest Sweetest

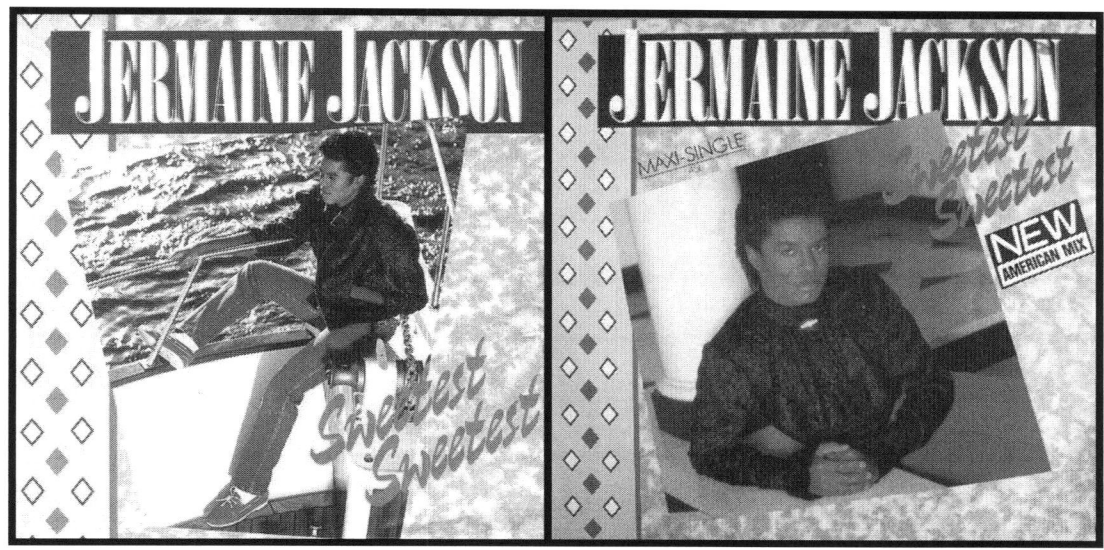

USA: Not Released.

UK: Arista JJK1 (May 1984).
B-side: *Come To Me (One Way Or Another)* (Jermaine Jackson).

12.05.84: 69-**52**-66-75

Australia
16.07.84: peaked at no.**57**, charted for 13 weeks

Belgium
19.05.84: 19-16-17-17-19-10-**9**-10-10-13-19-27

Finland
07.84: **30** (monthly chart)

Netherlands
16.06.84: 22-23-**20**-25-26-39

New Zealand
5.08.84: 33-25-28-**18**-19-20-27-28-43

Zimbabwe
20.10.84: 12-8-8-7-6-6-**3**-4-**3**-4-4-6-11

Whitney's first Top 40 single wasn't as a credited artist in her own right, but as a backing singer for Jermaine Jackson.

Sweetest Sweetest was written by Arthur Jacobson, Ellison Chase and Robin Lerner, and was recorded by Jermaine for the first album he released after leaving Motown, which was titled *JERMAINE JACKSON* in North America and *DYNAMITE* internationally.

Outside North America, *Sweetest Sweetest* was released as the album's lead single, and enjoyed moderate success, charting at no.3 in Zimbabwe, no.9 in Belgium, no.18 in New Zealand, no.20 in the Netherlands, no.30 in Finland, no.52 in the UK and no.57 in Australia.

Sweetest Sweetest was released as a picture disc single in the UK.

Whitney went on to record five duets with Jermaine, but only four have been released:

- *Nobody Loves Me Like You Do*
- *Take Good Care Of My Heart*
- *If You Say My Eyes Are Beautiful*
- *Shock Me*

Their fifth duet, *Don't Look Any Further*, was shelved after Dennis Edwards & Siedah Garrett's version was issued first, and remains unreleased.

1 ~ All At Once

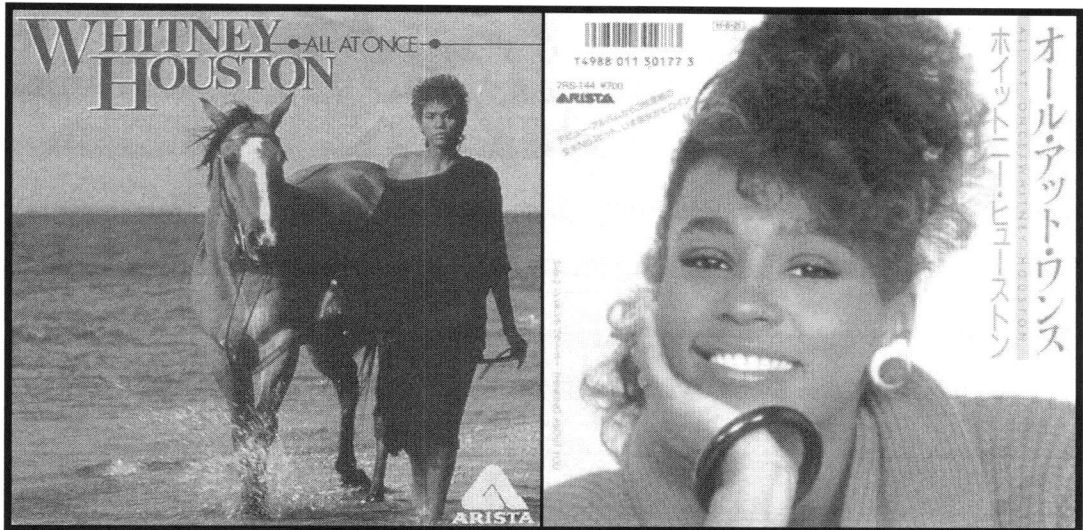

USA & UK: Not Released.

Europe: Arista 107 185 (1985).
  B-side: *Greatest Love Of All*

Belgium
30.03.85: 33-16-11-11-**2-2**-3-5-5-9-16-16-23-40

Italy
10.02.87: peaked at no.**3**, charted for 13 weeks

Japan
5.08.96: peaked at no.**42**, charted for 9 weeks

Netherlands
30.03.85: 29-16-**6-6-6-6**-10-13-21-29-44
18.02.12: 39-87

All At Once was written by Michael Masser and Jeffrey Osbourne, and recorded by Whitney for her self-titled debut album, released in 1985. Michael Masser also produced the recording.

In Japan and several continental European, including Belgium, Germany, Italy and the Netherlands, *All At Once* was chosen as Whitney's debut single from four songs on offer, including *Someone For Me* and *You Give Good Love*. In the USA and UK, it was later released as the B-side of *Saving All My Love For You*.

'Normally, we'll wait until an artist has a Top 30 single here (in the States) before launching them overseas,' said Rick Blaskey, Arista Record's international vice-president. 'Ironically, we wanted to present Whitney as the youthful, contemporary twenty-one year old artist she is, but the ballad (*All At Once*) was the one that got the best reaction over there (in Europe).'

All At Once charted at no.2 in Belgium, no.3 in Italy and no.6 in the Netherlands, but it wasn't a hit in Germany. In Japan, it wasn't until 1996 when the single finally charted, peaking at no.42.

Whitney performed *All At Once* at the American Music Awards, staged at the Shrine Auditorium, Los Angeles, on 26th January 1987.

Two years later, on 11th February 1999, she performed the song with show host Gianni Morandi, on the Italian TV show, *C'era Un Ragazzo* on. Morandi was the winner at the 37th *Festival di Sanremo*, where she sang *All At Once* twice.

2 ~ You Give Good Love

USA: Arista 9274 (1985).
  B-side: *Greatest Love Of All.*

11.05.85: 67-52-44-34-26-20-17-13-7-7-4-**3**-4-10-20-30-50-67-78-96-99

UK: Arista ARIST 625 (1985).
  B-side: *Thinking About You.*

24.08.85: **93**

Australia
26.08.85: peaked at no.**58**, charted for 17 weeks

Canada
8.05.85: 96-94-89-86-80-67-57-43-32-25-19-12-11-10-9-**7**-10-16-33-38-43-56-70-79-82

New Zealand
1.09.85: 46-x-**44**

You Give Good Love was written by La Forrest 'La La' Cope, and recorded by Whitney for her self-titled debut album, released in 1985. The recording was produced by Kashif.
  The song was originally offered to Roberta Flack ~ however, Kashif felt the song was better suited to Whitney, and she it was who recorded the song.
  You Give Good Love was chosen as the lead single from Whitney's debut album in North America.

'We wanted to establish her (Whitney) in the black market place first,' said Clive Davis, explaining why the song was chosen as Whitney's first solo single in the United States. 'Otherwise, you can fall between cracks, where Top 40 won't play you and R&B won't consider you their own. We felt that *You Give Good Love* would be, at the very least, a major black hit, though we didn't think that it would cross over as it did. When it did crossover, with such velocity, that gave us great encouragement.'

Whitney promoted *You Give Good Love* with a music video directed by Karen Bellone, which featured her performing the song at a nightclub.

'She came there like a real polished professional,' observed Kenneth Reynolds, head of Arista's R&B product management, at Whitney's first video shoot, 'which is a quality that I noticed in everything she did. She may have been new to the business, but she conducted herself like someone who had really been around from day one. I don't think I have met anyone initially who was so young in their career, and yet so sure about themselves, and so sure of what they wanted.'

The song's title and lyrics were deemed suggestive and sexually provocative by Ann Landers, a well know advice columnist with the *Chicago Sun-Times*, who called *You Give Good Love* 'pretty trashy stuff'.

Whitney responded, in an interview with the *Chicago Tribune*, by stating: 'I don't think that the title is suggestive at all. It didn't say anything but "you give good love", and it didn't say anything that was sexual or outrageous. I think Miss Landers just looked at the title and didn't view the song itself.'

You Give Good Love hit no.1 on the R&B chart in the States, and achieved no.3 on the Hot 100. Elsewhere, the single peaked at no.7 in Canada and no.44 in New Zealand. The singles was less successful in Australia and the UK, where it peaked at no.58 and no.93, respectively.

Whitney picked up two Grammy nomination for *You Give Good Love*: Best R&B Song and Best R&B Vocal Performance, Female ~ however, both awards went to the Aretha Franklin hit, *Freeway Of Love*.

Whitney did win an American Music Award for *You Give Good Love*, for Favourite Soul/R&B Single.

3 ~ Saving All My Love For You

USA: Arista 9381 (1985).
  B-side: *All At Once.*

17.08.85: 53-39-31-23-18-14-9-6-4-2-**1**-3-6-14-24-38-51-66-86-92-92-93

UK: Arista ARIST 640 (1985).
  B-side: *All At Once.*

16.11.85: 60-23-9-2-**1**-**1**-2-2-2-2-9-19-28-44-56-71-72-x-78-97
25.02.12: 59

Australia
4.11.85: peaked at no.**20**, charted for 29 weeks
26.02.12: 90

Austria
1.01.86: **12**-27-23 (bi-weekly)

Belgium
28.12.85: 28-17-12-11-**9**-13-19-33

Canada
7.09.85: 84-57-43-34-28-22-16-14-10-**8**-9-9-12-19-25-33-49-49-49-53-63-73-79

28

France
29.03.86: 50-x-49-36-30-21-16-13-13-12-**11**-12-13-14-17-24-31-39-43-x-49-47
11.02.12: 72-39

Germany
6.01.86: 67-31-22-20-**18**-24-29-38-39-34-30-35-55-60-71

Ireland
8.12.85: 16-2-**1**-4-4-2-8

Japan
9.12.85: peaked at no.**83**, charted for 11 weeks

Netherlands
16.11.85: 28-26-29-36-36-35-29-29-**16**-17-24-23-38-46
18.12.12: 62

New Zealand
3.11.85: 45-23-13-6-8-**5**-6-6-6-6-6-16-32-37-45-41

Norway
18.01.86: **10**

Switzerland
15.12.85: 29-15-15-15-12-6-**5-5**-11-14-18-22-17-26-23-21
26.02.12: 54

Saving All My Love For You was written by Michael Masser and Gerry Goffin, and was recorded by Whitney for her self-titled debut album, released in 1985.

The song was originally recorded by Marilyn McCoo & Billy Davis, Jr., for their 1978 album, *MARILYN & BILLY*.

Saving All My Love For You was brought to Whitney's attention by producer Michael Masser, who was impressed by her interpretation of his song, *Greatest Love Of All*. 'This is going to make women cry,' he told her. 'It is a woman's song.'

Masser had also produced the Marilyn McCoo & Billy Davis, Jr. version of the song. 'I altered the song somewhat (for Whitney),' he revealed, 'took out the second bridge, changed a few things, then when it was finished told Gene Harvey (a member of Whitney's management team) that's the single ~ that's going to be your first number one.'

Cissy Houston wasn't happy about her daughter singing about adultery but, after giving it some thought, Whitney agreed to record the song.

'When I did *Saving All My Love For You*,' she admitted, 'I was going through a terrible love affair. He was married, and that will never work out for anybody. Never. No way. Forget about it.'

Early takes of the song by Whitney were scrapped, as Clive Davis felt they were 'too black'.

'Clive had a formula already,' said Kenneth Reynolds, Arista's marketing director. 'Whitney was just a talent to mould. She had to lose her gospel roots. The early version of *Saving All My Love For You* sounded like the new Aretha Franklin. But Clive didn't like it.'

The music video for *Saving All My Love For You*, filmed in London, was directed by Stuart Orme, and explored the song's theme of adultery, with Ricco Ross playing the married man Whitney is singing about.

'I could never see myself in that position,' said Whitney, responding to the controversy the song and music video caused. 'I wouldn't just take whatever someone wants to give me, especially if I am giving a lot to him but not getting that much back.'

Saving All My Love For You gave Whitney her first no.1 on the Hot 100 in the USA. The single also went to no.1 in Ireland and the UK, and achieved no.5 in New Zealand and Switzerland, no.8 in Canada, no.9 in Belgium, no.10 in Norway, no.11 in France, no.12 in Austria, no.16 in the Netherlands, no.18 in Germany and no.20 in Australia.

Whitney performed *Saving All My Love For You* at the Grammy Awards, staged at the Shrine Auditorium, Los Angeles, on 25th February 1986. She went on to win her first Grammy for the song, for Best Pop Vocal Performance, Female.

Her performance at the Grammy Awards won her an Emmy, for Outstanding Individual Performance in a Variety or Music Program.

Saving All My Love For You also picked up an American Music Award, for Favourite Soul/R&B Video.

4 ~ How Will I Know

USA: Arista 9434 (1985).
  B-side: *Someone For Me.*

7.12.85: 60-50-42-36-33-31-23-17-11-5-**1-1**-2-3-5-12-18-26-35-47-59-74-97
3.03.12: 49

UK: Arista ARIST 656 (1986).
  B-side: *Someone For Me.*

25.01.86: 36-23-19-10-**5**-6-7-12-24-31-39-48
25.02.12: 56

Australia
8.07.85: peaked at no.**2**, charted for 27 weeks
26.02.12: 67-94

Austria
1.05.86: **28** (bi-weekly)

Belgium
22.06.85: 32-**28**

Canada
14.12.85: 80-56-48-48-48-29-22-19-15-9-6-**1**-2-2-3-4-8-12-17-32-35-42-50-60-78

Denmark
10.04.86: 13-**12**-x-13-**12**-x-15

Finland
03.86: peaked at no.**5**, charted for 2 months

Germany
31.03.86: 29-31-**26**-28-32-42-44-43-69

Ireland
16.02.86: 21-5-**3**-4-18-24-26

Italy
6.05.86: peaked at no.**23**, charted for 3 weeks

Japan
17.03.86: peaked at no.**77**, charted for 3 weeks

Netherlands
22.02.86: 27-20-**12-12**-18-24-30-42
18.02.12: 100

New Zealand
26.05.85: 35-25-22-30-38-34-41-44
2.02.86: 32-28-23-33-29-22-23-**19**-21-21-29-33

Norway
1.03.86: 7-3-**2-2-2-2**-6-6

Sweden
5.03.86: 13-4-**2-2**-4-5-10 (bi-weekly)

Switzerland
23.03.86: 16-13-**11**-20-14-19-25-25-26

How Will I Know was written by George Merrill and Shannon Rubicam ~ originally, for Janet Jackson.

'They asked us to write for Janet Jackson's next record,' George Merrill confirmed, 'so Shannon and I went to work and came up with our song, *How Will I Know*, which was sent to Janet Jackson's people. They passed on it because it wasn't right for her at the time ~ she was in the midst of doing her *CONTROL* album … We were pretty upset because we thought it was perfect for her at the time. We had written it with her completely in mind.'

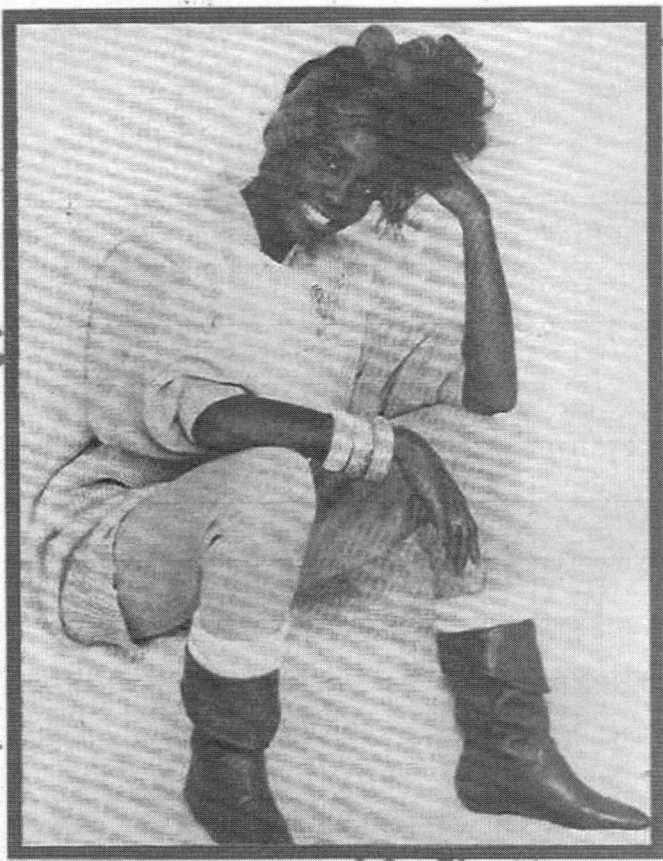

'It wasn't right for that,' Rubicam concurred, 'but then our publishing company played it for Gerry Griffith when he was in Los Angeles, gathering material for the unknown Whitney Houston. He loved it, sent it to Clive (Davis), and Clive said, "We must have it". And we said, Whitney who? Clive who?'

'We had a lot of R&B based tunes,' said Griffith, 'we had a few ballads, but we didn't really have a pop crossover song. But when I heard *How Will I Know*, I said "This is absolutely perfect". I played it to Clive Davis and he fell in love with it as well.'

Whitney's lead vocal was recorded in one day at a New York studio. The following day, Whitney and her mother Cissy recorded the backing vocals.

'I asked Whitney to sing on the background session,' said producer Narada Michael Walden. 'She was reluctant, though, because she wanted to enjoy hearing her mother sing. I said, "No ~ get out there, too, and sing!" so she did. The background sounds incredible.'

'Our good friends, brother team Alan and Preston Glass, called us where they were working with Narada Michael Walden,' said George Merrill. 'They were recording Whitney Houston on *How Will I Know*, and they said, "Guys, you've got to hear this". They played it over the phone, and I swear, her voice ~ hearing the first take of *How Will I Know* on the phone, we knew we were on to something special, too.'

The music video for *How Will I Know*, directed by Brian Grant, featured a cameo appearance by Aretha Franklin.

How Will I Know, like *Saving All My Love For You* before it, went all the way to no.1 on the Hot 100 in the USA. The single it deposed was *That's What Friends Are For*, by Whitney's cousin, Dionne Warwick.

The single also topped the singles chart in Canada, and charted at no.2 in Australia, Norway and Sweden, no.3 in Ireland, no.5 in the UK, no.11 in Switzerland, no.12 in Denmark and the Netherlands, no.23 in Italy, no.26 in Germany, and no.28 in Austria and Belgium.

5 ~ Hold Me

USA: Asylum 69720 (1984).
  B-side: *Love* (Teddy Pendergrass).

9.06.84: 89-75-67-60-55-50-48-**46-46**-54-63-65-73-78-79-83-89-96

UK: Asylum EKR 32 (1986).
  B-side: *Love* (Teddy Pendergrass).

18.01.86: 93-70-46-51-**44**-50-83

Belgium
22.02.86: **30**-32

Ireland
16.02.86: **25**

Netherlands
15.02.86: **24**-33-39

Hold Me was written by Michael Masser and Linda Creed, and was recorded by Whitney as a duet with Teddy Pendergrass, for his 1984 album, *LOVE LANGUAGE*. It was released as a single in 1984, and was the first single to credit Whitney Houston. It rose to no.5 on the R&B chart, but stalled at no.46 on the Hot 100 in the USA, and failed to chart anywhere else.

Hold Me was subsequently included on Whitney's self-titled debut album, released early the following year. Only after the album had already produced four Top 40 singles in various countries did *Hold Me* finally achieve Top 40 status, charting at no.24 in the Netherlands, no.25 in Ireland, no.30 in Belgium and no.44 in the UK.

Whitney would almost certainly have picked up a Grammy as Best New Artist, following the success of her debut album and the singles from it. However, the fact she had recorded and released *Hold Me* a year before she found success in her own right, meant she wasn't even eligible to be nominated.

Whitney performed *Hold Me* with Teddy Pendergrass at the Linda Creed Memorial Scholarship Fund concert, staged at Penn Hall Civic Center, Philadelphia, on 10th May 1987. Linda Creed, who co-wrote *Hold Me* and numerous other well-known songs, died of breast cancer on 10th April 1986.

6 ~ Greatest Love Of All

USA: Arista 9466 (1986).
  B-side: *Thinking About You.*

9.03.86: 54-40-29-22-12-7-3-**1-1-1**-3-6-11-22-37-50-63-87
25.02.12: 41-36

UK: Arista ARIST 658 (1986).
  B-side: *Thinking About You.*

12.04.86: 46-33-16-10-10-**8**-11-24-44-56-71-x-88
25.02.12: 58

Australia
2.06.86: peaked at no.**1** (1), charted for 19 weeks
26.02.12: 56-85

Austria
1.07.86: 26-**25** (bi-weekly)

Belgium
17.05.86: **31**-34-39

Canada
5.04.86: 81-63-39-30-25-20-9-4-2-**1**-3-4-5-11-22-27-42050-59-64-71

Finland
05.86: peaked at no.**16**, charted for 1 month

France
18.02.12: **70**

Germany
26.05.86: 56-39-**30**-32-39-52-57-61-69-74

Ireland
27.04.86: 17-6-**4**-9-21-7-13

Italy
29.07.86: peaked at no.**18**, charted for 10 weeks

Netherlands
17.05.86: 38-33-26-25-**24**-31-36-35-49
18.02.12: 28-60

New Zealand
15.06.86: 22-**12**-14-14-**12**-19-19-15-39-36-37
20.02.12: 40

Spain
19.02.12: **39**

Sweden
28.05.86: 16-**14** (bi-weekly)

Switzerland
1.06.86: 24-22-**20**-29
26.02.12: 55

The Greatest Love Of All, as it was originally titled, was written by Michael Masser and Linda Creed, for the 1977 film *The Greatest*, a film biography of the heavyweight boxer, Mohammed Ali. At the time, Linda Creed was battling breast cancer, and her lyrics describe her emotions, on being a young mother fighting a terminal illness (Linda died in 1986, aged just 36 years).

The song was recorded by George Benson, and he also recorded a live version of the song for his 1978 live album, *WEEKEND IN L.A.*.

George Benson's version of *The Greatest Love Of All* charted at no.2 on the R&B chart and no.24 on the Hot 100 in the States, no.25 in Canada and no.27 in the UK.

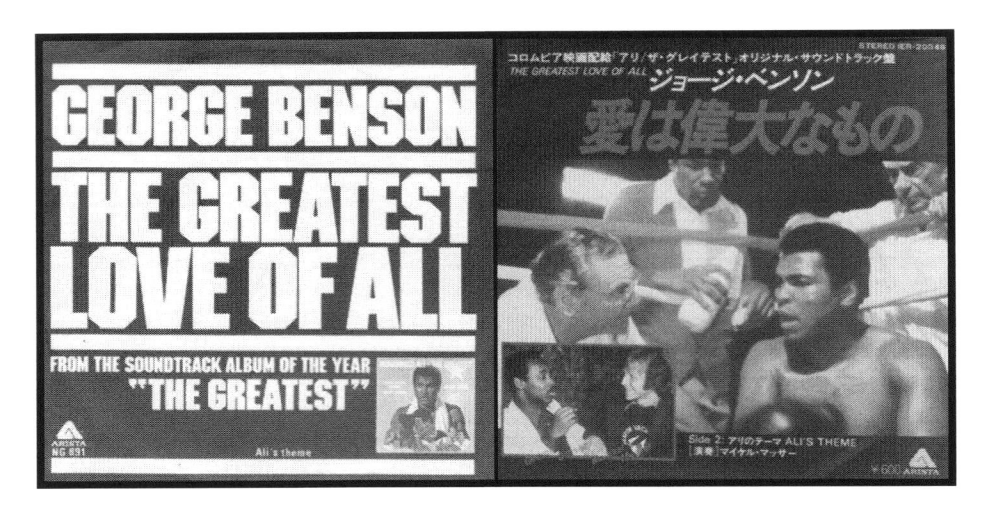

Whitney Houston was still a young, unknown singer when Clive Davis, the then President of Arista Records, and Michael Masser first heard her sing at Sweetwater's, a New York club on Amsterdam Avenue.

'I went down there instead of having her audition in a studio,' said Davis. 'I was seeing her before an audience. She did backup singing and you could see she was a beautiful young girl. But then she stepped out and she did two solo numbers, one of which was the song *The Greatest Love of All*. Whitney sang the song with such fervour, with such a natural vocal gift, with such passion, that I was stunned. I knew really right then and there that this was a special talent and I was blown away by her. As I reflect back on this, I can relive the experience for the very first time. There was no hesitation. I wanted to sign Whitney.'

The song's co-writer Michael Masser was equally impressed. 'I went into Sweetwater's,' he said, 'and I thought I must be totally out of it. I said, "I must be going crazy, I think I'm hearing one of my songs." She was singing *The Greatest Love of All* just as I walked in, and that meant something to me. Two and a half years later when I was doing Teddy Pendergrass there was a duet and everybody wanted me to use this or that known person. Only because I had heard Whitney singing *The Greatest Love of All*, I chose her.'

Whitney recorded *Greatest Love Of All*, as it was re-titled, for her debut album.

'Our young people need to hear that song,' she said, 'and realise it's about loving yourself. If you can love yourself through all your rights and wrongs and faults, then that's the greatest love of all. That's the message.'

Whitney's original album version of the song had a piano introduction, which was replaced by a keyboard introduction on later pressings. However, the original version was included on the deluxe 25th anniversary edition of *WHITNEY HOUSTON*, released in 2010.

An alternate version, with just piano and vocals, featured on a limited number of copies ~ 200,000 ~ of the album.

THE GREATEST LOVE OF ALL

Words by Linda Creed
Music by Michael Masser
Recorded by Whitney Houston on Arista Records

Chappell & Intersong Music

Greatest Love Of All was originally released as the B-side of *You Give Good Love* in the United States, and of *Someone For Me* in the UK, but strong radio airplay led to a decision to release the song as a single in its own right.

The accompanying music video, which featured Whitney's mother, Cissy, was filmed at the Apollo Theater in Harlem, New York City. The promo went on to pick up an American Music Award, for Favourite Soul/R&B Video.

Greatest Love Of All gave Whitney a hat-trick of no.1 singles on the Hot 100 in the USA. The single also went to no.1 in Australia and Canada, and charted at no.4 in Ireland, no.8 in the UK, no.12 in New Zealand, no.14 in Sweden, no.16 in Finland, no.18 in Italy, no.20 in Switzerland, no.24 in the Netherlands, no.25 in Austria, no.30 in Germany and no.31 in Austria.

Whitney performed *Greatest Love Of All* at the gala concert staged at Radio City Music Hall, New York, on 9th March 1990, to celebrate Arista Record's 15th anniversary. This live performance was one of the bonus tracks featured on the special deluxe edition of Whitney's debut album, issued in 2010. It also featured on the posthumous CD/DVD, *LIVE – HER GREATEST PERFORMANCES*, released in 2014.

Following Whitney's passing in February 2012, *Greatest Love Of All* proved to be one of her most loved songs, and re-entered in charts in several countries, peaking at no.28 in the Netherlands, no.36 in the USA, no.39 in Spain, no.55 in Switzerland, no.56 in Australia and no.58 in the UK.

Greatest Love Of All song has been recorded by numerous other artists over the years, including Shirley Bassey and Kevin Rowland (of Dexy's Midnight Runners fame).

7 ~ I Wanna Dance With Somebody (Who Loves Me)

USA: Arista 9598 (1987).
  B-side: *Moment Of Truth*.

16.05.87: 38-28-18-10-5-3-**1**-**1**-2-3-4-9-17-28-41-52-65-97
25.02.12: 35-25

UK: Arista RIS 1 (1987).
  B-side: *Moment Of Truth*.

23.05.87: 10-2-**1**-**1**-2-2-4-8-12-18-21-33-42-50-62-75
25.02.12: 20-62

Australia
25.05.87: peaked at no.**1** (5), charted for 23 weeks
26.02.12: 25-36-66-80-96

Austria
15.06.87: 29-5-**3**-**3**-**3**-12-15-24 (bi-weekly)
24.02.12: 70

Belgium
30.05.87: 13-5-4-3-2-**1**-**1**-**1**-2-3-5-12-18

Canada
9.05.87: 74-59-41-21-9-8-5-3-**1**-2-2-2-2-2-6-8-12-15-28-36-46-64-84

Denmark
15.05.87: 5-3-2-**1**-**1**-**1**-**1**-2-2-2-3-4-5-6-7-10-13

Finland
05.87: peaked at no.**1**, charted for 4 months

France
11.07.87: 49-40-35-29-20-17-17-**15**-25-19-18-25-31-37-39-46
11.02.12: 73-31

Germany
18.05.87: 74-35-3-3-**1**-**1**-**1**-**1**-**1**-2-4-6-7-10-13-13-17-27-40-64-62

Ireland
24.05.87: 3-**2**-**2**-3-3-7-13-25-28
16.02.12: 32-51-99

Italy
12.05.87: peaked at no.**1** (2), charted for 18 weeks

Japan
25.05.87: peaked at no.**95**, charted for 5 weeks

Netherlands
16.05.87: 53-11-3-3-2-**1**-**1**-**1**-**1**-4-5-6-15-23-33-47-59-90
18.02.12: 42-84

New Zealand
21.06.87: 3-**1**-**1**-**1**-**1**-2-2-5-5-14-17-31-36
20.02.12: 17

Norway
16.05.87: 5-2-**1**-**1**-**1**-**1**-**1**-**1**-**1**-3-5

Spain
20.07.87: peaked at no.**4**, charted for 41 weeks
19.02 12: 28

Sweden
20.05.87: 3-**1**-**1**-**1**-4-7 (bi-weekly)

Switzerland
31.05.87: 3-4-**1**-**1**-**1**-**1**-**1**-**1**-3-3-3-7-11-11-16-24-25
26.02.12: 28-60

Zimbabwe
3.10.87: peaked at no.**5**, charted for 13 weeks

I Wanna Dance With Somebody (Who Loves Me) was written by George Merrill and Shannon Rubicam, and recorded by Whitney for her second album, *WHITNEY*, released in 1987.

'That song got written pretty quickly, as I recall,' said Shannon Rubicam. 'We had a funky little garage studio at the time, and we just hung out in there one afternoon and wrote the song, and I know we tweaked it the next day, and started recording it on our little TX 4-track deck that we were using … a friend of ours had a larger, more comprehensive studio, so we recorded the demo there, and the demo we made of *I Wanna Dance With Somebody* was kind of a rock version.

'We recorded the song, mixed it, and then George literally ran to the airport with it and met Clive (Davis), who was getting on a plane, because he wanted it … so he took it with him and listened to it on the plane.'

'I (George Merrill) said, "You know, Clive, we're feeling great about this, and we're in the midst of doing a Boy Meets Girl album, and if you could get back to us on it and let us know if you don't want it for Whitney, we'd like it for the Boy Meets Girl album". He had had a quick listen to it, he just looked at me, and he said something I can't repeat.'

Initially, producer Narada Michael Walden wasn't convinced the song was right for Whitney. 'At first,' he said, 'I thought it was too country and western sounding. It reminded me of a rodeo song with Olivia Newton-John singing. I love Olivia Newton-John, but for Whitney Houston it didn't seem right. I felt the song needed a much more funkier feel. I slept, dreaming about it, woke up in the morning thinking about it, wondering what I was gonna do with this dance song. So, we just jumped in the water and lo-and-behold, a magic record was born. We just knocked it out, and then I knew we had a good record.'

I Wanna Dance With Somebody (Who Loves Me) was chosen at the lead single from Whitney's second, much anticipated album. It was sent out to radio stations with a note from Arista's legal department, which forbade anyone from playing the single before 7.30am on 29th April 1987. Of course, this meant radio stations across the States all gave the single its first spin at exactly the same time.

In the USA, the single gave Whitney her fourth consecutive no.1 single on the Hot 100; it also hit no.1 on Billboard's Hot Dance Club Play chart and no.2 on the R&B chart.

I Wanna Dance With Somebody (Who Loves Me) was a massive hit just about everywhere, hitting no.1 in Australia, Belgium, Canada, Denmark, Finland, Germany, Italy, the Netherlands, New Zealand, Norway, Sweden, Switzerland and the UK. The single also charted at no.2 in Ireland, no.3 in Austria, no.4 in Spain, no.5 in Zimbabwe and no.15 in France.

Whitney performed *I Wanna Dance With Somebody (Who Loves Me)* on *Top Of The Pops* in the UK, her first appearance on the show, which aired on 21st May 1987. Unlike many acts who appeared on the show, who mimed and lip-synched, Whitney's performance was live.

She also performed the song when she opened the Grammy Awards, staged at New York's Radio City Music Hall on 2nd March 1988. She went on to pick up a Grammy for Best Pop Vocal Performance, Female, for *I Wanna Dance With Somebody (Who Loves Me)*.

I Wanna Dance With Somebody (Who Loves Me) returned to many charts in February 2012, following Whitney's passing. It charted at no.17 in New Zealand, no.20 in the UK, no.25 in Australia and the USA, no.28 in Spain and Switzerland, no.31 in France, no.32 in Ireland and no.42 in the Netherlands.

8 ~ Didn't We Almost Have It All

USA: Arista 9616 (1987).
  B-side: *Shock Me.*

1.08.87: 50-40-25-16-8-5-3-2-**1**-**1**-6-15-24-35-52-79-97

UK: Arista RIS 31 (1987).
  B-side: *Shock Me.*

22.08.87: 22-**14**-**14**-21-28-36-60-68
25.02.12: 92

Australia
24.08.87: peaked at no.**27**, charted for 13 weeks
26.02.12: 96

Belgium
29.08.87: 36-**16**-17-17-29

Canada
15.08.87: 73-38-22-13-9-9-8-3-**2**-3-11-16-28-36-43-65-75-99

Denmark
14.08.87: 15-13-**11**-12

Whitney Gives It All...

DIDN'T WE ALMOST HAVE IT ALL* "REMIX"

The Perfect Second Single From That Perfect 2nd Album

12 INCH INCLUDES "I WANNA DANCE WITH SOMEBODY" ACAPPELLA MIX

*AS FEATURED ON THE No. 1 ALBUM/CASSETTE/COMPACT DISC "WHITNEY"

ARISTA
A BERTELSMANN MUSIC GROUP COMPANY

Germany
31.08.87: 21-25-**20**-33-35-39-49-61-65

Ireland
23.08.87: 22-**4**-5-22

Netherlands
15.08.87: 85-44-25-19-**17**-23-28-41-51-61
18.02.12: 65-97

New Zealand
1.11.87: 50-x-**49**

Spain
28.09.87: peaked at no.**12**, charted for 12 weeks

Switzerland
6.09.87: **18**-22-21-25

Didn't We Almost Have It All was written by Will Jennings and Michael Masser, and was recorded by Whitney for her second album, *WHITNEY*.

'*Didn't We Almost Have It All* is a song about wishing for reunion with someone, and making the case for it by recalling past good times,' said Will Jennings. 'I think that probably took longer than any other song. Michael (Masser) was travelling and he was in the studio and doing this and that, so I think it was about a year or two after we started it that it was finished. And I sort of lost track of the whole thing. It was one of those never-to-be-repeated experiences, because he was producing the record and he wanted to really nail it down. He kept feeling it wasn't finished and so he'd put it away, and I was off working on something. I'd lost track of what went on with it.'

It has been alleged the song was written about Whitney's relationship with the American football star, Randall Cunningham, however, this has never been confirmed.

Didn't We Almost Have It All was released as the follow-up to *I Wanna Dance With Somebody (Who Loves Me)*, ahead of the original choice, *For The Love Of You*. It gave Whitney her fifth consecutive no.1 single on the Hot 100 in the States, but was less successful in other countries, charting at no.2 in Canada, no.4 in Ireland, no.11 in Denmark, no.12 in Spain, no.14 in the UK, no.16 in Belgium, no.17 in the Netherlands, no.18 in Switzerland, no.20 in Germany, no.27 in Australia and no.49 in New Zealand.

Didn't We Almost Have It All picked up a Grammy nomination, for Song of the Year, but the award went to the Linda Ronstadt & James Ingram hit, *Somewhere Out There*.

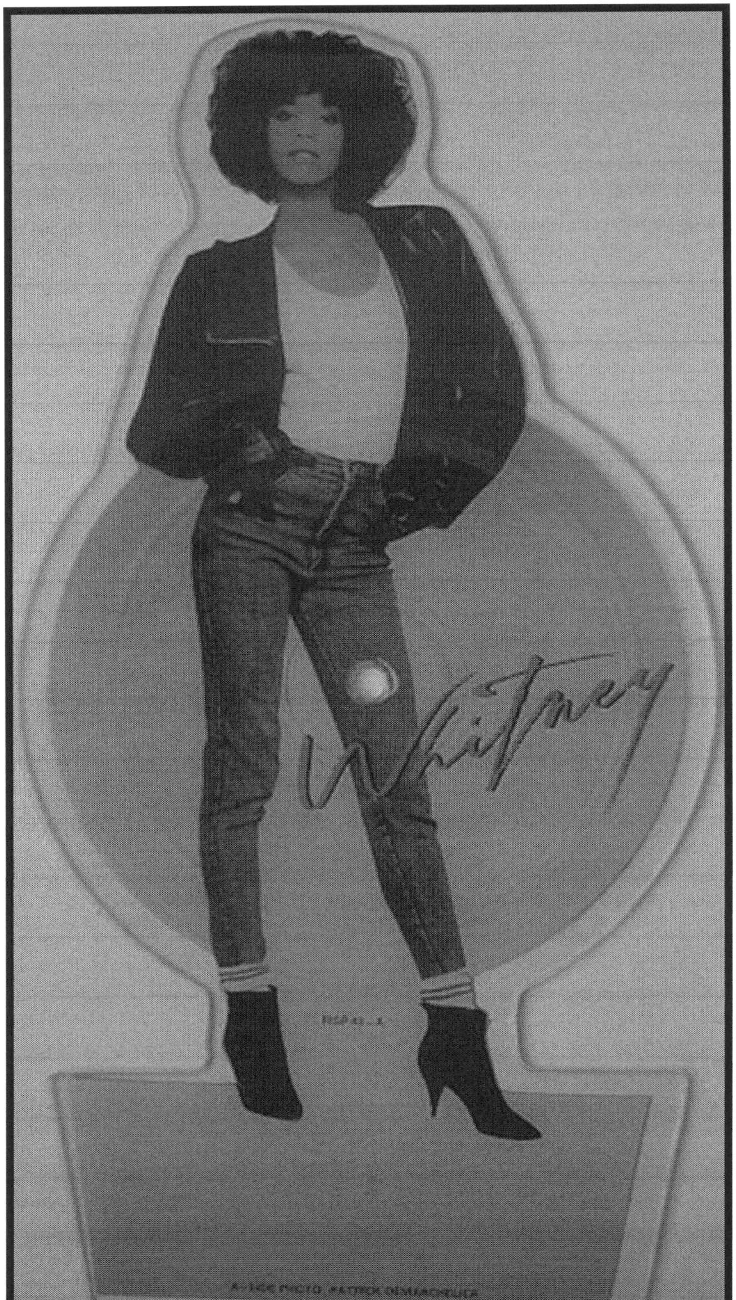
Whitney

9 ~ So Emotional

USA: Arista 9642 (1987).
  B-side: *For The Love Of You.*

31.10.87: 47-38-29-19-16-8-7-3-2-2-**1**-2-9-20-30-44-58-76-99

UK: Arista RIS 43 (1987).
  B-side: *For The Love Of You.*

14.11.87: 20-9-**5**-6-12-16-22-25-25-44-72

Australia
23.11.87: peaked at no.**26**, charted for 19 weeks

Belgium
21.11.87: 39-21-**18**-22-37-31

Canada
7.11.87: 79-65-38-24-19-13-10-**9-9-9**-10-10-13-32-43-59-61-71-80

Finland
11.87: peaked at no.**9**, charted for 1 month

France
2.04.88: 47-43-44-27-27-27-**21**-22-23-25-29-41

Ireland
15.11.87: 12-**3**-**3**-24

Italy
5.01.88: **25**

Netherlands
7.11.87: 56-30-20-**18**-24-25-49-52-52-53-57

New Zealand
20.12.87: 47-47-47-47-21-**16**-25-18-28-28-36

Spain
28.12.87: peaked at no.**15**, charted for 18 weeks

Switzerland
13.12.87: **30**

So Emotional was written by Tom Kelly and Billy Steinberg, and recorded by Whitney for her 1987 album, *WHITNEY*.

'A lot of songwriters,' said Billy Steinberg, 'get together and the first question they ask each other is, "Who do you want to write for?" Tom (Kelly) and I had never done that because I find it restricting, and we both like to write a song for the song's sake, and not try to aim at a particular recording artist. In the case of *So Emotional*, Tom and I had a regular dialogue with Clive Davis, and he advised us that he was looking for an up-tempo song for Whitney Houston, so we really tried to write for that.

'We were both big fans of Prince. If you were to hear the demo of *So Emotional*, you would hear that it sounds quite a bit like Prince. We did the demo and Clive really loved it. When we presented it to Narada Michael Walden to produce it, he changed it completely from the sound of our demo. I don't think anyone would ever hear Whitney's version of the song and hear anything Prince-like about the production. Originally, our demo had a certain Prince feel to it, in the verse in particular.'

So Emotional was the third single released from *WHITNEY*, and became Whitney's sixth consecutive no.1 on the Hot 100 in the States; she was only the third act to have achieved this feat, after the Beatles and the Bee Gees.

Elsewhere, the single achieved no.3 in Ireland, no.5 in the UK, no.9 in Canada and Finland, no.15 in Spain, no.16 in New Zealand, no.18 in Belgium and the Netherlands, no.21 in France, no.25 in Italy, no.26 in Australia and no.30 in Switzerland.

So Emotional was issued as a Whitney-shaped picture disc in the UK only.

The music video for *So Emotional*, directed by Wayne Isham, featured footage filmed at a concert staged in Bethlehem, Pennsylvania.

10 ~ Where Do Broken Hearts Go

USA: Arista 9674 (1988).
  B-side: *Where You Are.*

27.02.88: 47-38-28-19-16-10-5-3-**1**-**1**-4-11-19-33-49-63-82-98

UK: Arista 109 793 (1988).
  B-side: *Where You Are.*

12.03.88: 30-16-15-**14**-17-33-52-68
25.02.12: 74

Australia
18.04.88: peaked at no.**48**, charted for 14 weeks

Belgium
2.04.88: **28**-39-38-38-36

Canada
5.03.88: 76-44-?-30-25-19-16-?-10-9-**6**-8-26-36-50-60-82-91-100

Ireland
13.03.88: 22-**2**-7-15-23

Italy
10.05.88: peaked at no.**22**, charted for 2 weeks

Netherlands
9.04.88: 87-53-**47-47**-48-55-67

New Zealand
5.06.88: 33-**23**-42-34

Spain
11.04.88: peaked at no.**32**, charted for 2 weeks

Where Do Broken Hearts Go was written by Chuck Jackson and Frank Wildhorn, and was recorded by Whitney for her 1987 album, *WHITNEY*.

Initially, Whitney wasn't keen on recording the song, as she felt the lyrics had no special message to convey. Clive Davis, however, felt the song was a potential chart topper, and he wisely persuaded her to record it.

Time proved Clive Davis right: *Where Do Broken Hearts Go* gave Whitney her seventh consecutive no.1 on the Hot 100 in the States ~ a new record, ahead of the Beatles and Bee Gees, who both enjoyed six straight chart toppers.

'Whitney's seventh number one in a row is not only a great achievement in the outer world,' said producer Narada Michael Walden, 'but a most significant achievement in the inner worlds as well. There are seven lower worlds and seven higher worlds, with Whitney's seventh number one in a row, she takes us all to that seventh higher world. This is the place that all broken hearts go to for inner nourishment, inner satisfaction, inner and outer peace.'

Like *Didn't We Almost Have It All* and *So Emotional* before it, *Where Do Broken Hearts Go* couldn't match its success in the USA in other countries. The single charted at no.2 in Ireland, no.6 in Canada, no.14 in the UK, no.22 in Italy, no.23 in New Zealand, no.28 in Belgium, no.32 in Spain, no.47 in the Netherlands and no.48 in Australia.

Whitney performed *Where Do Broken Hearts Go* at the American Music Awards, staged at the Shrine Auditorium, Los Angeles, on 25th January 1988. Whitney also co-hosted the show with the Bee Gees, Mick Fleetwood, Barbara Mandrell & Smokey Robinson.

11 ~ Love Will Save The Day

USA: Arista 9720 (1988).
  B-side: *How Will I Know*.

2.07.88: 52-40-35-26-21-15-11-11-**9**-11-24-38-63-89-89-100

UK: Arista 111 516 (1988).
  B-side: *Hold Me*.

28.05.88: 27-**10**-16-31-42-51-71

Australia
8.08.88: peaked at no.**77**, charted for 3 weeks

Belgium
25.06.88: 31-21-9-**7**-12-12-17-17-23-30

Canada
9.07.88: 79-68-57-40-29-24-20-9-9-**8**-20-49-84

France
8.10.88: 49-**48**

Germany
12.07.88: 39-42-39-**37**-38-48-43-49-59-62-57-55-x-75

Ireland
29.05.88: 24-**8**-17

Netherlands
11.06.88: 74-53-11-9-8-**6**-7-9-16-22-27-62-73-94

Spain
4.07.88: peaked at no.**9**, charted for 14 weeks

Switzerland
10.07.88: 20-22-**18**-21-20-24

Love Will Save The Day written by Toni C., and recorded by Whitney for her 1987 album, *WHITNEY*.

The fifth single lifted from the album, *Love Will Save The Day* achieved no.1 on Billboard's Hot Dance Club Play chart, but it ended Whitney's record run of seven Hot 100 chart toppers, when it peaked at no.9. However, given how many people had already bought WHITNEY, so were familiar with the song, Top 10 for the fifth single from the album was still a creditable achievement.

Outside the USA, *Love Will Save The Day* charted at no.6 in the Netherlands, no.7 in Belgium, no.8 in Canada and Ireland, no.9 in Spain, no.10 in the UK, no.18 in Switzerland, no.37 in Germany and no.48 in France.

Love Will Save The Day was issued as a 7" picture disc single in the UK.

Whitney performed *Love Will Save The Day* at the Special Olympics Summer Games Opening Ceremonies, staged at the University of Notre Dame in South Bank, Indiana, on 31st July 1987. Her performance was later used in the music video used to promote the single, and won a Sports Emmy Award for the Outstanding Musical Performance in a Sports Program.

12 ~ One Moment In Time

USA: Arista 9743 (1988).
  B-side: *Love Is A Contact Sport.*

10.09.88: 57-42-35-29-22-18-12-9-6-**5**-10-20-39-54-63-100-100

UK: Arista 111 613 (1988).
  B-side: *Olympic Joy (Instrumental)* (Kashif).

24.09.88: 24-8-3-**1**-**1**-3-6-13-19-38-52-69-x-81-81
25.02.12: 40-89

Australia
3.10.88: peaked at no.**49**, charted for 17 weeks

Austria
1.11.88: 22-25-21-11-**5**-14-13-21 (bi-weekly)
24.02.12: 34-52

Belgium
24.09.88: 31-13-12-11-5-5-**3**-5-7-15-25-30

Canada
24.09.88: 81-62-38 …? ~ peaked at no.**3**

ONE MOMENT IN TIME

Whitney HOUSTON

Words and Music by Albert Hammond/John Bettis
Recorded by Whitney Houston on Arista Records
Empire Music Limited/Albert Hammond Inc./Warner Bros Music

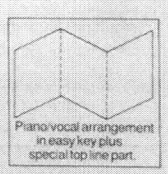

Piano/vocal arrangement in easy key plus special top line part.

Denmark
23.09.88: 10-11-**7**-8-14

Finland
09.88: peaked at no.**5**, charted for 1 month

France
31.12.88: 50-47-41-33-21-17-16-14-13-10-12-**8**-12-15-15-17-22-35-45
18.02.12: 61

Germany
26.09.88: 58-8-2-2-**1-1**-3-4-4-5-12-19-19-21-21-32-29-52-67
15.05.09: 67-90
24.02.12: 40-66

Ireland
2.10.88: 8-**2-2-2**-3-16
16.02.12: 42-64

Italy
4.10.88: peaked at no.**4**, charted for 24 weeks

Japan
1.10.88: peaked at no.**73**, charted for 3 weeks

Netherlands
17.09.88: 71-40-16-12-8-7-**6**-10-18-21-45-54-97
18.02.12: 30-54

New Zealand
13.11.88: 49-x-47-**34**

Norway
17.09.88: 7-**3**-4-4-**3-3-3**-5-10-x-7

Spain
3.10.88: peaked at no.**7**, charted for 16 weeks
19.02.12: 26

Sweden
21.09.88: 6-4-**3**-4-7-13 (bi-weekly)

Switzerland
25.09.88: 17-13-10-6-7-8-5-5-5-6-**4**-11-9-9-12-16-10-13-21-13-27
26.02.12: 18-51

Zimbabwe
3.12.88: peaked at no.**3**, charted for 20 weeks

One Moment In Time was written by Albert Hammond and John Bettis, and recorded by Whitney for the 1998 Summer Olympic Games, staged in Seoul, South Korea. The song featured on the album, *1988 SUMMER OLYMPICS ALBUM – ONE MOMENT IN TIME*.

One Moment In Time gave Whitney her third no.1 single in the UK, and also topped the chart in Germany. Elsewhere, the single charted at no.2 in Ireland, no.3 in Belgium, Canada, Norway, Sweden and Zimbabwe, no.4 in Italy and Switzerland, no.5 in Austria, Finland and the USA, no.6 in the Netherlands, no.7 in Denmark and Spain, no.8 in France, no.34 in New Zealand and no.49 in Australia.

The music video for *One Moment In Time* featured a montage of clips from previous Olympic ceremonies, but didn't include any footage of Whitney.

Whitney performed *One Moment In Time* at the Grammy Awards, staged at the Shrine Auditorium, Los Angeles, on 22nd February 1989. This performance was among the special features included on her 2000 home video, *THE GREATEST HITS*. It was also included on the posthumous CD/DVD, *LIVE – HER GREATEST PERFORMANCES*, released in 2014.

Following Whitney's passing in February 2012, *One Moment In Time* returned to the charts in a number of countries, rising to no.26 in Spain, no.30 in the Netherlands, no.34 in Austria, no.40 in Germany and the UK, and no.42 in Ireland.

13 ~ I Know Him So Well

USA & UK: Not Released.

Europe: Arista 111 904 (1988).
  B-side: *Just The Lonely Talking Again*.

Belgium
24.12.88: 29-37-x-x-39-23-**19**-21-24-28-40

Germany
9.01.89: **46**-51-50-68-57

Netherlands
17.12.88: 71-50-50-40-19-**16**-21-27-44-66-82

I Know Him So Well was written by Tim Rice with ABBA's Benny Andersson & Björn Ulvæus, and was originally recorded by Elaine Paige & Barbara Dickson for the 1984 concept album, *CHESS* (the theatrical production of *Chess* opened in London's West End in 1986).

Elaine & Barbara took *I Know Him So Well* to no.1 in the UK, no.7 in Switzerland, no.9 in New Zealand, no.13 in Belgium, no.16 in the Netherlands and no.22 in Germany.

'I love the song,' said Whitney. 'I thought it was a classic, actually. I was in Germany and these two young ladies who originally sang the song were in the dressing room next to me, and I could hear them singing it. And then, two years later, we were playing some material for the new album, and someone asked me, "Do you like this song?" And there it was!'

I KNOW HIM SO WELL
FROM CHESS
By
BENNY ANDERSSON, TIM RICE and BJÖRN ULVAEUS
Recorded by
ELAINE PAIGE AND BARBARA DICKSON
on RCA RECORDS
BOCU MUSIC LTD • sole selling agents • MUSIC SALES LTD • 8 & 9 Frith Street • London W1V 5TZ

Whitney recorded a cover of *I Know Him So Well*, as a duet with her mother Cissy, for her 1987 album, *WHITNEY*.

'I've worked with my Mom before,' she said, 'but to record with my mother was a dream come true, because I always wanted to do something with her. The experience of working with her was ~ I really can't begin to tell you how great that was!'

Whitney & Cissy's version of *I Know Him So Well* was released as a single in Japan and several continental European countries, but not in the UK or North America. The single achieved no.14 in the Netherlands, no.19 in Belgium and no.46 in Germany.

Whitney performed *I Know Him So Well* with Cissy at the Classic Whitney concerts, staged at the DAR Constitution Hall in Washington, D.C. on 3rd & 5th October 1997.

I Know Him So Well has proved popular with UK artists in more recent years, with Geraldine McQueen (*aka* Peter Kay) & Susan Boyle, Melanie C. & Emma Bunton and Steps all recording hit cover versions.

14 ~ It Isn't, It Wasn't, It Ain't Never Gonna Be

USA: Arista 9850 (1989).
 B-side: *If Ever A Love There Was* (Aretha Franklin).

1.07.89: 73-60-54-49-**41**-43-47-85

UK: Arista 112 545 (1989).
 B-side: *Think* (Aretha Franklin).

9.09.89: 55-40-**29**-33-48

Canada
17.07.89: ?-53-48-45-**43**-48-?

Ireland
1.10.89: **14**

Italy
26.09.89: peaked at no.**16**, charted for 6 weeks

Netherlands
26.08.89: 66-48-42-**40-40**-50-85-95

It Isn't, It Wasn't, It Ain't Never Gonna Be was written by Diana Warren and Albert Hammond, and was recorded by Whitney as a duet with Aretha Franklin for Aretha's 1989 album, *THROUGH THE STORM*.

'As it went down,' wrote Aretha about recording the duet, in her autobiography, *Aretha: From The Roots*, 'some things were misunderstood and we miscommunicated; we were very badly mismatched in terms of maturity and experience and sensitivity. It was something that never should have happened. I think Nippy (Whitney) felt unappreciated, and nothing could have been further from the truth.'

Given who recorded it, *It Isn't, It Wasn't, It Ain't Never Gonna Be* was an obvious single, but it wasn't well received by most people and wasn't as big as hit as Whitney and Aretha were more used to.

It Isn't, It Wasn't, It Ain't Never Gonna Be struggled to no.41 on the Hot 100 in the USA, and achieved no.14 in Ireland, no.16 in Italy, no.29 in the UK, no.40 in the Netherlands and no.43 in Canada.

15 ~ I'm Your Baby Tonight

USA: Arista 2108 (1990).
B-side: *I'm Knockin'*.

20.10.90: 42-29-18-13-5-3-**1**-2-3-7-7-10-13-19-30-47-58-79-92

UK: Arista 113 594 (1990).
B-side: *I'm Knockin'*.

20.10.90: 16-7-**5**-7-10-20-34-47-70-77-69

Australia
29.10.90: peaked at no.**4**, charted for 20 weeks

Austria
28.10.90: 30-20-15-7-4-**3**-7-8-7-7-8-11-11-17-18

Belgium
27.10.90: 36-24-16-12-5-3-**2-2**-4-8-14-21-34-43

Canada
27.10.90: 85-43-26-16-11-?-7-4-?-?-**2**-5-29-54-67-97

Denmark
19.10.90: 10-x-x-9-9-**7-7**

Finland
10.90: peaked at no.**2**, charted for 3 months

France
8.12.90: 35-19-20-**4**-8-**4**-10-11-15-20-23-22-23-22-27-41

Germany
29.10.90: 67-28-11-9-8-6-**5**-8-10-10-12-17-21-25-31-42-59-59-63-64-82-85-86

Ireland
21.10.90: 18-**6**-11-17-30

Italy
16.10.90: peaked at no.**1** (5), charted for 20 weeks

Japan
12.11.90: peaked at no.**96**, charted for 3 weeks

Netherlands
20.10.90: 62-30-12-5-3-**2**-3-10-12-22-34-49-71-91

New Zealand
25.11.90: 29-27-26-25-20-20-20-20-**16**-17-22-35-46-45

Norway
20.10.90: 8-**3**-4-4-4-7-10-10

Spain
10.12.90: peaked at no.**7**, charted for 17 weeks

Sweden
24.10.90: 8-**4**-5-6-9 (bi-weekly)

Switzerland
4.11.90: 9-6-8-**4**-5-**4**-**4**-5-**4**-6-18-18-10-14

Zimbabwe
26.01.91: peaked at no.**4**, charted for 2 weeks

I'm Your Baby Tonight was written by L.A. Reid & Babyface, and recorded by Whitney for her 1990 album of the same title.
   'We wrote *I'm Your Baby Tonight* among some other songs,' said L.A. Reid, 'and when we felt we had something we asked her (Whitney) to come and see us in Atlanta. We met with her and had dinner, played the song for her and she was very happy …

almost immediately after finishing, once all the material had been recorded, it was pretty much decided that would be the title song even then.'

I'm Your Baby Tonight gave Whitney her eighth no.1 on the Hot 100 in the States, and topped the R&B chart as well. The single entered the Top 10 in most countries, rising to no.1 in Italy, no.2 in Belgium, Canada, Finland and the Netherlands, no.3 in Austria and Norway, no.4 in Australia, France, Sweden, Switzerland and Zimbabwe, no.5 in Germany and the UK, no.6 in Ireland, no.7 in Denmark and Spain, and no.16 in New Zealand.

The music video for *I'm Your Baby Tonight*, directed by Julian Temple, had a retro feel. It paid tribute to Hollywood's Golden Age, and featured Whitney as all three of the Supremes, thanks to digital cloning imagery.

Whitney performed *I'm Your Baby Tonight* at her Welcome Home Heroes concert, staged at the Naval Air Station in Norfolk, Virginia, on 31st March 1991. The concert was dedicated to the Gulf War troops and their families. This performance was included on the posthumous CD/DVD, *LIVE – HER GREATEST PERFORMANCES*, released in 2014.

Whitney was nominated for a Grammy for *I'm Your Baby Tonight*, for Best Pop Vocal Performance, Female, but the award went to Mariah Carey for *Vision Of Love*.

16 ~ All The Man That I Need

USA: Arista 2156 (1990).
  B-side: *Dancin' On The Smooth Edge.*

22.12.90: 53-53-37-33-18-11-8-3-2-**1**-**1**-3-7-16-21-29-40-52-69-85-89-92-100

UK: Arista 114 000 (1990).
  B-side: *Dancin' On The Smooth Edge.*

22.12.90: 27-22-26-17-**13**-17-22-33-54-65

Australia
28,01.91: peaked at no.**45**, charted for 15 weeks

Austria
17.02.91: 29-29-**21**-24

Belgium
12.01.91: 29-27-21-**14**-16-18-20-34-37-50

Canada
12.01.91: 90-35-28-21-10-5-2-**1**-3-3-?-?-?-?-63-78

Finland
01.91: peaked at no.**17**, charted for 1 month

69

France
20.04.91: 37-33-29-**28**-29-37-42-31-46-41

Germany
21.01.91: 66-52-38-**37**-47-42-42-52-51-52-52-53-72-65-68-77-89-94

Ireland
6.01.91: 27-**16**-17-26

Netherlands
22.12.90: 94-94-44-24-12-**11**-17-25-39-56-86

New Zealand
24.02.91: 47-x-**36**

Switzerland
17.02.91: 30-x-29-x-**28**

Zimbabwe
1.06.91: peaked at no.**1** (3), charted for 5 weeks

All The Man That I Need was written by Dean Pitchford and Michael Gore. The song was originally titled *All The Man I Need*, and was first recorded by Linda Clifford.

'*All The Man I Need* was actually written for my husband and myself,' said Clifford. 'I recorded it in 1980, when I recorded *Red Light* for the movie, *Fame*.'

Linda Clifford's version featured on her 1982 album, *I'LL KEEP ON LOVING YOU*, but it wasn't a hit.

Also in 1982, Sister Sledge recorded a cover of *All The Man I Need*, for their album, *THE SISTERS*. Their version of the song was a minor R&B hit in the States, but it failed to enter the Hot 100.

'I figured that it was one of those songs,' said co-writer Dean Pitchford, 'that was going to get cut a number of times and not ever have its day.'

Pitchford was on friendly terms with Clive Davis, and heard it Davis liked the song, but at the time Whitney had just finished recording her second album. She did, however, go on to record the song for her third album, *I'M YOUR BABY TONIGHT*, changing the title to *All The Man That I Need*.

Issued as the follow-up to *I'm Your Baby Tonight*, *All The Man That I Need* gave Whitney her ninth no.1 on the Hot 100 in the USA. The single also topped the chart in Canada and Zimbabwe, but wasn't quite so successful in other countries, charting at no.11 in the Netherlands, no.13 in the UK, no.14 in Belgium, no.16 in Ireland, no.17 in Finland, no.21 in Austria, no.28 in France and Switzerland, no.36 in New Zealand, no.37 in Germany and no.45 in Australia.

Whitney picked up another Grammy nomination, for *All The Man That I Need*, but for the second year running she lost out in the Best Pop Vocal Performance, Female, category, this time to Bonnie Raitt, for *Something To Talk About*.

Whitney's Welcome Heroes performance of *All The Man That I Need* was included on her posthumous CD/DVD, *LIVE – HER GREATEST PERFORMANCES*, released in 2014.

17 ~ The Star Spangled Banner

USA: Arista 2207 (1991), Arista 15054 (2001).
  B-side: *America The Beautiful*.

9.03.91: 32-25-21-20-22-32-33-61-83-87-98
29.09.01: 50-97-72-13-**6**-18-38-59-80-85-85-90-82-89-80-97

UK: Not Released.

Canada
09.01: peaked at no.**5**

The Star Spangled Banner is America's national anthem.
   The song's lyrics were taken from the poem *Defence Of Fort McHenry*, written by Francis Scott Key in 1814, while the melody is from a popular British drinking song, *The Anacreontic Song*, written by John Stafford Smith.
   The song was renamed *The Star Spangled Banner*, and formally adopted as America's national anthem by congressional resolution, in March 1931.
   Whitney performed *The Star Spangled Banner* 'live' at Super Bowl XXV, staged at the Tampa Stadium, Tampa, Florida, on 27th January 1991.
   'I think it was a time when Americans needed to believe in our country,' said Whitney, '… I didn't want my (performance) to be the traditional *Star Spangled Banner*. I wanted an arrangement everyone could sing along with. It's a pretty tough song to sing. It goes from very low to very high, and it's very delicate.
   'At first, I just started to sing the song, and I was happy to be there. And then, I looked at the faces of the crowd and I saw the parents of the men and women who were over in

the Gulf, and it really made me think. It made me say: "This is for them". It made me very emotional and I cried. This is something that my children can look at in the future and proud ~ and I am proud of that.'

Controversy erupted a few days later, when it emerged Whitney's 'live' performance had actually been pre-recorded. A spokesman for Whitney confirmed, 'She sang, but the microphone was turned off. It was a technical decision, partially based on the noise factor. This is standard procedure for these events.'

Whitney's recording was released as a single in the United States only, produced by Whitney and Rickey Minor, to raise funds for the American Red Cross Gulf Crisis Fund and the Whitney Houston Foundation for Children. It debuted on the Hot 100 at no.32, and peaked at no.20 ~ however, on Billboard's Hot 100 Sales chart, it went all the way to no.1.

Whitney's performance was included on the posthumous CD/DVD, *LIVE – HER GREATEST PERFORMANCES*, issued in 2014.

The single was reissued in North America in 2001, following the 9/11 terrorist attacks. Whitney and her record company Arista donated their royalties to the New York Firefighters 9/11 Disaster Relief Fund and the New York Fraternal Order Of Police.

'When I first performed *The Star Spangled Banner* in 1991,' said Whitney, 'we were in the midst of the Gulf War and the country was united. This anthem has always been the musical symbol for the United States of America. I am proud to be able to participate in this way.'

'Whitney's decision to utilise her extraordinary talent as a means to inspire and heal,' said L.A. Reid, 'is only surpassed by her audience's eager desire to rise to the occasion. All of us are proud of the substantial contribution we will be able to make to the ongoing relief efforts, as a result of the single.'

Second time around, *The Star Spangled Banner* rose to no.6 on the Hot 100, and was also a no.5 hit in neighbouring Canada.

The first artist to take *The Star Spangled Banner* into the Hot 100 in the United States was José Feliciano, whose version charted at no.50 in 1969.

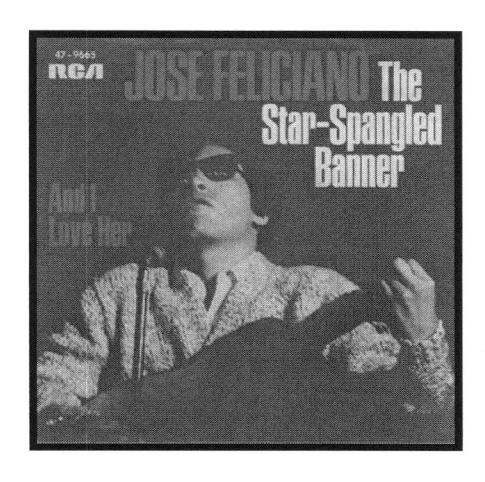

18 ~ Miracle

USA: Arista 2222 (1991).
B-side: *After We Make Love.*

13.04.91: 63-42-35-26-21-17-16-11-**9**-13-32-57-82-99

UK: Not Released.

Canada
27.04.91: 76-39-32-17-21-20-20- …? ~ peaked at no.**17**

Miracle was written by L.A. Reid & Babyface, and recorded by Whitney for her 1990 album, *I'M YOUR BABY TONIGHT*. It was chosen as the third single from the album, but only in North America and a small number of other countries, including Japan, Mexico and Spain.

Miracle achieved no. 9 on the Hot 100 in the USA and no.17 in Canada, but it wasn't a hit anywhere else.

Whitney refuted suggestions the song was pro-life or anti-abortion. 'I didn't sing it with that in mind,' she said. 'I think about the air we breathe, the Earth we live on. I think about our children. I think about a lot of things, things God put here for us to have, things that we need and take for granted. I think all of these things are miracles, and I think we should try to take better care of them.'

Miracle was one of three songs, performed by Whitney at her concert at Oakland, California on 11th May 1991, screened at *The Simple Truth: A Concert For Kurdish Refugees*, a five hour telethon broadcast around the world. The other two songs she performed were *My Name Is Not Susan* and *Greatest Love Of All*.

19 ~ My Name Is Not Susan

USA: Arista 12259 (1991).
   Tracks: *My Name Is Not Susan (Album Edit)/(UK Mix)/(Power Radio Mix w/Rap)/(Power Radio Mix w/o Rap).*

27.07.91: 67-46-36-29-24-23-**20**-30-56-95

UK: Arista 114 510 (1991).
   Tracks: *My Name Is Not Susan (Waddell 72 Mix)/(Album Edit).*

6.07.91: 32-**29**-39-52-74

Belgium
29.06.91: **43**-50

Canada
07.91: peaked at no.**43**

Germany
22.07.91: 64-72-57-68-70-75-73-70-87-93
13.07.98: 92-73-**52**-55-69-85-70-81-76

Ireland
14.07.91: **14**-28

Netherlands
15.06.91: 64-44-30-**28**-33-43-80

Sweden
3.07.91: 35-x-**31** (bi-weekly)

My Name Is Not Susan was written by L.A. Reid and Babyface, and recorded by Whitney for her 1990 album, *I'M YOUR BABY TONIGHT*. It was issued as the fourth single from the album in North America, and as the follow-up to *All The Man That I Need* in most other countries.

My Name Is Not Susan achieved no.14 in Ireland, no.20 in the USA, no.28 in the Netherlands, no.29 in the UK, no.31 in Sweden, no.43 in Belgium and Canada, and no.57 in Germany.

The Logic Remix of *My Name Is Not Susan* by Snap! returned the song to the German chart in 1998, achieving no.52, five places higher than its original peak.

The music video, directed by Lionel C. Martin, borrowed elements from Alfred Hitchcock's 1958 film, *Vertigo*, and featured Whitney playing both herself and the character Susan.

An alternated promo, a remix that featured rapper Monie Love, was posted on YouTube by Sony.

20 ~ I Will Always Love You

USA: Arista 12490 (1992).
  B-side: *Jesus Loves Me*.

14.11.92: 40-12-**1-1-1-1-1-1-1-1-1-1-1-1-1-1**-2-7-11-16-22-26-28-30-41-49
25.02.12: 7-3-30

UK: Arista 12065-7 (1992).
  B-side: *Jesus Loves Me*.

14.11.92: 12-4-2-**1-1-1-1-1-1-1-1-1-1**-2-4-9-17-23-28-36-50-63-69
29.05.93: 96
18.12.93: 50-40-25-31-58-69-x-88
25.02.12: 14-44-92

Australia
7.12.92: peaked at no.**1** (10), charted for 27 weeks
26.02.12: 8-24-52-77-75

Austria
13.12.92: 26-23-23-14-6-4-**1-1-1**-2-**1-1**-2-2-8-12-15

Belgium
28.11.92: 38-25-23-11-8-3-2-**1-1-1-1-1-1**-3-7-7-14-22-41
24.02.12: 10-20-50

Canada
21.11.92: 83-?-**1-1-1-1-1-1-1-1-1-1**-30-30-30-49-50-63-64-75-87

Denmark
9.01.93: 6-3-**1-1-1-1-1-1-1**-2-3-12-10-x-19-16-12-x-17
21.05.93: 20

Finland
12.92: peaked at no.**1**, charted for 6 months
14.02.12: 20-17

France
2.01.93: 19-8-5-3-**1-1-1-1-1-1-1-1**-2-3-4-6-8-7-15-17-26-24-33-38-43-41-35-45
11.02.12: 11-2-20-45-61-74
17.11.12: 89
23.02.13: 94
22.02.14: 68-73-96
21.02.15: 83

Germany
30.11.92: 63-54-28-20-20-10-5-3-**1-1-1-1-1-1**-3-5-6-10-12-15-19-24-31-36-40-47-85-x-82
24.02.12: 19-37-52-83

Ireland
16.11.92: 10-3-**1-1-1-1-1-1-1-1**-2-3-3-4-7-12-9-13-16-23-x-26
16.02.12: 13-21-53

Italy
17.11.92: peaked at no.**2**, charted for 17 weeks
23.02.12: 7

Japan
14.12.92: peaked at no.**5**, charted for 27 weeks

Netherlands
14.11.92: 60-33-19-7-3-2-2-**1-1-1-1-1-1**-3-3-4-6-6-14-18-24-29
18.02.12: 5-20-73

New Zealand
13.12.92: 2-**1-1-1-1-1-1-1-1-1-1-1-1-1**-4-3-6-5-9-18-17-22-45
20.02.12: 7-31

Norway
15.12.92: 9-2-2-**1-1-1-1-1-1-1-1**-2-3-4-8

25.02.12: 12

Spain
14.12.92: peaked at no.**1** (1 wk), charted for 17 weeks
12.02.12: 17-2-2-11-15-35-42-40-40-43-48

Sweden
25.11.92: 15-6-3-**1-1-1**-2-5-9-24 (bi-weekly)
17.02.12: 56-56

Switzerland
6.12.92: 18-21-19-4-4-**1-1-1-1-1-1-1-1**-3-6-16-15-15-16-23-19-28-25-31-21-38-21
24.05.09: 92
13.09.09: 93
26.02.12: 3-14-44-67-74

Zimbabwe
16.01.93: peaked at no.**1** (3), charted for 13 weeks

I Will Always Love You was written and originally recorded by Dolly Parton in 1973, following her split with her musical partner, country singer Porter Wagoner. The song featured on her 1974 album, *JOLENE*. Released as a single, *I Will Always Love You* hit no.1 on Billboard's Country chart in the States.

'I think stories like that,' said Parton, referring to reports that Elvis Presley wanted to record the song, but she refused as he also wanted half the publishing rights, 'are the reason why younger female artists say I've influenced them.'

ORIGINAL SHEET MUSIC EDITION
I WILL ALWAYS LOVE YOU
WHITNEY HOUSTON
Photography: Randee St. Nicholas
Recorded by Whitney Houston on Arista Records
Words and Music by Dolly Parton

Dolly Parton re-recorded *I Will Always Love You* in 1982, for the film, *The Best Little Whorehouse In Texas* ~ again, the song went to no.1 on the Country chart in the States, making it the first song to top that chart twice by the same artist. The re-recording also achieved no.53 on the Hot 100.

Whitney recorded *I Will Always Love You* for the soundtrack album, *THE BODYGUARD*, released in 1992.

Originally. Whitney recorded a version of Jimmy Ruffin's *What Becomes Of The Brokenhearted* for *The Bodyguard* ~ however, when she learned Paul Young had recorded the same song for another film, *Fried Green Tomatoes*, she requested a different song. Her co-star, Kevin Costner, brought Linda Ronstadt's version of *I Will Always Love You* to Whitney's attention, and liking it she recorded that song instead. And, despite her record company's reservations about the *a cappella* introduction, both Whitney and Costner insisted on keeping it.

I Will Always Love You was chosen as the lead single from *THE BODYGUARD* soundtrack album. It rose to no.1 on the Hot 100 in the States in just three weeks, to give Whitney her 10th chart topper. It held the no.1 spot for a record breaking 14 weeks, and spent a record 11 weeks at no.1 on the R&B chart.

The single went to no.1 around the world, topping the charts in most countries, including Australia, Austria, Belgium, Canada, Denmark, Finland, France, Germany, Ireland, the Netherlands, New Zealand, Norway, Spain, Sweden, Switzerland, the UK (where the single topped the chart for 10 consecutive weeks) and Zimbabwe.

I Will Always Love You was the no.1 best-selling single of 1992 in both the UK and USA, and is often cited at the no.1 biggest selling non-charity single of all-time. This is inaccurate, as that accolade almost certainly belongs to Bing Crosby's *White Christmas*. However, Whitney's version of *I Will Almost Love You* is the no.1 best-selling single of all-time by a female artist.

I Will Always Love You picked up two Grammy Awards, for Record Of The Year and Best Pop Vocal Performance, Female. The single also won two American Music Awards, for Favourite Pop/Rock Single, Female and Favourite R&B/Soul Single, Female.

At the World Music Awards, *I Will Always Love You* was named the World's No.1 Single Of 1993. A decade later, Whitney performed *I Will Always Love You* and *I Believe In You And Me* at the World Music Awards, staged in Las Vegas, Nevada, on 15th September 2004, as a tribute to her mentor Clive Davis, who was in attendance to pick up a Lifetime Achievement Award.

Not surprisingly, *I Will Always Love You* proved Whitney's most popular recording, following her passing in February 2012. The song re-entered the charts in many countries, rising to no.2 in France and Spain, no.3 in Switzerland and the USA, no.5 in the Netherlands, no.7 in Italy and New Zealand, no.8 in Australia, no.10 in Belgium, no.12 in Norway, no.13 in Ireland, no.14 in the UK, no.17 in Finland and no.19 in Germany.

The film version of *I Will Always Love You*, together with a live performance from The Bodyguard Tour and an alternate mix, all featured on Whitney's 2017 album, *I WISH YOU LOVE: MORE FROM THE BODYGYARD*.

21 ~ I'm Every Woman

USA: Arista 12519 (1993).
 B-side: *Who Do You Love*.

9.01.93: 66-66-32-22-14-10-**4**-**4**-6-5-5-7-6-13-18-22-23-26-33-39-39-44-45

UK: Arista 13150-7 (1993).
 B-side: *Who Do You Love*.

20.02.93: 5-**4**-6-6-12-17-25-39-40-52-74-x-x-x-100

Australia
1.03.93: peaked at no.**10**, charted for 20 weeks
26.02.12: 95

Austria
28.03.93: 23-28-**19**-23-29-27-29-29-26-29-25

Belgium
27.02.93: 42-13-9-4-3-**2**-**2**-3-6-9-21-32

Canada
23.01.93: 95-74-26-17-11-4-**2**-**2**-3-3-11-16-24-42-80

Denmark
19.02.93: **5**-7-x-13-x-17

Finland
02.93: peaked at no.**2**, charted for 2 months

France
17.04.93: 31-14-26-13-19-**11**-22-21-37-26-36
18.02.12: 92

Germany
22.03.93: 43-33-**13-13-13**-14-19-24-28-32-33-39-46-66-75-75

Ireland
15.02.93: 18-**4-4**-5-5-8-9-15-23-27

Italy
23.02.93: peaked at no.**6**, charted for 9 weeks

Netherlands
20.02.93: 29-14-5-5-**4**-5-6-8-14-15-20-26
18.02.12: 87

New Zealand
21.03.93: **5**-6-7-7-7-16-19-31-21-28-30-38

Spain
29.03.93: peaked at no.**3**, charted for 10 weeks

Sweden
24.02.93: 16-10-**7**-16-38 (bi-weekly)

Switzerland
28.02.93: 23-**18**-19-20-26-25-23-29-24-32-40

Zimbabwe
8.05.93: peaked at no.**6**, charted for 11 weeks

I'm Every Woman was written by Nickolas Ashford and Valerie Simpson, and was originally recorded by Chaka Khan for her 1978 album, *CHAKA*, with backing vocals by Whitney & Cissy Houston.

Chaka Khan took *I'm Every Woman* to no.11 in the UK, no.15 in the Netherlands, no.16 in Ireland, no.18 in New Zealand, no.21 in the USA and no.37 in Australia.

I'm Every Woman
WHITNEY HOUSTON
from the soundtrack of the movie The Bodyguard.
Words & Music by Nickolas Ashford & Valerie Simpson.
Recorded by Whitney Houston on Arista
Published by Island Music Limited.
Piano/vocal arrangement
in easy key plus

Whitney recorded a version of the song for the soundtrack album, *THE BODYGUARD*, released in 1992. Towards the end of her version, Whitney paid tribute to Chaka Khan, by singing her name.

I'm Every Woman was Whitney's second single lifted from the soundtrack album. Unusually, it was released while Whitney's previous single, *I Will Always Love You*, was still no.1 in the States. The single hit no.1 on Billboard's Hot Dance Club Play chart, but only rose to no.4 on the Hot 100 and no.5 on the R&B chart.

Outside the USA, *I'm Every Woman* achieved no.2 in Belgium, Canada and Finland, no.3 in Spain, no.4 in Ireland, the Netherlands, the UK and USA, no.5 in Denmark and New Zealand, no.6 in Italy and Zimbabwe, no.7 in Sweden, no.10 in Australia and France, no.13 in Germany, no.18 in Switzerland and no.19 in Austria.

Whitney was clearly pregnant at the time the music video (daughter Bobbi Kristina was born on 4th March 1993), directed by Randee St. Nicholas, was filmed. As well as clips from the *The Bodyguard*, the video featured cameo appearances by Whitney's mother, Cissy, plus Chaka Khan and TLC.

Whitney was nominated for a Grammy for *I'm Every Woman*, for Best R&B Vocal Performance, Female, but the award went to Toni Braxton, for *Another Sad Love Song*.

Whitney performed *I'm Every Woman* at her trio of concerts for a new South Africa in November 1994. One of her performances was included on her posthumous CD/DVD, *LIVE – HER GREATEST HITS*, released in 2014.

Whitney, with Chaka Khan, performed *I'm Every Woman* at *VH1 Divas Live-2: An Honors Concert For VH1's Save The Music*, staged at New York's Beacon Theater on 13th April 1999, which aired live on TV in the States. She later reprised the song with Chaka Khan, Faith Hill, Brandy, Le Ann Rimes & Mary J. Blige, and both performances featured on the accompanying album and home video, *VH-1 DIVAS LIVE/99*, issued in November 1999.

22 ~ I Have Nothing

USA: Arista 12527 (1993).
B-side: *Where You Are*.

27.02.93: 42-23-11-9-6-**4-4-4-4-4**-5-5-9-9-16-26-33-42-51-53

UK: Arista 14614-7 (1993).
B-side: *All The Man That I Need*.

24.04.93: 9-**3-3**-6-11-18-28-39-57-71-80
25.02.12: 44

Australia
10.05.93: peaked at no.**30**, charted for 15 weeks
26.02.12: 47-68

Belgium
1.05.93: 42-22-22-**16**-18-26-28-30-50

Canada
13.03.93: 90-35-23-12-10-5-3-**1-1-1**-2-5-13-20-23-37-41-?

Denmark
14.05.93: **20**

France
28.08.93: 50
18.02.12: **29**

Germany
7.06.93: 51-54-**39**-57-57-63-81-92-82-89

Ireland
25.04.93: 8-**4**-5-8-14-12-21

Netherlands
15.05.93: 31-24-**23**-35
18.02.12: 48-88

New Zealand
25.04.93: 42-**20**-26-25-40-33-44

Spain
19.02.12: **23**

Switzerland
9.05.93: **39**-40
26.02.12: 69

Zimbabwe
17.04.93: peaked at no.**5**, charted for 12 weeks

I Have Nothing was written by David Foster and Linda Thompson, and was recorded by Whitney for the soundtrack album, *THE BODYGUARD*. It was Whitney's third single to be lifted from the album, but it couldn't match the success of the first two in most countries.

I Have Nothing did spend three weeks at no.1 in Canada, and charted at no.3 in the UK, no.4 in Ireland and the USA, no.5 in Zimbabwe, no.16 in Belgium, no.20 in Denmark and New Zealand, no.23 in the Netherlands and Spain, no.29 in France, no.30 in Australia, and no.39 in Germany and Switzerland.

I Have Nothing was nominated for an Academy Award, for Best Original Song, but the Oscar went to *A Whole New World*, written for *Aladdin* by Alan Menken and Tim Rice, and best known for the hit version by Peabo Bryson & Regina Belle.

The film version and a live performance of *I Have Nothing* featured on Whitney's 2017 album, *I WISH YOU LOVE: MORE FROM THE BODYGYARD*.

23 ~ Run To You

USA: Arista 12570 (1993).
  B-side: *After We Make Love*.

26.06.93: 83-60-49-**31-31-31-31-31**-37-43-49-49-61-63-67-69-73-76-90-99

UK: Arista 15333-7 (1993).
  B-side: *After We Make Love*.

31.07.93: 20-**15**-25-33-45-62
25.02.12: 67

Australia
2.08.93: peaked at no.**72**, charted for 4 weeks

Belgium
7.08.93: 32-**27**-39

Canada
10.07.93: 86-34-30-?-12-11-11-**10**-26-26-23-?-78-89

France
23.04.94: **47**
18.02.12: 55

Germany
30.08.93: **58-58**-62-64-62-65-79
24.02.12: 98

Ireland
8.08.93: **9**-20-19-25

Netherlands
31.07.93: **47-47**
18.02.12: 66

Spain
19.02.12: **44**

Run To You was written by Jud Friedman and Allan Rich, and was recorded by Whitney for the soundtrack album, *THE BODYGUARD*.

'The project was very wide open,' said Rich. 'It seemed like everyone and their mother was trying to place their songs with Whitney. Jud and I zeroed in on a specific scene towards the end of the film, which was a break-up type song, with the theme of "I love you, but you're going away" ... I was going through a break-up in my life at the time, which may have helped me write a lyric which reflected the feelings I was experiencing. I wrote the lyrics in a few days, then I presented the lyric to Jud (Friedman).'

'I thought Allan (Rich) wrote a beautiful lyric for *Run To You*,' said Friedman. 'It inspired me to run over to the keyboard and start writing the music. I wrote most of the music, then we finished the song together. When it was completed, we recorded a very simple demo, with just piano, guitar samples and strings. Then we brought in a wonderful vocalist, Valerie Pinkston, to sing the demo. She sang the song beautifully, and we were very happy with the way it came out.'

Allan Rich passed on the demo to his publisher, Carol Ware, who forwarded it to Arista's Gerry Griffith. He liked what he heard, so he played the demo for Clive Davis. Rich heard back from Davis via his answer phone.

'I got a wonderful phone message,' said Rich. 'I came home one day and the voice on the machine said, "I hope this is Allan Rich that I'm calling. This is Clive Davis, and I think you're going to like this message. Whitney and I love your song *Run To You*. Please call back as soon as possible". And I flipped out!'

Kevin Costner and Mick Jackson, the film's director, loved the song as well ~ but, a month later, Rich and Friedman received a phone call from Jackson.

'Jackson called,' said Friedman, 'and said, "We still love your song, but there's one little detail". Already my hands are starting to sweat. I'm bracing for the news. Jackson said, "We love the song so much, we want to use it earlier in the movie when they fall in love, instead of when they're breaking up. So could you change the lyric to make it a love song instead of a break-up song? It should be pretty easy, right?"

'My response was, no problem! Then we got off the phone and basically collapsed on the floor in shock. Our song-writing lives were passing before us.'

Rich and Friedman spoke to Clive Davis, who firmly believed their song was a hit. He advised they take a shot at re-writing the lyric, and suggested if the re-write didn't work, he might be able to use the song on a future Whitney project ~ her greatest hits album, maybe. But the re-write did work, and producer David Foster hired Friedman to do the programming and playing on the recording.

'It was on a Friday night that Whitney came into the studio,' recalled Friedman. 'It was great to meet her, and she was just a pleasure to work with. She was totally professional. Whitney actually had a cold that night, and her speaking voice was whispery and hoarse. But when she started singing, she sounded incredible. For Allan and I to be in the studio, to hear her sing our song so beautifully, it was one of the greatest moments in our lives.'

Run To You was the fourth of Whitney's songs to be lifted from *THE BODYGUARD* soundtrack, and it proved to be the least successful to date. It achieved no.9 in Ireland, no.10 in Canada, no.15 in the UK, no.27 in Belgium, no.31 in the USA, no.44 in Spain, and no.47 in France and the Netherlands.

Like *I Have Nothing*, *Run To You* was also nominated for an Academy Award, for Best Original Song, but the award went to *A Whole New World*.

'It was a fantastic time for us,' said Allan Rich. 'We went to the Academy Awards, the Academy Award Nominees luncheon, and the Grammy Awards … when they called my name, and I went to the podium to receive my nomination award, Carol (Ware) and I had tears in our eyes. We were both so happy.'

The film version and a live performance from The Bodyguard Tour of *Run To You* featured on Whitney's 2017 album, *I WISH YOU LOVE: MORE FROM THE BODYGYARD*.

24 ~ Queen Of The Night

USA: Arista 2650 (promo, 1993).
   Tracks: *Queen Of The Night (CJ's Single Edit)/(Album Version)*.

Queen Of The Night wasn't a hit in the USA.

UK: Arista 16930-7 (1993).
   Tracks: *Queen Of The Night (CJ's Single Edit)/(Album Version)*.

6.11.93: **14**-16-32-48-71-x-x-x-78-78-x-96

Australia
29.11.93: peaked at no.**80**, charted for 5 weeks

Belgium
20.11.93: 29-29-22-**20**-23-23-24-32-37

Canada
24.01.94: 73-43-40-39-**38**-64-79

France
1.01.94: **47**

Germany
13.12.93: 66-**64**-68-68-69-72-76-73-92-81

Ireland
7.11.93: 27-**26**-30

Netherlands
6.11.93: 38-25-**21**-32-46

Switzerland
21.11.93: 40-39-40-**36**-40

Queen Of The Night was co-written by Whitney with Babyface, L.A. Reid and Daryl Simmons, and was recorded by Whitney for the soundtrack album, *THE BODYGUARD*.

Queen of the Night was the fifth Whitney single released from *The Bodyguard*, and it gave Whitney her first hit as a credited songwriter. However, as it was only released as a promo single in the USA, chart rules at the time meant it wasn't eligible to enter the Hot 100, as it hadn't been commercially released. It did, however, hit no.1 on Billboard's Hot Dance Club Play chart, and gain enough airplay to rise to no.36 on Billboard's Hot 100 Airplay chart and no.47 on the R&B Airplay chart.

Elsewhere, *Queen Of The Night* more or less matched the success of *Run To You* in most other countries. It achieved no.14 in the UK, no.20 in Belgium, no.21 in the Netherlands, no.26 in Ireland, no.36 in Switzerland, no.38 in Canada and no.47 in France.

The film version and a live performance from The Bodyguard Tour of *Queen Of The Night* featured on Whitney's 2017 album, *I WISH YOU LOVE: MORE FROM THE BODYGYARD*.

25 ~ Something In Common

USA: MCA MCA5P 2912 (promo, 1994).
  Tracks: *Something In Common (Radio Edit w/out Rap)/(Quiet Storm w/out Rap)*.

Something In Common wasn't a hit in the USA.

UK: MCA MCSTD 1957 (1994).
  Tracks: *Something In Common (Radio Edit)/(Extended Vocal Version)/(Quiet Storm Version)/(Dub Version)*.

22.01.94: **16-16**-17-50-74

Australia
28.03.94: peaked at no.**87**, charted for 5 weeks

Canada
27.11.93: 68-?-45-42-31-31-**26-26**-41-60-60-67-97

Germany
7.03.94: **58**-63-63-65-71-71-68-81-75-81

Netherlands
19.02.94: 48-**40**-44

New Zealand
6.03.94: 34-38-**33**-39

Switzerland
27.02.94: **41**-43-42-42-43-x-44

Zimbabwe
13.02.94: peaked at no.**5**, charted for 6 weeks

Whitney co-wrote *Something In Common* with Bobby Brown, Teddy Riley and Bernard Belle, and recorded it as a duet with Bobby for his 1992 album, *BOBBY*. The track was recorded in Atlanta, Georgia, in September 1991, shortly after Whitney and Bobby became engaged.

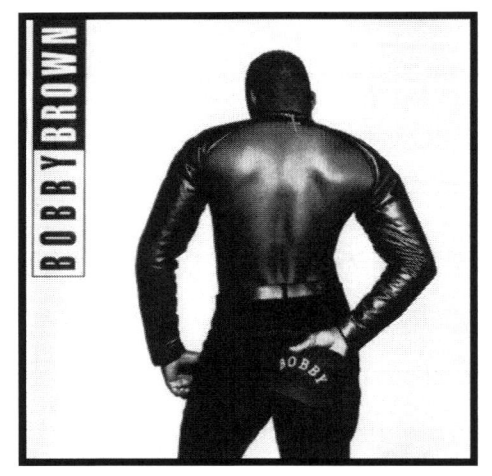

Like *Queen Of The Night*, *Something In Common* was only issued as a promo in the USA, so it wasn't eligible to enter Billboard's Hot 100.

Outside the USA, *Something In Common* was a hit, but not a major hit, charting at no.5 in Zimbabwe, no.16 in the UK, no.26 in Canada, no.33 in New Zealand, no.40 in the Netherlands and no.41 in Switzerland.

Whitney and Bobby performed *Something In Common* on her The Bodyguard World Tour in 1993-94, and at her concerts in Bangkok, Taipei & Hawaii in May 1997, part of her Pacific Rim Tour.

The couple also performed *Something In Common*, as a medley with *My Love*, at the *VH1 Diva Duets: An Honors Concert For VH1's Save The Music* show, staged at the MGM Grand in Las Vegas, Nevada, on 22nd May 2003, which aired live in the United States.

26 ~ Exhale (Shoop Shoop)

USA: Arista 12885 (1995).
  B-side: *Dancin' On The Smooth Edge.*

25.11.95: **1**-2-2-2-2-2-2-2-2-2-2-2-3-8-8-11-14-18-31-40-45

UK: Arista 32754-7 (1995).
  Tracks: *Dancin' On The Smooth Edge/It Isn't, It Wasn't, It Ain't Never Gonna Be.*

18.11.95: **11**-16-19-26-40-49-44-56-73-85-94

Australia
11.12.95: peaked at no.**19**, charted for 17 weeks

Austria
3.12.95: 27-20-**15**-21-21-24-30-27-34-36-38

Belgium
25.11.95: **22**-29-35-27-23-25-29-30-32-30

Canada
13.11.95: 90-80-53-36-14-10-10-10-**1-1**-2-2-8-8-12-?-?-?-12-12-14-23-35-53-71-96

Denmark
17.11.95: 13-8-13-17-18-x-11-**6**-8-12-12-13-14-15

EXHALE
(Shoop Shoop)

WHITNEY HOUSTON

Warner Chappell Music

Finland
11.11.95: **6**-9-12
13.01.97: 11

France
11.11.95: 37-43-42-26-30-40-36-35-30-25-31-30-24-**23**-28-40-44

Germany
20.11.95: 41-68-27-**26**-28-35-35-38-42-47-49-50-54-55-62-72-78

Ireland
9.11.95: 24-**16**-17-22-30

Italy
7.11.95: peaked at no.**5**, charted for 14 weeks

Japan
11.12.95: peaked at no.**61**, charted for 4 weeks

Netherlands
18.11.95: 30-16-13-**12**-17-24-24-24-27-31

New Zealand
3.12.95: 5-**4**-7-8-8-8-8-14-11-16-22-27-39-28-46-45-44

Norway
30.12.95: 18-**14-14**-16-17

Spain
6.11.95: peaked at no.**1** (2 wks), charted for 4 weeks

Sweden
17.11.95: 18-**10**-11-11-21-20-20-21-23-24-30-41-59-49

Switzerland
10.12.95: 16-14-15-**13**-16-19-26-23-27-27-32-26-43-43-49

Zimbabwe
8.01.96: peaked at no.**1** (1), charted for 23 weeks

Exhale (Shoop Shoop) was written by Babyface, and was recorded by Whitney for the soundtrack album, *WAITING TO EXHALE*, released in 1995.

 'When Whitney first heard the song,' said Babyface, 'she figured I'd lost it ~ I couldn't come up with words anymore. And actually, she's right. I couldn't think of anything for that particular part. It felt like it should groove there, but I knew it couldn't groove without any vocals. So I started humming along with it, and that's what happened. The 'shoops' came. But they felt so good, I thought, why not? It doesn't have to mean anything.'

Exhale (Shoop Shoop) was the lead single released from the *WAITING TO EXHALE* soundtrack, and became only the third single to debut on the Hot 100 in the United States at no.1 (Michael Jackson's *You Are Not Alone* was the first). It spent a solitary week at the top, followed by a record breaking 11 weeks at no.2, behind Boyz II Men & Mariah Carey's *One Sweet Day*.

The single also topped the chart in Canada, Spain and Zimbabwe, and charted at no.4 in New Zealand, no.5 in Italy, no.6 in Denmark and Finland, no.10 in Sweden, no.11 in the UK, no.12 in the Netherlands, no.13 in Switzerland, no.14 in Norway, no.15 in Austria, no.16 in Ireland, no.19 in Australia, no.22 in Belgium, no.23 in France and no.26 in Germany.

Exhale (Shoop Shoop) picked up one Grammy Award, for Best R&B Song, but lost out in a further three categories: Song Of The Year, Best Song Written for a Motion Picture Television or other Visual Media and Best R&B Vocal Performance, Female.

27 ~ Count On Me

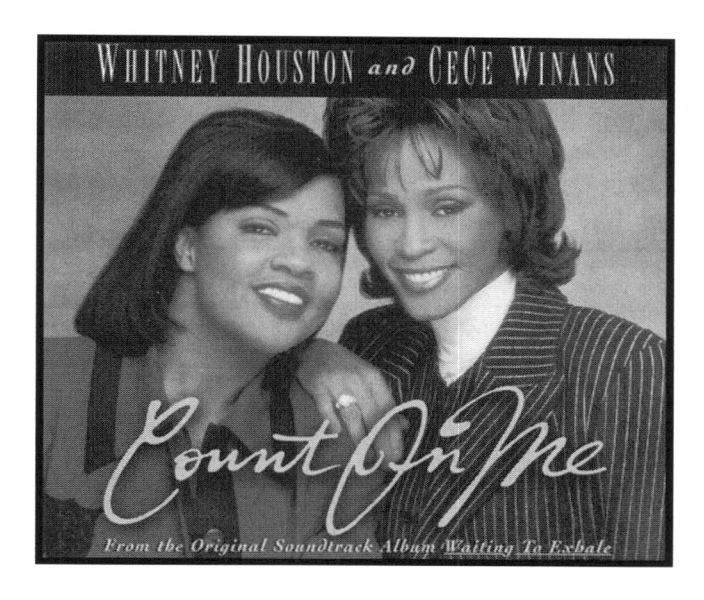

USA: Arista 12976 (1996).
  B-side: *One Moment In Time*.

23.03.96: 32-19-16-14-10-9-**8**-**8**-9-**8**-9-17-25-34-39-44-49-51-61-66

UK: Arista 34584-2 (1996).
  Tracks: *Exhale (Shoop Shoop)/Run To You*.

24.02.96: **12**-18-26-37-44-71-92-x-x-x-x-x-92-x-83

Australia
25.03.96: peaked at no.**72**, charted for 8 weeks

Austria
24.03.96: **28**

Canada
8.04.96: 79-70-60-56-50-50-49-36-**26**-27-39-54-71-96

Germany
11.03.96: 97-96-**75**-83-82-78-82-95

Netherlands
2.03.96: 42-38-**34**-38

New Zealand
14.04.96: 42-42-28-**26**-28-37-46

Switzerland
24.03.96: **31**-38-x-35

Count On Me, like *Exhale (Shoop Shoop)*, was co-written by Whitney with Babyface and Michael Houston for the film, *Waiting To Exhale*. Whitney recorded the song as a duet with CeCe Winans, and it was the second track to credit Whitney to be released from the soundtrack album.

While it couldn't match the success of *Exhale (Shoop Shoop)*, *Count On Me* did achieve Top 10 status on the Hot 100 in the United States, rising to no.8. Elsewhere, the single charted at no.12 in the UK, no.26 in Canada and New Zealand, no.28 in Austria, no.31 in Switzerland and no.34 in the Netherlands.

Count On Me picked up two Grammy nominations, for Best Pop Collaboration with Vocals and Best Song Written for a Motion Picture, Television or other Visual Media, but won neither. The awards went to Natalie & Nat 'King' Coles *When I Fall In Love* and Dianne Warren's *Because You Loved Me*, a hit for Celiné Dion from *Up Close & Personal*, respectively.

28 ~ Why Does It Hurt So Bad

USA: Arista 13214 (1996).
Tracks: *Why Does It Hurt So Bad (Album Version)/(Live Version)/I Wanna Dance With Somebody (Who Loves Me) (Junior's Happy Hand Bag Mix)/(Junior's X-Beat Dub).*

3.08.96: 60-38-38-36-**26**-29-30-30-34-46-56-65-68-72-80-81-87-87-84-84

UK: Not Released.

Australia
16.09.96: peaked at no.**94**, charted for 5 weeks

Canada
22.07.96: 98-91-86-80-76-69-?-56-**45-45**-58-93

Why Does It Hurt So Bad was the third single to credit Whitney, which was written by Babyface, for the film, *Waiting To Exhale*.

Unlike *Exhale (Shoop Shoop)* and *Count On Me*, *Why Does It Hurt So Bad* wasn't released as a single in Europe, but it was issued in North America, Australasia, South Africa and Japan. The single rose to no.26 in the Hot 100 in the United States, but failed to enter the Top 40 in Canada, where it stalled at no.45.

A live version of *Why Does It Hurt So Bad* was included on the American CD single. This was recorded when Whitney performed at the MTV Movie Awards on 8th June 1996. This performance was also among the special features included on her 2000 home video, *THE GREATEST HITS*, and was used to promote the single, in the absence of a specially made music video.

29 ~ Step By Step

USA: Arista 13313 (1997).
  Tracks: *Step By Step (Tony Moran Remix)/(Junior's Arena Anthem Mix)/(Soul Soluntion Diva Vocal)/(K-Klassic Remix)/(Teddy Riley Remix).*

15.03.97: 22-**15**-17-17-22-31-37-43-56-60-65-80-79-86-88-97-100

UK: Arista 44933-2 (1996).
  Tracks: *Step By Step (Album Version)/(Teddy Riley Remix)/(K-Klassic Mix).*

21.12.96: 17-15-15-**13**-18-17-16-22-26-25-37-41-63-87

Australia
20.01.97: peaked at no.**11**, charted for 15 weeks

Austria
12.01.97: 33-32-15-10-8-**6**-8-**6-6**-10-8-9-18-13-19-27

Belgium
28.12.96: 47-27-37-35-21-15-19-20-**13-13-13**-17-39-44-41-43

Canada
3.03.97: 89-77-71-66-43-37-29-25-**23**-30-40-59-62-79

Denmark
20.12.96: 14-7-**6-6-6-6**-7-11-12-13-15-14-14-20

Finland
18.01.97: 12-**11**

France
18.01.97: 36-42-40-34-34-33-**30**-32-47-38

Germany
16.12.96: 67-41-41-34-28-20-10-**8-8**-10-9-11-13-15-17-18-20-29-32-42-50-54-55

Ireland
2.01.97: 26-19-**14**-17-19-19-23-23-29

Italy
7.01.97: peaked at no.**14**, charted for 4 weeks

Netherlands
21.12.96: 75-53-52-40-27-20-17-**13**-16-18-18-18-19-23-24-31-38-49-64-74-78-81-95

New Zealand
16.02.97: 49-x-**46**-49

Spain
6.01.97: peaked at no.**3**, charted for 3 weeks

Sweden
20.12.96: 45-36-34-20-18-**15**-34-27-37-47-46-52

Switzerland
2.02.97: 20-20-19-**15-15**-21-19-19-20-26-31-33-42-49-43

Step By Step was written and originally recorded by Annie Lennox, and featured on the B-side of her 1992 solo single, *Precious*.

With some new lyrics, and with Annie Lennox contributing backing vocals, Whitney recorded *Step By Step* for the 1996 film, *The Preacher's Wife*, which saw Whitney playing the title role. Two versions, including a remix by Teddy Riley, featured on the accompanying soundtrack album.

Outside North America and Australasia, *Step By Step* was chosen as the lead single from *THE PREACHER'S WIFE*. It achieved no.3 in Spain, no.6 in Austria and Denmark, no.8 in Germany, no.11 in Finland, no.13 in Belgium, the Netherlands and the UK, no.14 in Ireland and Italy, no.15 in Sweden and Switzerland, no.30 in France and no.46 in New Zealand.

In North America and Australasia, the lead single from *THE PREACHER'S WIFE* was *I Believe In You And Me*, with *Step By Step* issued as the follow-up. *Step By Step* rose to no.15 on the Hot 100 in the USA, and peaked at no.11 in Australia and no.23 in Canada.

30 ~ I Believe In You And Me

USA: Arista 13293 (1996).
  B-side: *Step By Step*.

28.12.96: 7-6-5-5-5-**4**-5-6-7-11-11-15-26-37-45-44-52-54-59-59

UK: Arista 46715-2 (1997).
  Tracks: *Step By Step (Radio Remix)/(K-Klassic Mix)*.

29.03.97: **16**-33-53-61-73-95

Australia
14.04.97: peaked at no.**48**, charted for 7 weeks

Canada
10.02.97: 83-71-69-65-**59**-94

Germany
19.05.97: **98**

Netherlands
22.03.97: 89-76-**74**-76-80-82-84-81-86

Sweden
4.04.97: **46**-59

I Believe In You And Me was written by Sandy Linzer and David Wolfert, and was originally recorded by the Four Tops for their 1982 album, ONE MORE MOUNTAIN.

Whitney recorded a cover of *I Believe In You And Me* for the 1996 soundtrack album, THE PREACHER'S WIFE ~ she also co-produced the recording with Mervyn Warren. Two versions of the song, including the single version, were featured on the album; the single version was produced by David Foster.

In North America and Australasia, *I Believe In You And Me* was chosen as the lead single from THE PREACHER'S WIFE, and gave Whitney a no.4 hit on the Hot 100 in the United States. The single was less successful in Canada and Australia, where it struggled to no.59 and no.48, respectively.

In most other countries, *I Believe In You And Me* was issued as the follow-up to *Step By Step*, but it failed to match the success of its predessessor. *I Believe In You And Me* charted at no.16 in the UK and no.46 in Sweden, but it was only a minor hit in Germany and Netherlands, and didn't chart at all in many countries.

31 ~ When You Believe

USA: Dreamworks/Arista/Columbia 59022 (1998).
  Tracks: *When You Believe (Album Version)/(Instrumental)*.

5.12.98: 51-53-53-56-64-72-64-25-**15-15**-18-22-24-31-43-50-65

UK: Columbia 666520-2 (1998).
  Tracks: *When You Believe (Album Version)/(TV Track)/I Am Free* (Mariah Carey)/
    You Were Loved.

19.12.98: **4**-14-17-19-23-32-38-43-53-60-67-77-79-86-68-70
29.12.07: 65

Australia
7.12.98: peaked at no.**12**, charted for 19 weeks

Austria
13.12.98: 25-19-16-16-18-17-14-9-10-7-7-8-**6**-7-13-15-14-15-20-26

Belgium
5.12.98: 31-21-17-6-6-**5**-6-7-8-8-10-15-13-15-25-29-38-46-46

Canada
7.12.98: ?-?-?-?-55-48-**20**-65-93-?-?-?-59-74-94-77

Denmark
11.12.98: 18-12-12-12-12-11-10-8-10-10-**7-7**-11-14-14-19

Finland
2.01.99: **10**

France
5.12.98: 14-8-**5**-6-7-10-6-6-8-8-8-10-22-34-51-56-56-65-78-90
18.02.12: 90

Germany
14.12.98: 20-16-12-12-10-9-9-10-**8**-11-16-15-17-20-24-25-32-41-55-75

Ireland
10.12.98: 12-14-13-10-9-8-**7**-9-13-21-24-38

Italy
15.12.98: peaked at no.**4**, charted for 11 weeks

Japan
7.12.98: peaked at no.**45**, charted for 8 weeks

Netherlands
5.12.98: 54-17-7-**4-4**-5-6-9-10-14-14-15-22-29-35-42-52-61-69-74-83

New Zealand
7.02.99: 21-**8**-9-12-11-21-26-32-x-41

Norway
27.12.97: 3-5-3-3-**2-2-2-2**-4-3-4-5-13-12-19

Spain
21.12.98: peaked at no.**2**, charted for 5 weeks

Sweden
10.02.98: 9-4-4-4-3-**2-2-2**-5-4-6-6-7-16-18-23-25-29-44-51

Switzerland
13.12.98: 7-6-3-3-3-3-3-**2**-3-**2-2**-3-3-3-6-8-11-16-20-31-47-49-49

When You Believe was written by Stephen Schwartz, and was recorded by Whitney as a duet with Mariah Carey for the soundtrack album, *THE PRINCE OF EGYPT*. The duet also featured on Whitney's album, *MY LOVE IS YOUR LOVE*, and Mariah's compilation, *#1's*, both released in 1998.

In *The Prince Of Egypt*, *When You Believe* was performed by Michelle Pfeiffer and Sally Dworsky, with Whitney and Mariah's version playing over the film's closing credits. Whitney and Mariah recorded their duet on 7th August 1998 in New York.

'Jeffrey Katzenberg from Dreamworks showed us both the movie separately,' said Mariah Carey, 'and got us both excited about the project. It's sort of a message song. It's what *Prince Of Egypt* is about. Moses. If we were ever going to come together on any kind of record, this is definitely the right one, and really the coolest thing to me is that after all the drama and everybody making it like we had a rivalry, she (Whitney) was just really cool, and we had a really good time in the studio.'

'I thought, Wow! What an incredible idea,' said Whitney, explaining her reaction to Katzenberg's proposal. 'I love inspirational songs that mean something and I don't think they could have chosen two better people, two better voices, to come together and do it … singing with a voice like Mariah's, it can only be complementary, because the girl can go … I really enjoyed working with her, and we had a great relationship. I'd love to work with her in the future. We talked a lot of crap, a lot about what we can do together as two forces in the music industry, and being women, it makes it even more potent.'

'I don't know where this whole rivalry thing came from,' said Babyface, who produced *When You Believe*. 'I admit, when I agreed to do the song, I was nervous about it, but when we all got together we just laughed! The two of them were … almost awe-struck in each other's presence. We had a great time. They both gave it everything they had, and at times I was blown away by the sheer power of their voices together. At times they were giggling together like schoolgirls, and talking about what direction they wanted the song to go. I think, and I don't know if they want me saying this, but I think they were surprised by how much they had in common.'

Whitney admitted, when she arrived for the recording session, she didn't know the song at all. 'I just said, "Face, I don't know nothing". But 'Face and I go way back. When we do a record, we can do it in a couple of hours. It's like a partnership, a sister and brother kind of thing.'

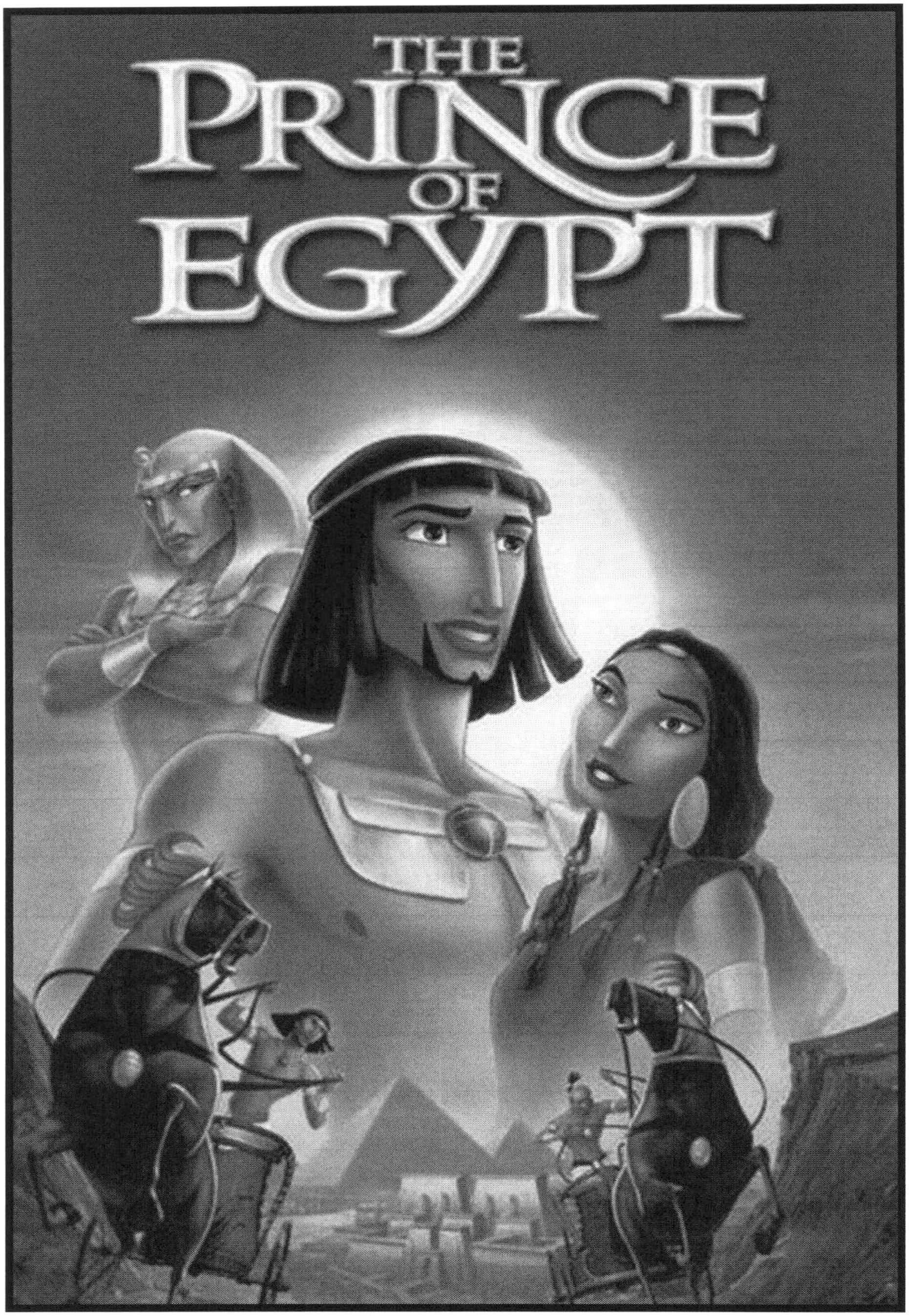
THE
PRINCE
OF
EGYPT

To avoid any conflict over who should have top billing, it was agreed Whitney would be named first on the North American release, and Mariah would be named first on the European release. The music video was filmed at the Brooklyn Academy Of Music; it featured both Whitney & Mariah, with a setting inspired by the film's Egyptian theme.

In the United States, despite all the hype surrounding the pairing of Whitney and Mariah, the single stalled at no.15 on the Hot 100 and no.33 on the R&B chart, and it peaked at no.20 in Canada.

Outside North America, the single generally performed much better, hitting no.2 in Norway, Spain, Sweden and Switzerland, no.4 in Italy, the Netherlands and the UK, no.5 in Belgium and France, no.6 in Austria, no.7 in Denmark and Ireland, no.8 in Germany and New Zealand, no.10 in Finland, no.12 in Australia and no.45 in Japan.

When You Believe went on to win an Academy Award for writer Stephen Schwartz, for Best Original Song. Controversially, Schwartz left Babyface's name off the submission sheet for the Academy, even though Babyface had added additional music to the Whitney/Mariah version, compared with the film version. Academy rules stated only one version of a song may be nominated.

'It wasn't that I was angry, I was just hurt,' said Babyface. 'It's my problem. I just hope the Academy will now look at changing the rules.'

Despite the controversy, Whitney and Mariah were permitted to perform their version of the song at the awards ceremony, staged at the Los Angeles County Music Center on 21st March 1999. Schwartz wasn't able to attend the ceremony, to pick up his Oscar, as he was in New York, rehearsing for a show.

Whitney and Mariah's performance at the awards ceremony was included on Whitney's posthumous DVD (but not accompanying CD), *LIVE – HER GREATEST PERFORMANCES*, released in 2014.

When You Believe also picked up a Golden Globe nomination, for Best Original Song, but lost out to *The Prayer*, from the film, *Quest For Camelot*.

When You Believe also failed to win either of the two Grammy Awards it was nominated for: Best Pop Collaboration with Vocals and Best Song Written for a Motion Picture, Television or other Visual Media. The awards went to Rob Thomas & Santana's *Smooth* and Madonna's *Beautiful Stranger*, from *Austin Powers: The Spy Why Shagged Me*, respectively.

Whitney performed *When You Believe* with Mariah Carey, when they appeared on *The Oprah Winfrey Show* on 25th November 1998. This was their first TV performance of the song, and they also talked about the song's recording.

Whitney and Mariah also co-hosted *The Prince Of Egypt TV Special*, which aired on WNBC TV in the States, on 13th December 1998. As well as talking about the film and songs, the special also saw the first showing of an alternate version of the *When You Believe* music video.

A cover of *When You Believe*, by *The X-Factor* winner Leon Jackson, hit no.1 in the UK in 2007. The track also featured on his debut album, *RIGHT NOW*, as a bonus track.

'I didn't include it on the album proper,' said Jackson, 'because it was then and this is now. It was made for four people who could have been the winner of *X-Factor*, and I did the best I could with it.'

32 ~ Heartbreak Hotel

USA: Arista 13619 (1998).
   Tracks: *Heartbreak Hotel (Original Radio Mix)/(Dance Mix)/It's Not Right But It's Okay (Dance Mix)*.

26.12.98: 84-77-73-77-58-55-29-7-4-3-3-3-**2-2-2**-5-5-6-6-7-7-8-11-15-23-26-34-44

UK: Arista 820572-2 (2000).
   Tracks: *Heartbreak Hotel (R.I.P. Radio Edit)/(Undadoggz Radio Edit)/(Album Version)/ (Undadoggz Club Rub Part 1)*.

30.12.00: 26-**25**-36-53-65-84-81-86

Australia
7.06.99: peaked at no.**16**, charted for 19 weeks

Canada
5.04.99: 71-60-37-18-**16**-24-25-28-29-22-31-37-39-52-65-72-77-96

France
20.03.99: 10-**7-7**-11-14-19-20-32-35-42-57-54-62-69-71-96
18.02.12: 96

Germany
19.03.01: **61**-85-83-91

Ireland
21.12.00: 43-**41**

Netherlands
23.12.00: 95-95-**41**-45-55-57-68-81

New Zealand
11.04.99: **33**-38-34-40-39-50

Switzerland
7.01.01: **77**-95-94-87-84

Heartbreak Hotel was written by C. Schack, K. Karlin and T. Savage, and was recorded by Whitney with Faith Evans and Kelly Price for her 1998 album, *MY LOVE IS YOUR LOVE*.

'These artists (Faith Evans & Kelly Price) can sing,' said Whitney. 'As for the title, I've stayed in that place before, but I checked out.'

'Working with Whitney was a lot of fun,' said Kelly Price. 'It was a great experience to carry me throughout the rest of my career. She gave me a lot of good advice.'

According to Whitney, *Heartbreak Hotel* is 'basically talking about the destruction of the world for the most part, and when it all ends. When it all comes right down to it, somehow we're all intertwined, in some way or another. Every human being is intertwined. So my love is your love and yours is mine ... we're still here, everybody. Black, white, green, yellow ~ we're all still loving here together. So we're doing something right, I think.'

Heartbreak Hotel was released as the follow-up to *When You Believe* in North America, Australasia and some continental European countries. The single spent three weeks at no.2 on the Hot 100 in the USA, and achieved no.7 in France, no.16 in Australia and Canada, and no.33 in New Zealand.

Elsewhere, including the UK, *Heartbreak Hotel* wasn't issued as a single until nearly two years after its North American release. Bizarrely, in the UK it was released just a week after it was the lead track on Whitney's *GREATEST HITS PREVIEW* CD, a freebie given away with the *Mail On Sunday* newspaper. Around two million free copies were given away, seriously damaging the single's sales potential, so not surprisingly it peaked at a lowly no.25.

Around the same time, *Heartbreak Hotel* charted at no.41 in Ireland and the Netherlands, and was a minor hit in Germany and Switzerland.

Heartbreak Hotel received two Grammy Award nominations, for Best R&B Song and Best R&B Performance by a Duo or Group with Vocal, but in both categories the award went to TLC's *No Scrubs*.

33 ~ It's Not Right But It's Okay

USA: Arista 13680 (1999).
   Tracks: *It's Not Right But It's Okay (Rodney Jerkins Smooth Mix)/(Rodney Jerkins Smooth Mix Instrumental)/(Thunderpuss 2000 Radio Mix)/(Club 69 Radio Mix)/(Club 69 Future Mix)/(Club 69 Future Dub)/I Will Always Love You (Hex Hector Club Mix).*

8.05.99: 87-71-50-50-32-21-17-11-**4**-5-7-7-9-11-12-13-17-25-40-41

UK: Arista 65240-2 (1999).
   Tracks: *It's Not Right But It's Okay (Original Radio Mix)/(Club 69 Club Mix)/(Johnny Vicious Radio Mix).*

6.03.99: **3**-5-6-7-12-18-21-19-24-29-35-38-41-58-65-83
25.02.12: 61

Australia
22.03.99: peaked at no.**76**, charted for 5 weeks

Austria
18.04.99: 27-27-21-25-21-**20**-21-25-28

Belgium
3.04.99: 50-45-45-41-**40**

Canada
05.99: peaked at no.**3**

France
21.11.99: 57-34-24-22-24-**21**-25-25-31-35-37-43-51-56-73-84-91
18.02.12: 97

Germany
1.03.99: 88-36-35-17-**14**-15-16-17-20-25-26-30-31-43-50-64-70

Ireland
25.02.99: 37-31-27-**21**-22-27-27-28-29-33

Italy
20.04.99: peaked at no.**18**, charted for 4 weeks

Netherlands
6.03.99: 68-25-16-14-**12**-16-19-24-27-28-31-37-40-43-53-68-80

Spain
13.03.99: 2-3-8-**1**-3-6-7-10-x-9-9-15-17

Sweden
25.02.99: 36-20-14-**12**-14-17-19-19-22-28-33-37-42

Switzerland
28.03.99: 24-25-24-22-24-**18**-19-27-41-37-37-38-44-43-47-47-49-45-49-36-42

It's Not Right But It's Okay was written by Rodney Jerkins, Fred Jerkins III, LaShawn Daniels, Isaac Phillips and Toni Estes, and was recorded by Whitney for her 1998 album, *MY LOVE IS YOUR LOVE*.

The track was originally released as the B-side of *Heartbreak Hotel* in the United States, which preceded it as a single. Despite this, *It's Not Right But It's Okay* rose to no.4 on the Hot 100, and hit no.1 on Billboard's Hot Dance Club Play chart.

In most other countries, *It's Not Right But It's Okay* was chosen as the follow-up to *When You Believe*. The single went to no.1 in Spain, and charted at no.3 in Canada and the UK, no.12 in the Netherlands and Sweden, no.14 in Germany, no.18 in Italy and Switzerland, no.20 in Austria, no.21 in France and Ireland, and no.40 in Belgium.

Whitney performed *It's Not Right But It's Okay* on *VH-1 Divas Live 2: An Honors Concert For VH-1's Save The Music*, staged at New York's Beacon Theater on 13th April 1999, which aired live on TV in the USA. Whitney's performance was omitted from the accompanying album and home video, *VH-1 DIVAS LIVE/99*, issued in November 1999, but it was later made available to download from US iTunes.

During a promotional visit to Europe, Whitney performed *It's Not Right But It's Okay* on a number of different TV shows, including:

- *The Surprise Show*, a Dutch TV show, on 8th February 1999.
- *C'era Un Ragazzo*, an Italian TV show, on 11th February 1999.
- *Sorpresa, Sorpresa*, a Spanish TV show, on 13th February.
- The BRIT Awards in London on 16th February 1999.
- *Sen Kväll Med Luuk*, a Swedish TV show, which aired on 18th February 1999.
- *Top Of The Pops*, filmed at Elstree Studios, London, on 19th February 1999, and aired at a later date.
- *Wetten Dass…?*, the popular German TV show, on 20th February 1999.

Whitney won another Grammy Award for *It's Not Right But It's Okay*, for Best R&B Vocal Performance, Female.

Like *Heartbreak Hotel*, *It's Not Right But It's Okay* also picked up a Grammy nomination for Best R&B Song, but the award went to TLC's *No Scrubs*.

THE FIRST SINGLE BECAME AN ACADEMY AWARD WINNING SONG.

THE SECOND SINGLE REIGNED AT #1 FOR 7 CONSECUTIVE WEEKS.

NOW COMES THE THIRD OFF-THE-HOOK SINGLE, AND IT'S ALL HER.

Whitney Houston
it's not right but it's okay

From her critically-acclaimed Double Platinum new album, *My Love Is Your Love*.

The New York Times reviewing *VH-1 Divas Live '99*, the highest rated show in VH-1's history, said: "Ms. Houston recognized no obstacles. On "It's Not Right But It's OK," she made every sound bite register. On "Ain't No Way," both Whitney & Mary J. Blige let loose, their voices entwining and rippling through the octaves. Then Ms. Houston reclaimed "I Will Always Love You" making its virtuoso flourishes heartfelt. On every song giving her room, she was invincible."

ARISTA
www.arista.com

34 ~ My Love Is Your Love

USA: Arista 13730 (1999).
  Tracks: *My Love Is Your Love (Album Version)/(Wyclef Remix)/(Jonathan Peters' Radio Mix)*.

4.09.99: 81-68-44-16-11- 9-8-7-8-7-8-8-6-6-5-5-5-**4-4**-6-10-10-11-20-22-27-34-49

UK: Arista 67286-2 (1999).
  Tracks: *My Love Is Your Love (Radio Edit)/(Wyclef Remix)/(Marvel & Eily Vocal Mix)*.

3.07.99: **2**-4-4-7-6-8-11-10-16-27-46-64-76-96
25.02.12: 42

Australia
4.10.99: peaked at no.**25**, charted for 11 weeks

Austria
20.06.99: 39-33-9-8-3-**2-2-2**-3-3-**2-2-2-2**-3-4-4-9-11-14-18-20-25-27

Belgium
3.07.99: 34-25-17-9-6-5-**3-3-3-3-3**-5-10-10-11-18-20-26-40-48

Canada
09.99: peaked at no.**10**

Denmark
9.07.99: 16-9-6-6-7-8-7-6-**5**-6-6-9-13-18

Finland
24.07.99: 19-13-**12**-13

France
10.07.99: 45-22-22-17-18-15-14-11-11-12-13-**10**-16-14-16-26-26-31-34-31-46-50-63-86-90-97
18.02.12: 52

Germany
14.06.99: 39-14-5-4-**2-2-2-2**-4-4-4-4-5-4-5-7-9-13-17-23-29-42-44-54-63
24.02.12: 64

Ireland
24.06.99: 6-4-**2-2-2**-4-5-8-14
16.02.12: 80-97

Italy
22.06.99: peaked at no.**36**, charted for 2 weeks

Netherlands
10.07.99: 6-5-3-**2**-3-3-4-4-6-8-10-19-21-28-29-32-39-49-58-67-68-66-74-78
18.02.12: 80

New Zealand
15.08.99: 5-6-**1**-3-5-6-9-12-11-12-23-36-39-46-44-46

Norway
10.07.99: 19-x-18-17-14-12-5-**4**-8-11-15-16

Spain
19.06.99: 20-x-**13**-15
19.02.12: 33

Sweden
10.06.99: 24-9-6-**2-2**-3-4-3-4-5-8-14-16-17-22-25-29-29-42

Switzerland
20.06.99: 12-9-7-4-3-3-**2**-3-3-3-3-3-3-3-3-3-3-5-6-8-12-15-20-24-24-31-44-50-39-58-64-67-68-80-86
26.02.12: 66

Whitney Houston
my love is your love

My Love Is Your Love was written by Wyclef Jean and Jerry Duplessis, and was recorded by Whitney for her similarly titled 1998 album.

Released as the follow-up to *It's Not Right But It's Okay*, *My Love Is Your Love* proved to be the album's most successful single to date. It gave Whitney her third straight no.1 on Billboard's Hot Dance Club Play chart in the United States, where it also charted at no.2 on the R&B chart and no.4 on the Hot 100.

My Love Is Your Love hit no.1 in New Zealand, and achieved no.2 in several countries, including Austria, Germany, Ireland, the Netherlands, Sweden, Switzerland and the UK. Elsewhere, the single charted at no.3 in Belgium, no.4 in Norway, no.5 in Denmark, no.10 in Canada and France, no.12 in Finland, no.13 in Spain, no.25 in Australia and no.36 in Italy.

Whitney promoted *My Love Is Your Love* at a number of high profile events or on TV shows, including:

- *The Rosie O'Donnell Show*, with brother Gary backing her, on 23rd November 1998.
- *The David Letterman Show*, with Wyclef Jean, on 10th December 1998. This performance was included on Whitney's posthumous CD/DVD, *LIVE – HER GREATEST PERFORMANCES*, released in 2014.
- *The NBC Today Show* on 11th December 1998.
- American Music Awards, with Wyclef Jean & Babyface, as a medley with *Until You Come Back*, on 11th January 1999.
- *Top Of The Pops* ~ filmed on 19th February 1999, but aired at a later date.
- *The Oprah Winfrey Show* on 21st June 1999.

Whitney performed *My Love Is Your Love* at *VH-1 Divas Live 2: An Honors Concert For VH1's Save The Music*, staged at New York's Beacon Theater on 13th April 1999. But, like *It's Not Right But It's Okay*, *My Love Is Your Love* was omitted from the accompanying album and home video, *VH-1 DIVAS LIVE/99*, issued in November 1999, but was later made available to download from US iTunes.

Whitney's performance of *My Love Is Your Love* in Mannheim, Germany, on 25th August 1999, was among the special features included on her 2000 home video, *THE GREATEST HITS*.

Whitney performed *My Love Is Your Love* with Bobby Brown, Deborah Cox and Monica, when she headlined a show at the Shrine Auditorium, Los Angeles, on 10th April 2000, to celebrate Arista Record's 25th anniversary.

My Love Is Your Love is generally cited as Whitney's no.3 best-selling single globally, after *I Will Always Love You* and *I Wanna Dance With Somebody (Who Loves Me)*.

35 ~ I Learned From The Best

USA: Arista 13790 (2000).
   Tracks: *I Learned From The Best (Original Version)/(HQ2 Uptempo Remix)/(Junior Vasquez Disco Mix)*.

19.02.00: 83-83-83-40-28-**27**-28-36-53-73-82

UK: Arista 72399-2 (1999).
   Tracks: *I Learned From The Best (Radio Edit)/I Will Always Love You (Hex Hector Club Mix)/It's Not Right But It's Okay (Thunderpuss 2000 Radio Mix)*.

11.12.99: **19**-26-38-33-30-29-33-40-54-65-68-85-x-100-97

Finland
20.11.99: 17-12-**6**-8-x-20-x-14-17

France
22.04.00: 73-60-53-45-45-**44**-50-70-69-80-87

Germany
29.11.99: 54-53-50-54-53-53-**48**-59-57-58

Ireland
2.12.99: 22-**18**-19-21-21-**18**-21-24-33-42

Netherlands
4.12.99: 63-42-38-39-39-**34**-38-36-41-46-55-59-66-73-84

Spain
18.12.99: 9-13-**8**-14

Sweden
25.11.99: 59-41-24-25-33-31-28-**23**-29-34-51

Switzerland
12.12.99: 34-32-**28**-30-32-32-35-31-37-42-48-69-73-77-91-98

I Learned From The Best was written by Diane Warren, and was recorded by Whitney for her 1998 album, *MY LOVE IS YOUR LOVE*.

I Learned From The Best was the final single released from the album in North America, and it gave Whitney another no.1 on Billboard's Hot Dance Club Play chart. However, it was less successful on the Hot 100, where it peaked at no.27.

I Learned From The Best also charted at no.6 in Finland, no.8 in Spain, no.18 in Ireland, no.19 in the UK, no.23 in Sweden, no.28 in Switzerland, no.34 in the Netherlands, no.44 in France and no.48 in Germany.

The music video for *I Learned From The Best*, directed by Kevin Bray, was filmed in Cologne, Germany.

Whitney promoted *I Learned From The Best* on several TV shows, including:

- *The Oprah Winfrey Show* on 25th November 1998.
- *The NBC Today Show*, from the Rockefeller Centre in New York, on 11th December 1998.
- *The Tonight Show with Jay Leno* on 13th January 1999.
- *C'era Un Ragazzo*, an Italian TV show, on 11th February 1999.
- *Sorpresa, Sorpresa*, a Spanish TV show, on 13th February 1999.
- *Top Of The Pops* ~ filmed at Elstree Studios, London, on 19th February 1999 and aired at a later date.

36 ~ If I Told You That

USA: Arista 3834 (promo, 2000).
  Tracks: *If I Told You That (Radio Edit)/(Call Out Research Hook)*.

If I Told You That wasn't a hit in the USA.

UK: Arista 76628-2 (2000).
  Tracks: *If I Told You That (Album Version)/(Johnny Douglas Mix)/Fine*.

17.06.00: **9**-19-25-34-48-47-49-54-63-93-62-51

Australia
18.09.00: peaked at no.**31**, charted for 8 weeks

Belgium
17.06.00: **41**

Denmark
9.06.00: **16**

Germany
19.06.00: 60-66-**58**-60-62-62-69-77-87

Ireland
8.06.00: **25**-35-40-45

Italy
15.06.00: peaked at no.**9**, charted for 6 weeks

Netherlands
3.06.00: 62-**31**-35-51-61-61-52-53-68-82

Spain
17.06.00: **18**

Sweden
22.06.00: 46-x-**44**-56

Switzerland
11.06.00: 44-36-38-35-**33**-41-43-47-49-58-60-77-84-90-88

If I Told You That was written by Rodney Jerkins, Fred Jerkins III, LaShawn Daniels and Toni Estes, and was originally recorded by Whitney for her 1998 album, *MY LOVE IS YOUR LOVE*.

A duet version of the song, featuring George Michael, featured on Whitney's compilation, *THE GREATEST HITS*, released in 2000. This version was co-produced by George Michael, whose vocals were added to Whitney's after she had recorded it for her *MY LOVE IS YOUR LOVE* album.

If I Told You That was originally written as a duet for Whitney and Michael Jackson. 'That song was meant for Whitney and Michael,' Rodney Jerkins confirmed in 1998. 'We didn't make it happen, and the next person was George Michael.'

The duet with George Michael was only released as a promotional single in the USA, so it wasn't eligible to chart on the Hot 100. Elsewhere, the single was released commercially, and apart from the no.9 it achieved in Italy and the UK, sales were generally disappointing, with *If I Told You That* peaking at no.16 in Denmark, no.18 in Spain, no.25 in Ireland, no.31 in Australia and the Netherlands, no.33 in Switzerland, no.41 in Belgium, no.44 in Sweden and no.58 in Germany.

The music video for *If I Told You That*, directed by Kevin Bray, was filmed in a nightclub setting. The promo was included on Whitney's *Fine* DVD single, which was only released in the United States.

37 ~ Same Script, Different Cast

USA: Arista 3846 (promo, 2000).
   Tracks: *Same Script, Different Cast (Radio Edit)/(Full Version)/(Call Out Research Hook)*.

17.06.00: 71-71-71-71-**70**-75-77-88-91

UK: Not Released.

Canada
06.00: peaked at no.**38**

Same Script, Different Cast was written by Montell Jordan, Shep Crawford, Shae Jones and Stacey Daniels, and was recorded by Whitney as a duet with Deborah Cox, for her 2000 compilation, *THE GREATEST HITS*.
   Same Script, Different Cast was released as a digital single in North America only. It rose to no.15 on Billboard's R&B chart, but could only manage a very disappointing no.70 on the Hot 100.
   The single achieved Top 40 status, just, in Canada where it peaked at no.38.

38 ~ Could I Have This Kiss Forever

USA: Arista 78207 (2000).
   Tracks: *Could I Have This Kiss Forever ((Metro Mix)/(Original Version)/(Tin Tin Out Mix)/(Tin Tin Out Mix Edit)/If I Told You That (Johnny Douglas Remix)/I'm Every Woman (Clivilles & Cole Mix).*

17.06.00: 74-68-68-67-59-59-60-**52**-54-56-59-70-69-81-87-95-98-100-x-97

UK: Arista 79599-2 (2000).
   Tracks: *Could I Have This Kiss Forever (Metro Mix)/(Tin Tin Out Mix)/I'm Your Baby Tonight (Dronez Mix).*

14.10.00: **7**-9-11-16-21-28-42-63-83-98

Australia
2.07.00: 24-20-22-20-19-15-20-18-**12**-18-13-18-32-49   (Top 50)

Austria
17.09.00: 23-17-12-10-9-9-9-9-**8**-9-16-16-21-26-34-36-52-54-58-69

Belgium
16.09.00: 30-18-13-9-**8**-9-10-**8**-9-9-16-22-29-31-40

Canada
06.00: peaked at no.**3**

ORIGINAL SHEET MUSIC EDITION
COULD I HAVE THIS KISS FOREVER
Recorded by WHITNEY HOUSTON & ENRIQUE IGLESIAS on Arista Records
Words and Music by DIANE WARREN
WHITNEY HOUSTON & ENRIQUE IGLESIAS
COULD I HAVE THIS KISS FOREVER

Finland
16.09.00: 18-x-x-**17**

France
30.09.00: 96-89-85-84-83-22-**16**-20-**16**-**16**-23-24-26-22-28-26-30-38-39-45-45-45-57-56-67-72-97

Germany
18.09.00: 13-11-9-8-**5**-8-8-9-9-12-18-21-30-29-40-40-40-51-64

Ireland
5.10.00: **8**-10-11-10-14-18-25-40

Italy
21.09.00: peaked at no.**6**, charted for 20 weeks

Netherlands
16.09.00: 14-4-**2**-**2**-**2**-3-5-7-11-12-17-25-31-31-35-35-50-55-69-77

New Zealand
25.06.00: 45-43-32-26-14-17-**7**-9-8-10-9-14-12-13-21-17-23-22

Norway
23.09.00: 13-8-9-**7**-9-9-10-12-16-15-18

Spain
9.09.00: 20-7-**4**-7-8

Sweden
14.09.00: 5-3-3-**2**-4-6-8-9-12-13-15-23-25-29-29-35-35-37-x-43

Switzerland
17.09.00: 16-15-7-**1**-**1**-2-2-2-2-3-4-4-4-8-10-11-17-21-21-29-39-39-51-53-70-76

Could I Have This Kiss Forever was written by Diane Warren, and was recorded by Whitney as a duet with Enrique Iglesias for her 2000 compilation, *THE GREATEST HITS*. The duet also featured on Enrique Iglesias's debut English language album, titled simply *ENRIQUE*, released in 1999.

'Me and Clive (Davis) were talking about this song that I'd heard a demo of and loved,' said Enrique Iglesias, 'and he says, "Why don't you do it with Whitney?" So we did, and it turned out fantastic. Clive was very nice about letting Whitney sing with me – I'm not even an Arista artist.'

Whitney and Enrique originally recorded the song in different studios, Whitney in Hamburg, Germany, and Enrique in Los Angeles, California. However, they did come together to re-record the song's single version.

Could I Have This Kiss Forever was chosen as the lead single from Whitney's *THE GREATEST HITS* in North America, whereas in most of Europe, *If I Told You That* was preferred. Disappointingly, the single only managed no.52 on the Hot 100 in the United States, but it did rather better in Canada, where it rose to no.3.

Could I Have This Kiss Forever enjoyed far greater in other countries, going all the way to no.1 in Switzerland, and charting at no.2 in the Netherlands and Sweden, no.4 in Spain, no.5 in Germany, no.6 in Italy, no.7 in New Zealand, Norway and the UK, no.8 in Austria, Belgium and Ireland, no.12 in Australia, no.16 in France and no.17 in Finland.

The music video for *Could I Have This Kiss Forever*, directed by Francis Lawrence, featured both Whitney and Enrique Iglesias, and had its world premiere on 22nd June 2000.

39 ~ Whatchulookinat

USA: Arista 5170 (promo, 2002).
Tracks: *Whatchulookinat (Album Version)/(Instrumental)*.

24.08.02: **96**-96-96

UK: Arista 97306-1 (double pack, 2002).
Tracks: *Whatchulookinat (Radio Mix)/(P. Diddy Remix – Radio Edit)/(Full Intention Club Mix)/(Radio Edit)/Love To Infinity Megamix*.

9.11.02: **13**-32-50

Australia
8.12.02: **48**-76-87-83-93-89-90-94 (b/w *One Of Those Days*)

Austria
29.09.02: 55-**53**-64-68

Belgium
12.10.02: **48**

Canada
08.02: peaked at no.**3**

France
23.11.02: 74-**65**-75-88-91-92

Germany
30.09.02: **47**-66-82-85-96-99

Ireland
31.10.02: **33**

Italy
12.09.02: peaked at no.**17**, charted for 10 weeks

Netherlands
12.10.02: 34-**29**-40-57-77

Spain
22.09.02: 11-**6**-13-14-15-x-19

Sweden
19.09.02: **29**-37-49-60-60

Switzerland
29.09.02: **22**-30-32-39-45-40-52-67

Whitney co-wrote *Whatchulookinat* with Tammie Harris, Jerry Muhammad and Andre Lewis, and recorded it for her 2002 album, *JUST WHITNEY*.... The song was seen by many as a response to all the negative media attention Whitney was attracting around this time.

Whatchulookinat was released as the album's lead single, but it wasn't especially well received in most countries. In the United States, although it did give Whitney another no.1 on Billboard's Hot Dance Club Play chart, the single made its debut on the Hot 100 at no.96 ~ Whitney's lowest debuting single at the time, as a solo artist. Even worse, it rose no higher, stalling at no.96 for three weeks, before dropping off the chart.

Globally, with a few notable exceptions, *Whatchulookinat* didn't fare much better. The single did achieve no.3 in Canada, no.6 in Spain and no.13 in the UK, and it charted at no.17 in Italy, no.22 in Switzerland, no.29 in the Netherlands and Sweden, no.33 in Ireland, no.47 in Germany, no.48 in Belgium, no.53 in Austria and no.65 in France.

In Australia, *Whatchulookinat* was released as a double A-side with *One Of Those Days*, and peaked at its debut position of no.48.

The music video for *Whatchulookinat*, directed by Kevin Bray, featured a cameo appearance by Faith Evans.

40 ~ Try It On My Own

USA: Arista 50138 (2003).
   Tracks: *Try It On My Own (Radio Edit)/(Thunderpuss Radio Mix)/(Thunderpuss Radio Mix Instrumental)*.

26.04.03: 99-93-93-**84-84**-95-93-x-99-99-97-95-95

UK: Arista 82876-50666-2 (2003, promo).
   Tracks: *On My Own (Radio Edit)*.

On My Own, as it was titled in Europe, wasn't a hit in the UK.

Canada
04.03: peaked at no.**24**

Switzerland
6.07.03: **79**

Try It On My Own was written by Babyface, Carole Bayer Sager, Jason Edmonds, Nathan Walton and Aleese Simmons, and was recorded by Whitney for her 2002 album, *JUST WHITNEY*....
   Try It On My Own was the third single released from the album; the second, *One Of Those Days*, failed to achieve Top 40 status anywhere.
   Try It On My Own topped Billboard's Dance Club Play chart, but entered the Hot 100 at a lowly no.99, before stalling at no.84. The single did rather better in Canada, where it rose to no.24.

In Europe, *Try It On My Own* was re-titled *On My Own*. A promo single was released in the UK, before a decision was taken to cancel the single's release. *On My Own* was released in most continental European countries, but the best it could manage chart-wise was no.79 in Switzerland.

The music video for *Try It On My Own*, directed by David LaChappelle, was filmed at the Lyric Theater in Miami, Florida, and featured a cameo appearance by Whitney's husband, Bobby Brown. It was released as a DVD single in the States, with *One Of Those Days*, and achieved no.21 on Billboard's Music Videos chart.

Whitney performed *Try It On My Own* at several high profile events and TV shows, including:

- the 'Keeper Of The Dream Awards' dinner, to honour of L.A. Reid, at New York's Sheraton Hotel on 3rd April 2003. Whitney also sang *I Will Always Love You*.
- the American drama show, *Boston Public*, when Whitney made a guest appearance on Episode 22 of Season 3, which aired on FOX TV on 12th May 2003.

- the *VH-1 Diva Duets: An Honors Concert For VH-1's Save The Music* show, staged at the MGM Grand in Las Vegas, Nevada, on 22nd May 2003. This show aired live in the United States.

41 ~ Million Dollar Bill

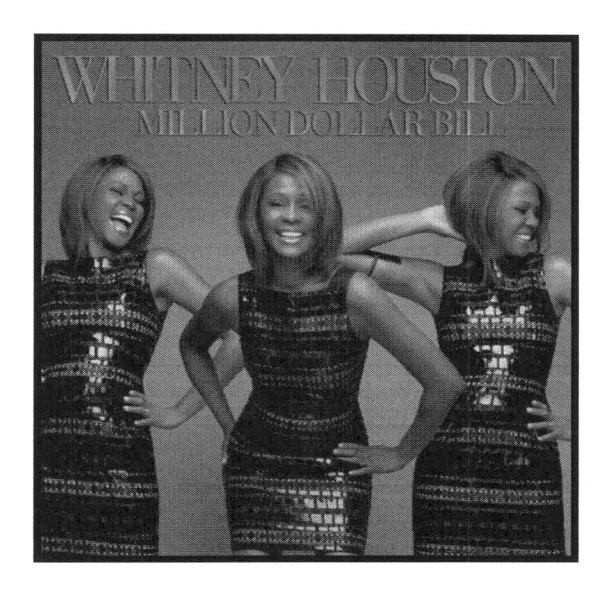

USA: Arista (promo, 2009).
 Tracks: *Million Dollar Bill (Radio)/(Instrumental)*.

19.09.09: **100**

UK: RCA 759908-2 (2009).
 Tracks: *Million Dollar Bill/(Freemasons Remix)*.

17.10.09: 12-14-**5**-8-14-19-28-28-35-44-64-62-46-69-95
25.02.12: 62

Canada
09.09: peaked at no.**62**

Finland
7.11.09: **18**

Germany
16.10.09: **41**-46-52-65-73-81-86-99 (b/w *I Look To You*)

Ireland
8.10.09: 45-40-11-**8**-15-24-35-38-40-49

Italy
29.10.09: peaked at no.**15**, charted for 2 weeks

Netherlands
29.08.09: 74-65-**58**-68-86

Sweden
4.09.09: **22**-26-27-30-43

Switzerland
13.09.09: **40**-65-66

Million Dollar Bill was written by Alicia Keys, Swizz Beatz and Norman Harris, and was recorded by Whitney for her 2009 album, *I LOOK TO YOU*. The track sampled Loletta Holloway's 1977 hit, *We're Getting Stronger*.

'At the time I was working on some stuff with Alicia (Keys),' said Swizz Beatz. 'I was like, "We need to bring Whitney back ~ we need to do some stuff to support Whitney", then Alicia was like, "I love Whitney, she's an icon. I would love to be part of that". I started vibing on different things. I didn't want to come with anything that would make her sound too old or too young. That's when I got the vibe to do something that had, like, a disco feel, but still with the hard drums on it, still musical but moving. I wanted to do something that was instant when it came on. Then I played the idea for Alicia, to make sure I wasn't bugging out. Am I going too far with this? She was, like, "Nah, that can be a big smash".'

Swizz Beatz and Alicia Keys wrote the lyrics together. 'Whitney is an artist who inspired me from a little girl,' said Alicia. 'Fast-forwarding to now and being able to work with her to help create this song that took off was fun. We had a lot of laughs. It was like being with a long-time friend … I love being part of Whitney Houston's comeback. She is such a dynamic force. It was really an honour and a pleasure.'

Whitney felt the song was a turning point for her. 'I worked with Alicia Keys on that one,' she said, 'and it was probably the most fun, but it also felt like I was working with someone who understood me, who could relate to me, singer to singer. At that point, I knew that it was coming together, that this was the album that I wanted, and that it was going to get done after two and a half years in the making.'

Million Dollar Bill was chosen as the lead single from *I LOOK TO YOU* outside the North America, where the album's title track was issued first. The single debuted on the Hot 100 at no.100, and fell off the chart the following week, making it Whitney's least successful charting single to date in the United States. However, impressively, *Million Dollar Bill* did give Whitney her 13th no.1 on Billboard's Hot Dance Club Songs chart.

In the UK, the single was released as a CD single, as well as digitally. Further, Whitney promoted *Million Dollar Bill* with a performance on the popular TV show, *The X-Factor*, on 18th October 2010.

'I have always loved my UK fans,' she said, prior to her appearance, 'and I'm thrilled to perform for them on *The X-Factor*. I'm also a fan of Simon Cowell's and look forward to meeting him. It should be a fun night.'

Three days later, Whitney reprised her performance on the Italian version of *The X-Factor*.

Boosted by her *The X-Factor* appearance, *Million Dollar Bill* rose to no.5 in the UK ~ Whitney's biggest UK hit single for more than ten years. The single also charted at no.8 in Ireland, no.15 in Italy, no.18 in Finland, no.22 in Sweden, no.40 in Switzerland and no.58 in the Netherlands.

In Germany, *Million Dollar Bill* was released as a double A-side with *I Look To You*, and achieved no.41.

The music video for *Million Dollar Bill*, directed by Melina Matsoukas, premiered on Whitney's official website on 16th September 2009.

42 ~ I Look To You

USA: Arista (promo, 2009).
  Tracks: *I Look To You (Johnny Vicious Warehouse Radio Edit)/(Johnny Vicious Warehouse Club Mix)/(Johnny Vicious Warehouse Mixshow)/(Johnny Vicious Club Radio Edit)/(Johnny Vicious Club Mixshow Mix)/(Johnny Vicious Club Mix)/ (Christian Dio Radio Mix)/(Christian Dio Mixshow Mix)/(Christiam Dio Club Mix)/ (Guiseppe D. Radio Mix)/(Guiseppe D. Club Mix)/(Guiseppe D. Mixshow Mix.*

22.08.09: 74-x-99-98-**70**-88-83

UK: RCA (promo, 2009).
  Tracks: *I Look To You (Guiseppe D. Radio Mix)/(Guiseppe D. Club Mix)/(Original Radio Edit).*

I Look You failed to enter the Top 100 in the UK, but did spend three weeks on the Top 200, peaking at no.115.

Canada
09.09: peaked at no.**68**

Austria
16.10.09: **47**-52-70

Germany
16.10.09: **41**-46-52-65-73-81-86-99 (b/w *Million Dollar Bill*)
24.02.12: 84

Netherlands
15.08.09: 97-x-x-82-66-**65**

Sweden
11.09.09: **33**-51

Switzerland
13.09.09: **16**-32-30-63-x-47-46-37-36-32-48-51-74-99
26.02.12: 56

I Look To You was written by Robert Kelly (*aka* R. Kelly), and was recorded by Whitney for her 2009 album with the same title. The song was brought to Whitney's attention by Clive Davis.

'When Clive heard *I Look To You*,' she said, 'because he knows my background in gospel, he knew that song would put it all in check for me ... I heard the song, and I loved that it was so short and sweet. And then I got to Chicago, and Robert (Kelly) told me there was still another verse to write, and a bridge. So he stood there with me in the studio, and wrote the second verse right off the top of his head. He closed his eyes, we kinda leaned on each other ~ as he was singing, I was praying, and the words just came out.'

'This song says all I wanted to say,' stated Whitney. 'There are times in life when we go through certain situations ~ some not so good. You have to reach for a higher strength. You have to reach deep inside yourself, spend time with yourself, to make some corrections that go beyond your own understanding and lean on a higher understanding. For me the song puts it all in check. If I did not have my faith, I wouldn't be as strong today.'

I Look To You was chosen as the album's lead single in North America, but it wasn't the big hit Whitney hoped it would be, peaking at no.68 in Canada and no.70 on the Hot 100 in the United States.

In Europe, *I Look To You* was promoted as the follow-up to *Million Dollar Bill*. It charted at no.16 in Switzerland, no.33 in Sweden, no.47 in Austria and no.65 in the Netherlands, but failed to enter the Top 100 in the UK.

In Germany, *I Look To You* was released as a double A-side with *Million Dollar Bill*, and achieved no.41.

The music video for *I Look To You*, directed by Melina Matsoukas, premiered on Whitney's official website and on the American TV show, *Entertainment Tonight*, on 10th September 2010.

R. Kelly performed *I Look To You* at Whitney funeral on 18th February 2012, at New Hope Baptist Church in Newark, New Jersey.

Later the same year, a duet version of *I Look To You* by Whitney and R. Kelly was released, to promote Whitney's posthumous compilation, *I WILL ALWAYS LOVE YOU – THE BEST OF*, but it wasn't a hit.

43 ~ I Didn't Know My Own Strength

USA: Arista (2009, no physical release).

I Didn't Know My Own Strength failed to enter the Hot 100 in the USA, but it did spend one week at no.19 on the 'Bubbling Under' chart.

UK: Arista (2009, no physical release).

31.10.09: **44**

Ireland
22.10.09: **38**-40

I Didn't Know My Own Strength was written by Diane Warren, and was recorded by Whitney for her 2009 album, *I LOOK TO YOU*.
　'I tried to get inside her head,' said Diane, who wrote the song especially for Whitney.
　'It really speaks for Whitney,' stated Clive Davis. 'She tumbled but she didn't crumble.'
　Recording the song reunited Whitney with producer David Foster, who had worked with her on songs for *The Bodyguard*. As his home had been damaged in the Malibu fires of 2007, Foster was working out of a small apartment, when it was time for Whitney to record her vocal.
　'Basically, I recorded in an office, next to the bathroom,' she said, 'with some sheets up near the microphone. It was totally different from doing *I Will Always Love You* in a beautiful studio, or *I Learned From The Best* in David's beautiful home. But when I

listened to my vocal, it was real, it was passionate ~ which is most unusual when you're singing next to a bathroom!'

As for the song itself, Whitney said, 'I wasn't thinking only in terms of myself. I was thinking about other people and other struggles. I thought about becoming a single mother. I thought about my mother, my cousin Dionne, my sisters-in-law. I thought about people with sicknesses, people who triumph in the face of adversity. The simplicity and strength that came out in my singing made me know how strong that song could be for a lot of people.'

'The thing about Whitney,' said David Foster, 'is that the expectation is absolutely too high for her, because nobody can live up to the hype of ~ you know, everybody. She's been gone for so long, and everybody wants that 'bodyguard' voice. Everybody wants that feeling, and when you're 18 and when you're 46, or 45, or however old, you can't be that same person. Nobody can be. You know, Barbra Streisand at 18 was not Barbra Streisand at 45. Celiné (Dion) at 40 is not who she was at 18. It's just different now, and I think she's made a really good record.'

Originally, *I Didn't Know My Own Strength* was planned as the lead single from *I LOOK TO YOU*, before it was decided to go with the title track in North America and *Million Dollar Bill* in Europe, instead.

I Didn't Know My Own Strength wasn't released as a physical single, but thanks to digital sales it did chart at no.38 and no.44 in Ireland and the UK, respectively.

Whitney performed *I Didn't Know My Own Strength* at Clive Davis's Pre-Grammy Gala on 7th February 2009, and again when she gave her first major interview since 2002, on *The Oprah Show*.

'It will leave you gasping,' predicted Oprah, before the interview aired. 'She (Whitney) does not blame Bobby Brown, and she takes full responsibility for her engagement in drugs. At one point, she says: "I didn't get out of my pyjamas for seven months".

'She talks about doing drugs and sitting in the house, the two of them, going "What are we doing?" She said, "I want to tell my story, I want to tell the truth". She talks about when it started to go wrong after *The Bodyguard* ~ that was a long time ago ... the thing most shocking to me is that Whitney tried to make herself smaller, to fit in a marriage, so the man could be bigger. How many women have done that? I deeply felt for her. She was trying to be a good wife. She really, truly loved him.'

'He (Bobby Brown) was my drug,' admitted Whitney. 'I didn't do anything without him. I wasn't getting high by myself. It was me and him together. You know, we were partners. And that's what my high was. Him. He and I being together ... I wanted to stop at that point. I mean, the drugs, the whole thing. I wanted it all just to stop, and he just wanted to continue.'

The interview aired in two parts, on 14th & 15th September 2009. This performance was included on the posthumous CD/DVD, *LIVE – HER GREATEST PERFORMANCES*, issued in 2014.

44 ~ Higher Love

USA: Kygo/RCA (2019, no physical release).

13.07.19: **63**
14.09.19: 93-x-x-92-95-85-87-85-99-98

UK: Kygo/RCA (2019, no physical release).

11.07.19: 36-26-17-15-10-9-5-4-**2-2**-3-4-3-5-6-23-23-31-34-41-45-60-88-88-88-x-54-65-81-89-88-76-78-90-96-97-x-x-94-91-81-74- (still charting)

Austria
12.07.19: 29-26-32-29-27-24-23-**20**-21-26-25-25-29-31-28-33-31-35-39-47-52-56
10.01.20: 51-64

Australia
12.07.19: 34-25-28-**20**-28-21-27-31-37-31-38-36-34-35-37-37-34-50-50-50-50

Belgium
27.07.19: 37-35-28-20-14-14-10-8-5-4-4-4-4-5-5-7-10-10-15-15-19-24-21-28-29-41-45

Canada
13.07.19: 38-37-42-39-37-35-33-32-26-**22**-30-31-27-24-31-32-26-35-34-33-37-46

Denmark
10.07.19: **28**-33

France
6.09.19: 83-93-x-x-96-83-85-82-85-**72**-80-71-80-85

Germany
5.07.19: 30-39-50-30-29-24-**22-22**-25-25-29-33-40-40-42-48-52-50-62-75-74-86-x-65-87

Ireland
5.07.19: 36-29-19-15-11-10-8-5-**4**-6-6-6-6-7-11-28-20-32-39-38-44-66-85-x-x-76-77-82-
90-89-89-97-100-100-100-95-100-93-x-99-89- (still charting)

Netherlands
6.07.19: 66-60-60-38-34-36-33-**29**-30-33-35-35-32-32-27-27-29-45-44-42-42-45-49-80-
88-x-70-98

New Zealand
12.08.19: 37-33-32-32-**26**-31-32-30-33-35-39

Norway
6.07.19: **2-2**-6-7-8-8-7-7-7-10-16-16-12-16-18-16-24-28-29-36

Sweden
5.07.19: **9**-15-18-19-20-22-19-21-17-18-33-30-25-26-30-33-34-42-50-65-66-68-83-x-x-x-
x-52-69-80-88-78-79-84-87
3.04.20: 89-97- (still charting)

Switzerland
7.07.19: 14-27-32-35-19-17-11-**10**-11-13-11-14-15-15-16-15-15-21-23-30-29-32-42-47-
54-86-41-42-48-61-79-34-63-67-80-86-84-52-82-66- (still charting)

Higher Love was written by Steve Winwood and Will Jennings, and was originally recorded by Steve Winwood for his 1986 album, *BACK IN THE HIGH LIFE*.

Steve Winwood took *Higher Love* to no.1 in Canada and on the Hot 100 in the United States, and to no.8 in Australia, no.11 in Ireland and New Zealand, and no.13 in the UK.

Whitney recorded a cover of *Higher Love* for her *I'M YOUR BABY TONIGHT* album, but it failed to make the final track listing. However, it was included as a bonus track on the Japanese edition of the album, but few Whitney fans had heard it before the Norwegian producer Kygo (real name Kyrre Gorvell-Dahll) re-invented it in 2019.

Kygo's re-working of *Higher Love*, with Whitney's vocals, was released digitally and to streaming on 28th June 2019, and became Whitney's first new hit single for almost ten years.

In Kygo's homeland, *Higher Love* made its chart debut at no.2, where it spent two weeks, before slowly slipping down the chart. Elsewhere, the song proved to be a real grower in many countries, rising to no.2 in the UK, no.4 in Ireland, no.4 in Belgium, no.9 in Sweden, no.10 in Switzerland, no.20 in Austria and Australia, no.22 in Canada and Germany, no.26 in New Zealand, no.28 in Denmark and no.29 in the Netherlands.

Disappointingly, in the United States, *Higher Love* entered the Hot 100 at no.63, but dropped off the chart again the following week. Two months later, the song re-entered the Hot 100 at no.93 ~ this time, it spent eight non-consecutive weeks on the chart, but rose no higher than no.85. More impressively, *Higher Love* did give Whitney her 14th no.1 on Billboard's Dance Club Songs chart.

'Clive (Davis) said if *Higher Love* is successful,' said Narada Michael Walden, who produced Whitney's original recording of *Higher Love*, 'I should start thinking about an album, so that's what I'm doing right now. I would suggest we take some of the songs we've done that didn't get the single exposure, songs like *I Belong To You*, that those lead vocals, which are stellar, and make them current again. Whitney's vocals have fire and heat on them, and we could blow them up.'

THE ALMOST TOP 40 SINGLES

Two of Whitney's singles have made the Top 50 in one or more countries, but failed to enter the Top 40 in any.

Fine

Fine was written by Raphael Saadiq and Kamaal Fareed, and was recorded by Whitney for her 2000 compilation, *THE GREATEST HITS*. Released as the final single from the album, *Fine* spent a solitary week at no.50 in Sweden, but it wasn't a hit anywhere else. *Fine* was also released as a DVD single in North America, featuring the music videos for *Fine* and *If I Told You That*, plus behind the scenes footage of the *Fine* video shoot.

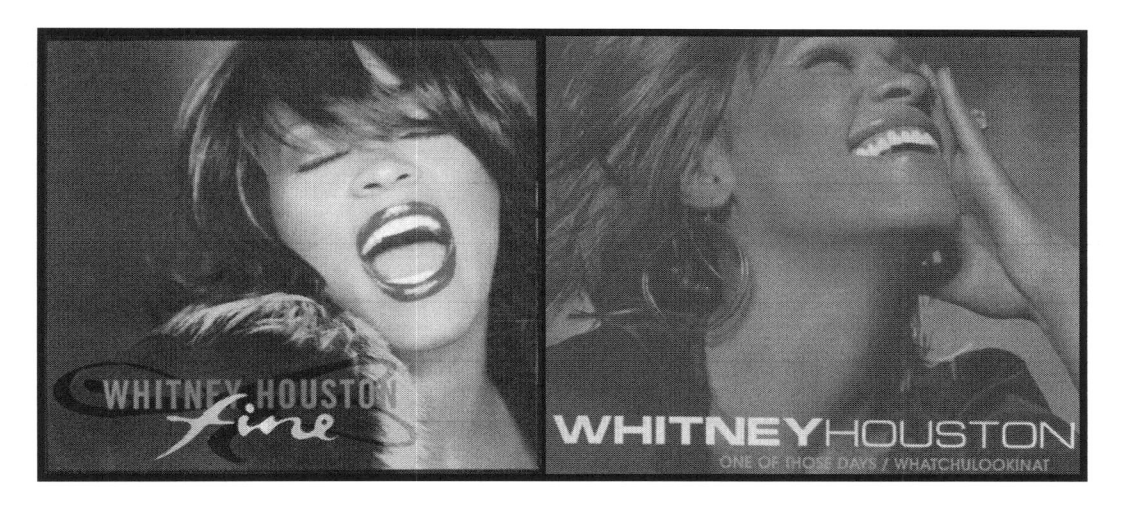

One Of Those Days

One Of Those Days was written by Kevin Briggs, Dwight Renolds and Patrice Stewart, and sampled the Isley Brothers 1983 hit, *Between The Sheets*. It was a minor hit in the Netherlands, Switzerland and the USA.

In Australia, *One Of Those Days* was issued as a double A-side single with *Whatchulookinat*. The single made its chart debut at no.48, but fell out of the Top 50 the following week.

WHITNEY'S TOP 30 SINGLES

In this Top 30, each of Whitney's singles has been scored according to the following points system.

Points are given according to the peak position reached on the albums chart in each of the countries featured in this book:

    No.1:   100 points for the first week at no.1, plus 10 points for each additional week at no.1.

    No.2:   90 points for the first week at no.2, plus 5 points for each additional week at no.2.

No.3:	85 points.
No.4-6:	80 points.
No.7-10:	75 points.
No.11-15:	70 points.
No.16-20:	65 points.
No.21-30:	60 points.
No.31-40:	50 points.
No.41-50:	40 points.
No.51-60:	30 points.
No.61-70:	20 points.
No.71-80:	10 points.
No.81-100:	5 points.

Total weeks charted in each country are added, to give the final points score.

Reissues, re-entries and remixes of a single are counted together.

Rank/Single/Points

1 *I Will Always Love You* – 3634 points

2 *I Wanna Dance With Somebody (Who Loves Me)* – 2582 points

3 *I'm Your Baby Tonight* – 1909 points

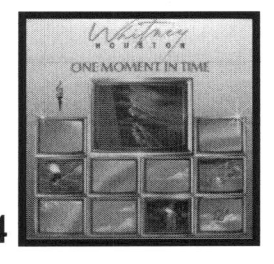

4 *One Moment In Time* – 1821 points

Rank/Single/Points

5   *My Love Is Your Love* – 1809 points

6. *When You Believe* – 1787 points
7. *Exhale (Shoop Shoop)* – 1753 points
8. *I'm Every Woman* – 1640 points
9. *Could I Have This Kiss Forever* – 1563 points
10. *How Will I Know* – 1470 points

11. *Step By Step* – 1390 points
12. *Higher Love* – 1309+ points
13. *Greatest Love Of All* – 1257 points
14. *Saving All My Love For You* – 1247 points
15. *All The Man That I Need* – 1127 points

16. *I Have Nothing* – 1106 points
17. *It's Not Right But It's Okay* – 1103 points
18. *So Emotional* – 1058 points
19. *Didn't We Almost Have It All* – 960 points
20. *Love Will Save The Day* – 796 points

21. *Whatchulookinat* – 771 points
22. *Where Do Broken Hearts Go* – 745 points
23. *I Learned From The Best* – 705 points
24. *If I Told You That* – 670 points
25. *Heartbreak Hotel* – 640 points

26. *Run To You* – 556 points
27. *Count On Me* – 519 points
28. *Million Dollar Bill* – 498 points
29. *Queen Of The Night* – 478 points
30. *My Name Is Not Susan* – 464 points

Predictably, Whitney's two most successful singles around the world are *I Will Always Love You* and *I Wanna Dance With Somebody (Who Loves Me)*, in that order. Not many points separate the next three singles, with *I'm Your Baby Tonight* taking a surprise no.3 spot, followed by *One Moment In Time* and *My Love Is Your Love*.

When You Believe, with Mariah Carey, emerges as Whitney's most successful duet, ahead of *Could I Have This Kiss Forever*.

Higher Love, Whitney's posthumous collaboration with Kygo, is her most recent single to make the Top 30, coming in at an impressive no.12.

SINGLES TRIVIA

To date, Whitney has achieved forty-four Top 40 singles in one or more of the countries featured in this book.

There follows a country-by-country look at the most successful Whitney hits, starting with her homeland.

Note: in the past, there was often one or more weeks over Christmas and New Year when no new chart was published in some countries. In such cases, the previous week's chart has been used to complete chart runs. Similarly, where a bi-weekly or monthly chart was in place, for chart runs these are counted as two and four weeks, respectively.

WHITNEY IN THE USA

Whitney has achieved 40 hit singles in the USA, which spent 588 weeks on the Hot 100.

No.1 Singles

1985	*Saving All My Love For You*
1986	*How Will I Know*
1986	*Greatest Love Of All*
1987	*I Wanna Dance With Somebody (Who Loves Me)*
1987	*Didn't We Almost Have It All*
1987	*So Emotional*
1988	*Where Do Broken Hearts Go*
1990	*I'm Your Baby Tonight*
1991	*All The Man That I Need*
1992	*I Will Always Love You*
1995	*Exhale (Shoop Shoop)*

Most Weeks at No.1

14 weeks	*I Will Always Love You*
3 weeks	*Greatest Love Of All*
2 weeks	*How Will I Know*
2 weeks	*I Wanna Dance With Somebody (Who Loves Me)*
2 weeks	*Didn't We Almost Have It All*
2 weeks	*Where Do Broken Hears Go*
2 weeks	*All The Man That I Need*

Singles with the most Hot 100 weeks

29 weeks	*I Will Always Love You*
28 weeks	*Heartbreak Hotel*
28 weeks	*My Love Is Your Love*
27 weeks	*The Star Spangled Banner*
24 weeks	*How Will I Know*
23 weeks	*All The Man That I Need*
23 weeks	*I'm Every Woman*
22 weeks	*Saving All My Love For You*
21 weeks	*You Give Good Love*
21 weeks	*Exhale (Shoop Shoop)*

RIAA (Recording Industry Association of America) Awards

The RIAA began certifying Gold singles in 1958 and Platinum singles in 1976. From 1958 to 1988: Gold = 1 million, Platinum = 2 million. From 1988 onwards: Gold = 500,000, Platinum = 1 million. Awards are based on shipments, not sales (unless the award is for digital sales).

8 x Platinum	*I Will Always Love You* (March 2019) = 8 million
3 x Platinum	*I Wanna Dance With Somebody* (February 2019) = 3 million
Gold & Platinum	*The Star Spangled Banner* (April 1991) (October 2001) = 1.5 million
Platinum	*Exhale (Shoop Shoop)* (January 1996) = 1 million
Platinum	*I Believe In You And Me* (February 1997) = 1 million
Platinum	*Heartbreak Hotel* (March 1999) = 1 million
Platinum	*My Love Is Your Love* (December 1999) = 1 million
Platinum	*Greatest Love Of All* (March 2019)) = 1 million
Platinum	*How Will I Know* (March 2019) = 1 million
Platinum	*I Have Nothing* (March 2019) = 1 million
Platinum	*It's Not Right But It's Okay* (March 2019) = 1 million
Platinum	*I'm Every Woman* (March 2019) = 1 million
Platinum	*Saving All My Love For You* (March 2019) = 1 million
Platinum	*You Give Good Love* (March 2020) = 1 million
Gold	*I'm Your Baby Tonight* (November 1980) = 500,000
Gold	*All The Man That I Need* (March 1991) = 500,000
Gold	*So Emotional* (December 1995) = 500,000
Gold	*Count On Me* (May 1996) = 500,000
Gold	*Step By Step* (April 1997) = 500,000
Gold	*When You Believe* (March 2019) = 500,000
Gold	*Run To You* (March 2019) = 500,000
Gold	*One Moment In Time* (March 2019) = 500,000
Gold	*Higher Love* (October 2019) = 500,000

WHITNEY IN AUSTRALIA

Whitney has achieved 31 hit singles in Australia, which spent 460 weeks on the chart.

No.1 Singles

1986	*Greatest Love Of All*
1987	*I Wanna Dance With Somebody (Who Loves Me)*
1992	*I Will Always Love You*

Most weeks at No.1

10 weeks	*I Will Always Love You*
5 weeks	*I Wanna Dance With Somebody (Who Loves Me)*

Singles with the most weeks

32 weeks	*I Will Always Love You*
30 weeks	*Saving All My Love For You*
29 weeks	*How Will I Know*
28 weeks	*I Wanna Dance With Somebody (Who Loves Me)*
21 weeks	*Greatest Love Of All*
21 weeks	*I'm Every Woman*
21 weeks	*Higher Love*
20 weeks	*I'm Your Baby Tonight*
19 weeks	*So Emotional*
19 weeks	*When You Believe*
19 weeks	*Heartbreak Hotel*

ARIA (Australian Recording Industry Association) Accreditations

The current ARIA accreditations are: Gold = 35,000, Platinum = 70,000.

4 x Platinum	*I Will Always Love You* = 280,000
3 x Platinum	*I Wanna Dance With Somebody (Who Loves Me)* = 210,000
2 x Platinum	*Higher Love* = 140,000
Gold	*I'm Every Woman* = 35,000
Gold	*Step By Step* = 35,000
Gold	*When You Believe* = 35,000
Gold	*Could I Have This Kiss Forever* = 35,000

WHITNEY IN AUSTRIA

Whitney has achieved 19 hit singles in Austria, which spent 229 weeks on the chart.

No.1 Singles

1993   *I Will Always Love You*

I Will Always Love You topped the chart for five non-consecutive weeks.

Singles with the most weeks

24 weeks	*My Love Is Your Love*
24 weeks	*Higher Love*
20 weeks	*I Will Always Love You*
20 weeks	*When You Believe*
20 weeks	*Could I Have This Kiss Forever*
18 weeks	*One Moment In Time*
17 weeks	*I Wanna Dance With Somebody (Who Loves Me)*
16 weeks	*Step By Step*
15 weeks	*I'm Your Baby Tonight*
11 weeks	*I'm Every Woman*
11 weeks	*Exhale (Shoop Shoop)*

WHITNEY IN BELGIUM (Flanders)

Whitney has achieved 29 hit singles in Belgium (Flanders), which spent 281 weeks on the chart.

No.1 Singles

1987	*I Wanna Dance With Somebody (Who Loves Me)*
1993	*I Will Always Love You*

Most weeks at No.1

6 weeks	*I Will Always Love You*
3 weeks	*I Wanna Dance With Somebody (Who Loves Me)*

Singles with the most weeks

27 weeks	*Higher Love*
20 weeks	*My Love Is Your Love*

19 weeks	*I Will Always Love You*
19 weeks	*When You Believe*
16 weeks	*Step By Step*
15 weeks	*Could I Have This Kiss Forever*
14 weeks	*All At Once*
14 weeks	*I'm Your Baby Tonight*
13 weeks	*I Wanna Dance With Somebody (Who Loves Me)*
12 weeks	*One Moment In Time*
12 weeks	*I'm Every Woman*

WHITNEY IN CANADA

Whitney has achieved 38 hit singles in Canada, which spent 462+ weeks on the chart.

No.1 Singles

1986	*How Will I Know*
1986	*Greatest Love Of All*
1987	*I Wanna Dance With Somebody (Who Loves Me)*
1991	*All The Man That I Need*
1992	*I Will Always Love You*
1993	*I Have Nothing*
1996	*Exhale (Shoop Shoop)*

Most weeks at No.1

10 weeks	*I Will Always Love You*
3 weeks	*I Have Nothing*
2 weeks	*Exhale (Shoop Shoop)*

Singles with the most weeks

26 weeks	*Exhale (Shoop Shoop)*
25 weeks	*You Give Good Love*
25 weeks	*How Will I Know*
23 weeks	*Saving All My Love For You*
23 weeks	*I Wanna Dance With Somebody (Who Loves Me)*
22 weeks	*Higher Love*
21 weeks	*Greatest Love Of All*
20 weeks	*I Will Always Love You*
19 weeks	*So Emotional*
19 weeks	*Where Do Broken Hearts Go*

Note: post-1999 information, especially, is incomplete.

WHITNEY IN DENMARK

Whitney has achieved 14 hit singles in Denmark, which spent 118 weeks on the chart.

No.1 Singles

1987	*I Wanna Dance With Somebody (Who Loves Me)*
1993	*I Will Always Love You*

Most weeks at No.1

6 weeks	*I Will Always Love You*
4 weeks	*I Wanna Dance With Somebody (Who Loves You)*

Singles with the most weeks

17 weeks	*I Wanna Dance With Somebody (Who Loves Me)*
17 weeks	*I Will Always Love You*
16 weeks	*When You Believe*
14 weeks	*Step By Step*
14 weeks	*My Love Is Your Love*
13 weeks	*Exhale (Shoop Shoop)*

WHITNEY IN FINLAND

Whitney has achieved 16 hit singles in Finland, which spent 107 weeks on the chart.

No.1 Singles

1987	*I Wanna Dance With Somebody (Who Loves Me)*
1993	*I Will Always Love You*

Singles with the most weeks

24 weeks	*I Will Always Love You*
16 weeks	*I Wanna Dance With Somebody (Who Loves Me)*
12 weeks	*I'm Your Baby Tonight*
8 weeks	*How Will I Know*
8 weeks	*I'm Every Woman*
7 weeks	*I Learned From The Best*

WHITNEY IN FRANCE

Whitney has achieved 25 hit singles in France, which spent 326 weeks on the chart.

No.1 Singles

1993   *I Will Always Love You*

I Will Always Love You spent eight weeks at no.1.

Singles with the most weeks

40 weeks	*I Will Always Love You*
27 weeks	*My Love Is Your Love*
27 weeks	*Could I Have This Kiss Forever*
22 weeks	*Saving All My Love For You*
21 weeks	*When You Believe*
20 weeks	*One Moment In Time*
18 weeks	*I Wanna Dance With Somebody (Who Loves Me)*
18 weeks	*It's Not Right But It's Okay*
17 weeks	*Exhale (Shoop Shoop)*
17 weeks	*Heartbreak Hotel*

WHITNEY IN GERMANY

Whitney has achieved 31 hit singles in Germany, which spent 442 weeks on the chart.

No.1 Singles

1987	*I Wanna Dance With Somebody (Who Loves Me)*
1988	*One Moment In Time*
1993	*I Will Always Love You*

Most weeks at No.1

6 weeks	*I Will Always Love You*
5 weeks	*I Wanna Dance With Somebody (Who Loves Me)*
2 weeks	*One Moment In Time*

Singles with the most weeks

32 weeks	*I Will Always Love You*
26 weeks	*My Love Is Your Love*

24 weeks	*Higher Love*
23 weeks	*One Moment In Time*
23 weeks	*I'm Your Baby Tonight*
23 weeks	*Step By Step*
21 weeks	*I Wanna Dance With Somebody (Who Loves Me)*
21 weeks	*When You Believe*
19 weeks	*My Name Is Not Susan*
19 weeks	*Could I Have This Kiss Forever*

WHITNEY IN IRELAND

Whitney has achieved 33 hit singles in Ireland, which spent 264 weeks on the chart.

No.1 Singles

1985	*Saving All My Love For You*
1992	*I Will Always Love You*

Most weeks at No.1

8 weeks	*I Will Always Love You*

Saving All My Love For You spent a single week at no.1.

Singles with the most weeks

38+ weeks	*Higher Love*
24 weeks	*I Will Always Love You*
12 weeks	*I Wanna Dance With Somebody (Who Loves Me)*
12 weeks	*When You Believe*
12 weeks	*My Love Is Your Love*
10 weeks	*I'm Every Woman*
10 weeks	*It's Not Right But It's Okay*
10 weeks	*I Learned From The Best*
10 weeks	*Million Dollar Bill*
9 weeks	*Step By Step*

WHITNEY IN ITALY

Whitney has achieved 20 hit singles in Italy, which spent 201 weeks on the chart.

No.1 Singles

1987	*I Wanna Dance With Somebody (Who Loves Me)*
1990	*I'm Your Baby Tonight*

Most weeks at No.1

5 weeks	*I'm Your Baby Tonight*
2 weeks	*I Wanna Dance With Somebody (Who Loves Me)*

Singles with the most weeks

24 weeks	*One Moment In Time*
20 weeks	*I'm Your Baby Tonight*
20 weeks	*Could I Have This Kiss Forever*
18 weeks	*I Wanna Dance With Somebody (Who Loves Me)*
18 weeks	*I Will Always Love You*
14 weeks	*Exhale (Shoop Shoop)*
13 weeks	*All At Once*
11 weeks	*When You Believe*
10 weeks	*Greatest Love Of All*
10 weeks	*Whatchulookinat*

WHITNEY IN JAPAN

Whitney has achieved 10 hit singles in Japan, which spent 74 weeks on the chart.

Her most successful single is *I Will Always Love You*, which peaked at no.5.

Singles with the most weeks

27 weeks	*I Will Always Love You*
11 weeks	*Saving All My Love For You*
9 weeks	*All At Once*
8 weeks	*When You Believe*
5 weeks	*I Wanna Dance With Somebody (Who Loves Me)*

WHITNEY IN THE NETHERLANDS

Whitney has achieved 39 hit singles in the Netherlands, which spent 448 weeks on the chart.

No.1 Singles

1987	*I Wanna Dance With Somebody (Who Loves Me)*
1993	*I Will Always Love You*

Most weeks at No.1

6 weeks	*I Will Always Love You*
4 weeks	*I Wanna Dance With Somebody (Who Loves Me)*

Singles with the most weeks

27 weeks	*Higher Love*
25 weeks	*I Will Always Love You*
25 weeks	*My Love Is Your Love*
23 weeks	*Step By Step*
21 weeks	*When You Believe*
20 weeks	*I Wanna Dance With Somebody (Who Loves Me)*
20 weeks	*Could I Have This Kiss Forever*
17 weeks	*It's Not Right But It's Okay*
15 weeks	*Saving All My Love For You*
15 weeks	*One Moment In Time*
15 weeks	*I'm Your Baby Tonight*
15 weeks	*I Learned From The Best*

WHITNEY IN NEW ZEALAND

Whitney has achieved 24 hits singles in New Zealand, which spent 236 weeks on the chart.

No.1 Singles

1987	*I Wanna Dance With Somebody (Who Loves Me)*
1992	*I Will Always Love You*
1999	*My Love Is Your Love*

Most weeks at No.1

14 weeks	*I Will Always Love You*
4 weeks	*I Wanna Dance With Somebody (Who Loves Me)*

Singles with the most weeks

26 weeks	*I Will Always Love You*
20 weeks	*How Will I Know*
18 weeks	*Could I Have This Kiss Forever*
17 weeks	*Exhale (Shoop Shoop)*
16 weeks	*Saving All My Love For You*
16 weeks	*My Love Is Your Love*
14 weeks	*I Wanna Dance With Somebody (Who Loves Me)*
14 weeks	*I'm Your Baby Tonight*
12 weeks	*Greatest Love Of All*
12 weeks	*I'm Every Woman*

WHITNEY IN NORWAY

Whitney has achieved 11 hit singles in Norway, which spent 117 weeks on the chart.

No.1 Singles

1987	*I Wanna Dance With Somebody (Who Loves Me)*
1993	*I Will Always Love You*

Most weeks at No.1

9 weeks	*I Will Always Love You*
7 weeks	*I Wanna Dance With Somebody (Who Loves Me)*

Singles with the most weeks

20 weeks	*Higher Love*
17 weeks	*I Will Always Love You*
15 weeks	*When You Believe*
11 weeks	*I Wanna Dance With Somebody (Who Loves Me)*
11 weeks	*My Love Is Your Love*
11 weeks	*Could I Have This Kiss Forever*
10 weeks	*One Moment In Time*

WHITNEY IN SPAIN

Whitney has achieved 21 hit singles in Spain, which spent 207 weeks on the chart.

No.1 Singles

1993 *I Will Always Love You*
1995 *Exhale (Shoop Shoop)*
1999 *It's Not Right But It's Okay*

Most weeks at No.1

2 weeks *Exhale (Shoop Shoop)*

I Will Always Love You and *It's Not Right But It's Okay* each spent one week at no.1.

Singles with the most weeks

42 weeks *I Wanna Dance With Somebody (Who Loves Me)*
28 weeks *I Will Always Love You*
18 weeks *So Emotional*
17 weeks *One Moment In Time*
17 weeks *I'm Your Baby Tonight*
14 weeks *Love Will Save The Day*
12 weeks *Didn't We Almost Have It All*
12 weeks *It's Not Right But It's Okay*
10 weeks *I'm Every Woman*

WHITNEY IN SWEDEN

Whitney has achieved 22 hit singles in Sweden, which spent 248 weeks on the chart.

No.1 Singles

1987 *I Wanna Dance With Somebody (Who Loves Me)*
1992 *I Will Always Love You*

Both singles topped the chart for six weeks.

Singles with the most weeks

33+ weeks *Higher Love*
22 weeks *I Will Always Love You*
20 weeks *When You Believe*
19 weeks *My Love Is Your Love*
19 weeks *Could I Have This Kiss Forever*
14 weeks *How Will I Know*

14 weeks	*Exhale (Shoop Shoop)*
13 weeks	*It's Not Right But It's Okay*
12 weeks	*I Wanna Dance With Somebody (Who Loves Me)*
12 weeks	*One Moment In Time*
12 weeks	*Step By Step*
12 weeks	*I Learned From The Best*

WHITNEY IN SWITZERLAND

Whitney has achieved 31 hit singles in Switzerland, which spent 406 weeks on the chart.

No.1 Singles

1987	*I Wanna Dance With Somebody (Who Loves Me)*
1993	*I Will Always Love You*
2000	*Could I Have This Kiss Forever*

Most weeks at No.1

8 weeks	*I Will Always Love You*
6 weeks	*I Wanna Dance With Somebody (Who Loves Me)*
2 weeks	*Could I Have This Kiss Forever*

Singles with the most weeks

40+ weeks	*Higher Love*
36 weeks	*My Love Is Your Love*
35 weeks	*I Will Always Love You*
26 weeks	*Could I Have This Kiss Forever*
24 weeks	*One Moment In Time*
24 weeks	*When You Believe*
21 weeks	*It's Not Right But It's Okay*
19 weeks	*I Wanna Dance With Somebody (Who Loves Me)*
17 weeks	*Saving All My Love For You*
16 weeks	*I Learned From The Best*
15 weeks	*I'm Your Baby Tonight*
15 weeks	*Exhale (Shoop Shoop)*
15 weeks	*Step By Step*
15 weeks	*If I Told You That*

WHITNEY IN THE UK

Whitney has achieved 37 hit singles in the UK, which spent 432 weeks on the chart.

No.1 Singles

1985	*Saving All My Love For You*
1987	*I Wanna Dance With Somebody (Who Loves Me)*
1988	*One Moment In Time*
1992	*I Will Always Love You*

Most Weeks at No.1

10 weeks   *I Will Always Love You*

Whitney's other chart toppers each spent two weeks at no.1.

Singles with the most weeks

39+ weeks	*Higher Love*
34 weeks	*I Will Always Love You*
19 weeks	*Saving All My Love For You*
18 weeks	*I Wanna Dance With Somebody (Who Loves Me)*
17 weeks	*When You Believe*
17 weeks	*It's Not Right But It's Okay*
16 weeks	*One Moment In Time*
16 weeks	*Million Dollar Bill*
15 weeks	*My Love Is Your Love*
14 weeks	*Step By Step*
14 weeks	*I Learned From The Best*

The BRIT Certified/BPI (British Phonographic Industry) Awards

The BPI began certifying Silver, Gold & Platinum singles in 1973. From 1973 to 1988: Silver = 250,000, Gold = 500,000 & Platinum = 1 million. From 1989 onwards: Silver = 200,000, Gold = 400,000 & Platinum = 600,000. Awards are based on shipments, not sales; however, in July 2013 the BPI automated awards, based on actual sales since February 1994.

2 x Platinum	*I Will Always Love You* (January 1983) = 1.2 million
Gold & Platinum	*I Wanna Dance With Somebody (Who Loves Me)* (August 1987) (February 2018) = 1.1 million
Platinum	*My Love Is Your Love* (April 2016) = 600,000
Platinum	*It's Not Right But It's Okay* (April 2017) = 600,000

Platinum	*Higher Love* (November 2019)	= 600,000
Gold	*Saving All My Love For You* (December 1985)	= 500,000
Gold	*I Have Nothing* (April 2019)	= 400,000
Gold	*How Will I Know* (September 2019)	= 400,000
Gold	*When You Believe* (March 2020)	= 400,000
Gold	*Million Dollar Bill* (March 2020)	= 400,000
Silver	*So Emotional* (? 1988)	= 250,000
Silver	*One Moment In Time* (October 1988)	= 250,000
Silver	*Step By Step* (February 1997)	= 200,000
Silver	*Greatest Love Of All* (June 2019)	= 200,000

WHITNEY IN ZIMBABWE

Whitney has achieved nine hit singles in Zimbabwe, which spent 105 weeks on the chart.

No.1 Singles

1991	*All The Man That I Need*
1993	*I Will Always Love You*
1996	*Exhale (Shoop Shoop)*

Most weeks at No.1

3 weeks	*All The Man That I Need*
3 weeks	*I Will Always Love You*

Singles with the most weeks

23 weeks	*Exhale (Shoop Shoop)*
20 weeks	*One Moment In Time*
13 weeks	*I Wanna Dance With Somebody (Who Loves Me)*
13 weeks	*I Will Always Love You*
12 weeks	*I Have Nothing*
11 weeks	*I'm Every Woman*

All The Top 40 Albums

1 ~ WHITNEY HOUSTON

You Give Good Love/Thinking About You/Someone For Me/Saving All My Love For You/ Nobody Loves Me Like You Do/How Will I Know/All At Once/ Take Good Care Of My Heart/Greatest Love Of All/Hold Me

Someone For Me, Nobody Loves Me Like You Do & Take Good Care Of My Heart produced by Jermaine Jackson, *Thinking About You & You Give Good Love* produced by Kashif, *Hold Me, Saving All My Love For You, All At Once & Greatest Love Of All* produced by Michael Masser, *How Will I Know* produced by Narada Michael Walden.

USA: Arista 8212 (1985).

27.04.85: 91-79-66-56-55-50-42-39-34-21-16-13-13-13-12-12-12-11-9-9-8-8-5-5-4-2-2-3-4-4-6-7-7-9-9-13-13-15-12-11-9-8-5-4-3-**1-1-1-1-1-1-1**-2-2-2-**1-1-1-1-1-1-1**-3-3-7-7-8-10-10-12-13-13-16-19-19-23-26-29-35-39-52-53-65-71-69-59-64-58-58-51-48-47-46-51-51-47-44-43-30-28-28-37-40-42-48-57-79-75-72-65-60-56-53-59-70-52-72-67-65-59-64-60-68-58-66-80-83-90
25.02.12: 72-37-9-10-21-29-59-88-99

UK: Arista 610 359 (1985).

14.12.85: 52-26-22-17-11-9-10-9-8-6-4-**2-2-2**-3-3-5-5-5-4-3-3-3-4-7-7-13-10-11-12-18-21-21-19-22-21-22-22-27-30-34-30-33-38-41-27-21-29-26-20-22-27-35-42-41-34-30-31-34-34-29-26-21-24-24-30-39-32-42-58-52-52-53-65-50-55-35-27-32-35-37-42-38-51-44-39-50-47-49-41-40-38-62-52-59-70-76-96-88-x-x-92-99
9.01.88: 99-98-x-x-100

Whitney
She's Making
An Amazing
First Impression.
Right from the start, she's generating the kind of excitement–in the press, at radio and retail, on stage–that marks her as a star.
Everyone who hears her knows one thing.
She's Got It!
WHITNEY HOUSTON.
Her debut album features the first hit single, "You Give Good Love."
The Beginning Of Something Special!
ARISTA

19.03.88: 94-74-97-100-x-x-x-x-84-90-82-84-95-x-72-86-82-94-x-96-96

Australia
17.06.85: peaked at no.**1** (11), charted for 125 weeks
26.02.12: 81

Austria
15.02.86: 24-27-16-18-22-24-29-24-**9**-12-11-16-16-22-21-27 (bi-weekly)
2.03.12: 44

Canada
25.05.85: 91-87-82-77-69-59-47-42-36-29-26-22-21-19-17-16-17-17-15-13-10-10-11-12-9-9-13-14-14-13-12-12-12-12-19-19-12-11-6-4-2-**1-1-1-1-1-1-1-1-1-1-1-1-1-1-1-1-1**-2-3-3-4-4-4-4-5-7-8-8-9-10-11-11-14-18-20-20-25-23-28-26-24-23-23-23-23-24-26-26-26-23-22-22-24-27-32-32-35-36-42-42-51-51-49-49-56-56-56-65-65-66-66-67-64-59-59-57-57-57-57-61-61-67-67-83-82-83-84

Finland
01/86: peaked at no.**2**, charted for 41 weeks

Germany
26.08.85: 32-26-24-34-29-28-35-39-45-38-39-38-32-36-40-36-31-21-21-19-15-7-5-4-6-8-6-7-5-3-3-**2**-5-5-4-5-3-4-3-3-5-6-8-8-8-10-13-15-14-14-15-17-17-17-21-19-21-28-28-31-41-43-54-61-57-52
2.03.12: 86

Italy
6.05.86: peaked at no.**1** (4), charted for 29 weeks
23.02.12: peaked at no.72, charted for 7 weeks

Japan
1.04.85: peaked at no.**4**, charted for 76 weeks

Netherlands
30.03.85: 35-15-9-9-12-11-13-18-25-30-29-37-37-45-48
4.01.86: 63-18-11-9-9-10-9-9-10-7-10-10-13-16-17-23-26-24-23-23-14-8-7-**5**-7-9-11-16-17-15-16-14-18-19-27-27-31-25-41-31-43-39-45-50-30-32-40-46-59-65-54-61-61-44-34-40-35-41-54-56-40-30-43-55-65-55-41-64-62-75-67-x-71-50-53-62-45-33-33-32-24-26-40-43-48-46-40-56-73-66-45-55

Whitney
She's Got It!
The power.
The emotion.
The magnetism.
The kind of talent
that's going
to blow you away.
Whitney Houston.
This is only
the beginning.
Featuring
the hit single
"You Give Good Love,"
produced by Kashif,
and her hit duets
with Teddy Pendergrass
and
Jermaine Jackson.
Proudly,
on Arista Records.
ARISTA

New Zealand
30.06.85: 22-19-27-34-45-36-39-41-35-29-35-47-41-38-32-27-21-19-12-12-9-9-9-11-13-13-13-13-13-20-16-20-20-14-17-16-13-18-13-13-13-16-14-15-13-11-11-**3**-8-5-7-4-5-**1**-3-3-4-5-7-10-13-12-15-16-12-12-21-18-20-18-21-24-32-30-29-26-26-30-30-30-30-46-38-39-33-41-40-x-34039-46-45-41-45-47-47-43-x-49-49-x-x-x-x-24-20-31-25-20-22-22-31-23-25-32-38-44-x-x-41

Norway
25.01.86: 16-18-9-6-5-2-**1-1-1-1-1-1-1-1-1**-2-2-1-2-4-4-8-8-13-11-16-15-20

Sweden
5.02.86: 29-13-4-**1-1-1-1-1-1**-3-3-6-13-19-27-45 (bi-weekly)

Switzerland
29.12.85: 17-17-12-8-**2**-4-4-4-6-4-**2**-4-3-5-9-8-9-10-8-13-7-7-9-10-9-15-16-22-14-20-18-19-x-29

The budget for Whitney's debut album was $175,000 ~ a generous sum at the time, for a new artist (which actually rose to nearer $400,000, before the album was completed).

Initially, Clive Davis wanted to team Whitney with four different producers, to record maybe three songs with each producer. However, two of the first potential producers ~ Ray Parker, Jr. and George Duke ~ Davis approached politely declined to work with Whitney.

Whitney's first live performance on TV, of *Home* on *The Merv Griffin Show* on 29th April 1985, was watched by Jermaine Jackson. Having stayed at Motown when his brothers signed for CBS/Epic, Jermaine was now signed with Arista, and he was interested in working with Whitney. This, ultimately, led to *Someone For Me*, which Jermaine produced, and the duets, *Nobody Loves Me Like You Do* and *Take Good Care Of My Heart*.

Finding the right songs for Whitney, and the right producers, took the best part of two years but, ultimately, it proved to be time well spent.

Whitney's self-titled debut album debuted on the Billboard 200 in the States, at the end of March 1985, at a lowly no.166. It took twelve months to rise to no.1, where it stayed for 14 non-consecutive weeks. The album also hit no.1 on the R&B chart, where it stayed at the top for six weeks.

The album also hit no.1 in Australia, Canada, Italy, New Zealand, Norway and Sweden, and charted at no.2 in Finland, Germany, Switzerland and the UK, no.4 in Japan, no.5 in the Netherlands and no.9 in Austria.

WHITNEY HOUSTON was the no.1 best-selling album of 1986, and no.8 best-selling album of 1987, in the United States. In the UK, the album was the no.3 best-selling album of 1986.

Eight singles were released from *WHITNEY HOUSTON* in various countries (including her duet with Teddy Pendergrass), six of which achieved Top 40 status in one or more countries:

- *All At Once*
- *You Give Good Love*
- *Hold Me*
- *Saving All My Love For You*
- *How Will I Know*
- *Greatest Love Of All*

Thinking About You was issued as the second single in the United States, and as a promo 12" single in the UK. It rose to no.10 on Billboard's R&B chart, but failed to enter the Hot 100.

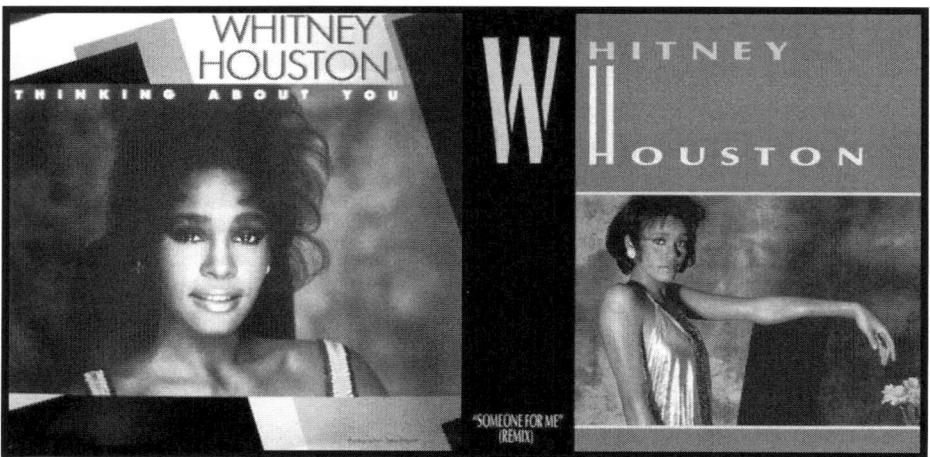

A remixed version of *Someone For Me* was chosen as Whitney's lead single from her debut album in the UK, but it wasn't a hit.

Whitney won her first Grammy Award, for Best Pop Vocal Performance, Female, for *Saving All My Love For You*, but missed out on the Grammy for Album of the Year, which went to *NO JACKET REQUIRED* by Phil Collins.

Whitney also picked up an impressive seven American Music Awards:

- Favourite Soul/R&B Single: *You Give Good Love*.
- Favourite Soul/R&B Video (1986): *Saving All My Love For You*.
- Favourite Soul/R&B Album.
- Favourite Soul/R&B Artist, Female.
- Favourite Pop/Rock Artist, Female (1987).
- Favourite Pop/Rock Album.
- Favourite R&B/Soul Video (1987): *Greatest Love Of All*.

WHITNEY HOUSTON was the first debut album, and first album by a female artist, to generate three no.1 singles on the Hot 100 in the States: *Saving All My Love For You*, *How Will I Know* and *Greatest Love Of All*.

Following the unprecedented success of her debut album, Whitney admitted, 'I had to catch up on all that Whitney Houston had become. It just took off so fast that I had to backtrack.'

Whitney persuaded her father, John, to become more involved in her career.

'First of all I was in trouble,' she said, 'and I knew that my father is a very wise man, a smart man. I figured that if there is anybody I can trust, it is my Daddy, because I know my Daddy loves me. And I know that before the business and the money came, it was just him and family. Plus, my Mom was on Daddy's case, to get him involved in my business … I feel secure that somebody is watching over me, and watching over everybody else, too. I trust him. He literally came in and saw the troubled areas and what needed to be done, what I needed to do, and we did it.'

'When I finished that first album, I felt successful,' admitted Whitney. 'I made some great songs, and people liked it. But with the second album coming, you know what people said to me? "Whitney, this is the most important album you will ever do." And I was like, huh?! I just sold thirteen, fourteen million albums, and now you tell me I have to work at success.'

THE DELUXE ANNIVERSARY EDITION

To celebrate the 25th anniversary of Whitney's debut album, a deluxe anniversary edition was released in January 2010, with five bonus tracks and a bonus DVD.

Bonus Tracks: *Thinking About You (12" Dance Remix)/Someone For Me (12" Dance Remix)/How Will I Know (Acappella)/How Will I Know (12" Dance Remix)/Greatest Love Of All (Live At Radio City Hall)*

Bonus DVD: *Home* (from *The Merv Griffin Show*)/*You Give Good Love*/*Saving All My Love For You*/*How Will I Know*/*Greatest Love Of All*/Interviews with Whitney & Clive Davis

The reissue entered the Billboard 200 in the United States for a solitary week at no.164, and peaked at no.21 on Billboard's Catalog albums chart, but it failed to chart in most countries.

2 ~ DANCIN' SPECIAL

How Will I Know (Dance Remix)/You Give Good Love (Extended Dance Version)/ Thinking About You (Extended Dance Version)/Someone For Me (Remix)/Thinking About You (Dub Version)/How Will I Know (Instrumental Version)

Japan: Arista 28RD-76 (1986).

1.11.86: peaked at no.**14**, charted for 12 weeks

This little known album, featuring remixes of tracks from Whitney's debut album, plus an instrumental version of *How Will I Know*, was exclusively released in Japan, where it rose to no.14.

3 ~ WHITNEY

I Wanna Dance With Somebody (Who Loves Me)/Just The Lonely Talking Again/Love Will Save The Day/Didn't We Almost Have It All/So Emotional/Where We Are/Love Is A Contact Sport/You're Still My Man/For The Love Of You/Where Do Broken Hearts Go/I Know Him So Well

Produced by Narada Michael Walden, except: *Love Will Save The Day* produced by Jellybean, *Didn't We Almost Have It All* & *You're Still My Man* produced by Michael Masser, *Where You Are* produced by Kashif.

USA: Arista 8405 (1987).

27.06.87: **1-1-1-1-1-1-1-1-1-1-1**-2-2-3-3-3-3-6-7-7-8-8-8-10-10-10-10-10-7-7-9-11-11-11-11-12-12-12-12-14-16-20-21-19-23-26-24-24-26-30-35-42-45-48-49-48-51-54-56-56-63-66-81-82-83-85-89-98
3.03.12: 87

UK: Arista 258 141 (1987).

13.06.87: **1-1-1-1-1-1**-3-3-6-4-4-6-4-6-7-13-15-16-17-21-23-31-36-23-18-14-14-20-16-11-10-13-18-19-22-24-27-32-25-24-16-15-14-13-11-14-19-10-10-9-6-9-9-13-4-11-13-14-16-17-18-20-23-25-31-28-33-29-27-28-24-30-27-33-39-44-47-53-64-76-68-57-51-36-38-39-43-45-56-44-53-52-56-61-60-62-73-74-71-64-70
18.09.99: 94

Australia
22.06.87: peaked at no.**1** (3), charted for 62 weeks

Austria
1.07.87: **1-1**-2-2-2-2-2-7-11-23-18 (bi-weekly)
15.07.88: 7-6-9-18-28-26-24-30-x-x-x-17-20-12-22-25-30 (bi-weekly)

Canada
6.06.87: 2-2-2-**1-1-1-1-1-1-1-1-1-1-1**-2-2-3-4-5-7-9-11-13-14-15-15-16-18-21-19-19-19-18-18-20-20-20-20-21-24-33-30-30-32-35-34-36-36-39-36-37-44-45-56-62-67-77-87-96

Finland
06.87: peaked at no.**1** (8wks), charted for 21 weeks

France
24.04.88: 24-**14**-18-23-27-23-30-29-30 (bi-weekly)

Germany
15.06.87: 2-**1-1-1-1-1-1-1-1-1-1-1**-2-2-3-4-7-11-15-22-30-27-35-35-49-44-47-55-55-57-55-63-64-62

Italy
2.06.87: peaked at no.**1** (5), charted for 21 weeks

Japan
1.06.87: peaked at no.**2**, charted for 26 weeks

Netherlands
13.06.87: 2-**1-1-1-1-1**-2-2-6-5-4-4-4-6-7-9-12-12-25-33-37-53-44-46-50-41-33-37-55-55-22-23-32-33-34-33-38-41-46-39-34-48-51-56-60
28.05.88: 31-21-28-43-26-13-14-9-8-9-10-10-9-12-13-14-12
18.02 89: 24-30-35-28-28-41-44-51-60-58-67-77

New Zealand
28.06.87: 7-**1-1**-2-2-2-5-4-6-5-5-5-9-9-11-16-19-25-30-35-23-34-36-37-27-41-41-41-41-20-26-24-44-39-31-34-40-35-37-41-43-43-43

Norway
13.06.87: **1-1-1-1-1-1-1-1-1-1-1**-3-4-7-12-20

Spain
31.08.87: peaked at no.**4**, charted for 51 weeks

Sweden
17.06.87: **1-1-1-1**-3-5-10-22-40 (bi-weekly)
8.06.88: 24-21-32 (bi-weekly)

Switzerland
14.06.87: **1-1-1-1-1-1-1-1-1-1-1**-2-4-7-9-8-12-15-16-30

Zimbabwe
16.08.87: peaked at no.1 (4)

'A lot of prayer helps,' said Whitney, when asked about how she handled the pressure of having to follow such a hugely successful debut album. 'I don't think about it in terms of trying to do better than before, or trying to outdo what I did before. It's a matter of just being the best you can be.

'You do have apprehension, but if you get into that "Oh, God, this has got to be this or this has got to be that", you sort of lose the magic and the creativity that goes along with it. You lose what it's all about. It's not mandatory that I sell thirteen or fourteen million copies worldwide. What is mandatory is that I continue to stay healthy, so that I can make records.'

'Sometimes she (Whitney) didn't know the songs,' said producer Walden, 'so it may have taken her a day to sing it through a bunch of times to learn it, but then on the next day, she would knock things out in one or two takes.'

'People have their own opinions about the record,' said Whitney, 'but it is basically me. A lot of more up-tempo things will be on this album. My ballads are still there, I can never do away with those. There are a few surprises and things.'

I Wanna Dance With Somebody (Who Loves Me), the album's lead single, gave Whitney her biggest hit to date, and the album was equally successful.

WHITNEY debuted on the Billboard 200 in the States at no.1 ~ the first album by a female artist to do so. Previously, only Elton John, Stevie Wonder and Bruce Springsteen had achieved this feat. The album topped the chart for an impressive 11 consecutive weeks.

The album also hit no.1 in Australia, Austria, Canada, Finland, Germany, Italy, the Netherlands, New Zealand, Norway, Sweden, Switzerland, the UK and Zimbabwe, and charted at no.2 in Japan, no.4 in Spain and no.14 in France.

WHITNEY was the no.2 best-selling album of 1987 in the United States, and no.3 best-selling album of the same year in the UK.

Six singles ~ all Top 40 hits ~ were released from *WHITNEY*:

- *I Wanna Dance With Somebody (Who Loves Me)*
- *Didn't We Almost Have It All*
- *So Emotional*
- *Where Do Broken Hearts Go*

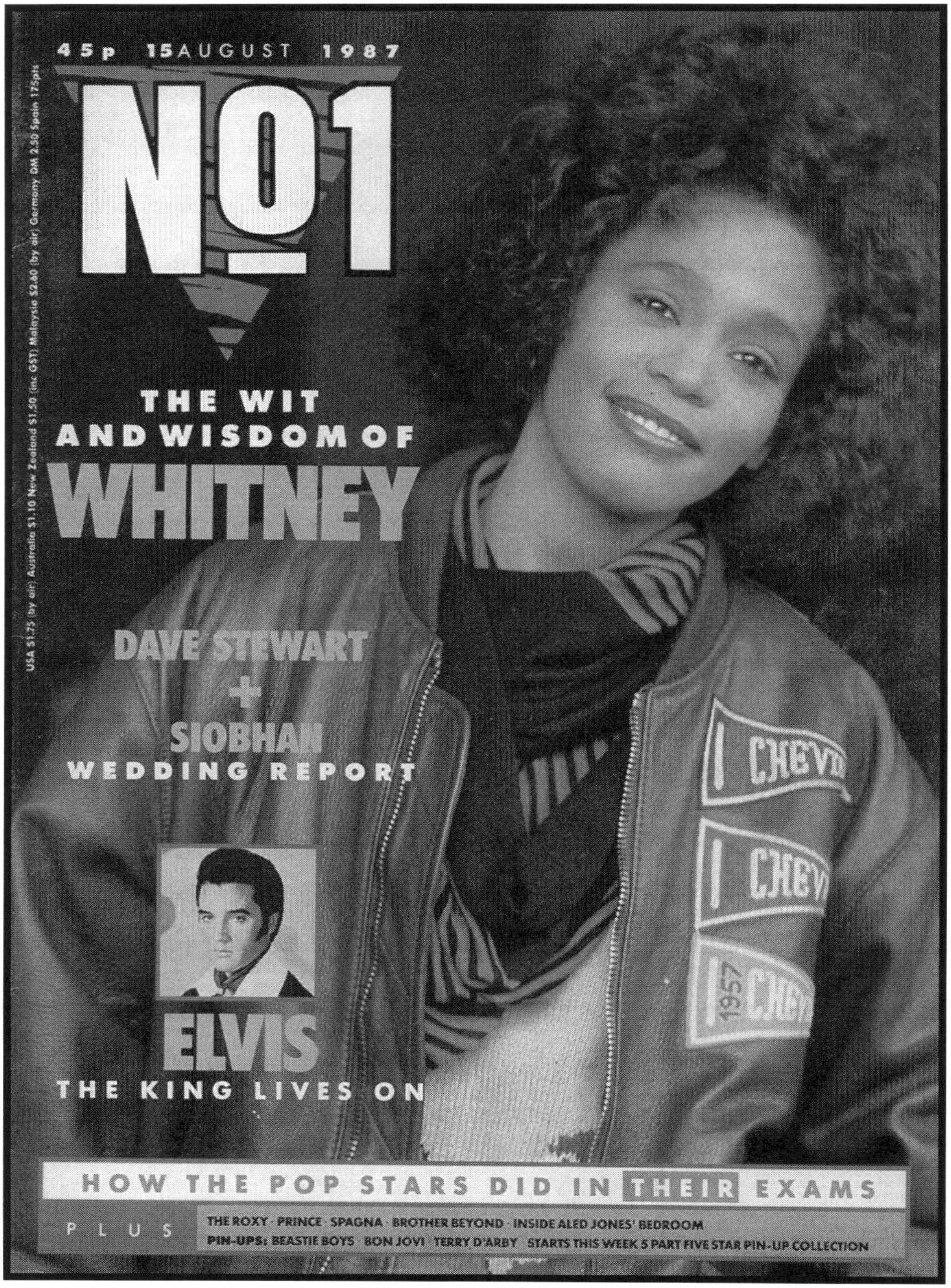
45p 15AUGUST 1987
No1
USA $1.75 (by air) Australia $1.10 New Zealand $1.50 (inc GST) Malaysia $2.60 (by air) Germany DM 2.50 Spain 175pts
THE WIT
AND WISDOM OF
WHITNEY
DAVE STEWART
+
SIOBHAN
WEDDING REPORT
ELVIS
THE KING LIVES ON
HOW THE POP STARS DID IN THEIR EXAMS
PLUS
THE ROXY · PRINCE · SPAGNA · BROTHER BEYOND · INSIDE ALED JONES' BEDROOM
PIN-UPS: BEASTIE BOYS · BON JOVI · TERRY D'ARBY · STARTS THIS WEEK 5 PART FIVE STAR PIN-UP COLLECTION
1957

- *Love Will Save The Day*
- *I Know Him So Well*

Whitney won a Grammy Award, for Best Pop Vocal Performance, Female, for *I Wanna Dance With Somebody (Who Loves Me)*, and picked up another four American Music Awards:

- Favourite Pop/Rock Artist, Female (1988 & 1989).
- Favourite Pop/Rock Single: *I Wanna Dance With Somebody (Who Loves Me)*.
- Favourite Soul/R&B Artist, Female (1987).

'Again and again,' said Whitney, following the success of her second album, 'I heard I was too white, because I had such huge success. I was accused of selling out, of being a black singer doing pop for white audiences ... I don't categorise either music or people on the basis of their colour, and there's no way I would attempt to make myself less black, whatever that entails, to be more commercial. I'm comfortable with myself, and I don't want to change anything.'

MUSIK EXPRESS SOUNDS

Nr. 7   JULI 1987   DM 4,50

DER IMPORT-REPORT PLATTEN PER POST

WHITNEY HOUSTON
Zur Sache, Schätzchen!

BRYAN ADAMS
„ICH HASSE BANDS"

BEASTIE BOYS & CO
DIE DRECKIGSTE PLATTENFIRMA DER WELT

THE CURE
INTERVIEW MIT ROBERT SMITH

4 ~ I'M YOUR BABY TONIGHT

I'm Your Baby Tonight/My Name Is Not Susan/All The Man That I Need/Lover For Life/Anymore/Miracle/I Belong To You/Who Do You Love/We Didn't Know/After We Make Love/I'm Knockin'

Japan Bonus Tracks: *Takin' A Chance/Higher Love*

Produced by L.A. Reid & Kenneth 'Babyface' Edmonds, except: *All The Man That I Need*, *Lover For Life* & *I Belong To You* produced by Narada Michael Walden, *Who Do You Love* produced by Luther Vandross, *We Didn't Know* produced by Stevie Wonder, *After We Make Love* produced by Michael Masser, *I'm Knockin'* produced by Whitney & Rickey Minor.

USA: Arista 8616 (1990).

24.11.90: 22-5-**3**-4-4-4-4-5-6-6-6-6-6-5-5-4-5-7-9-9-11-6-6-8-12-15-20-24-27-26-28-41-45-50-56-63-68-78-87-87-100-99
10.03.12: 39-32-61-76

UK: Arista 261 039 (November 1990).

17.11.90: 6-11-13-14-15-8-8-6-5-**4**-5-6-8-11-9-20-23-29-32-35-46-66-62-60-x-x-x-68
13.07.91: 74-67
14.09.91: 72-72

Australia
26.11.90: peaked at no.**9**, charted for 23 weeks

Austria
18.11.90: 13-11-**2**-**2**-3-3-5-5-9-7-10-12-14-18-15-12-14-14-26-25

Canada
17.11.90: 56-23-14-13-16-13-13-13-14-**12**-14-14-19-22-35-27-26-23-24-23-27-33-33-51-53-53-62-56-50-49-55-57-80

Finland
10.90: peaked at no.**2**, charted for 22 weeks

France
26.12.90: 27-**21** (bi-weekly)

Germany
19.11.90: 21-20-**3**-6-10-10-12-15-13-14-17-15-20-20-22-30-33-34-42-49-61-63-68-68-77-84

Italy
6.11.90: peaked at no.**5**, charted for 17 weeks

Japan
10.11.90: peaked at no.**6**, charted for 19 weeks

Netherlands
17.11.90: 64-11-5-5-**4**-6-8-13-13-12-9-8-8-8-9-11-18-18-22-34-43-53-67-83
29.06.91: 91-84-92

New Zealand
9.12.90: 45-35-39-39-39-39-27-36-23-34-36-42-30-**19**-26-22-48-48-29-43-50

Norway
10.11.90: 7-**5**-**5**-**5**-**5**-**5**-6-7-7-7-7-6-10-16-17

Spain
26.11.90: peaked at no.**6**, charted for 27 weeks

Sweden
21.11.90: 6-**3**-5-7-8-16-22-46 (bi-weekly)

184

Switzerland
18.11.90: **2**-6-**2**-**2**-4-5-7-8-5-7-11-13-14-16-9-13-20-30-39-31-34-38

Zimbabwe
11.02.91: peaked at no.7

'For three years I was everywhere,' said Whitney, prior to the release of her third album, *I'M YOUR BABY TONIGHT*. 'I kind of got sick of myself in the end, and that's why I took a break after the second album. I couldn't take it anymore. It got to the point where I'd lay down at night and I could feel people talking about me. In the end I had to get out of that fame aura for a while.'

Whitney acknowledged her third album was different from her first two, but said, 'I wouldn't say new, I would say an extension of what I've already done. I think that people will say it's new. They'll say it's something other than what I'm used to doing. I just think it was just a matter of time before this kind of music in me came out.'

'We wanted to come up with something that was different from anything Whitney had sung in the past,' said producer L.A. Reid, 'so we approached it from that angle. We wanted to give her a new direction and to pick the music up from where we felt she was lacking. We did feel that she needed more of a black base.'

'I loved working with L.A. (Reid) and Babyface,' said Whitney. 'L.A. and Babyface are actually known for their kind of R&B grooves, their funky grooves. But still, within the groove, we have songs, which to me is most important. Not only to dance and have the groove, but to have lyric content, something that says something. That's important to me, so I think that the music is not different, it's just growth.'

The number plate on the motorbike on the album's sleeve was 'NIPPY' ~ Whitney's childhood nickname.

I'M YOUR BABY TONIGHT couldn't match the success of Whitney first two albums, but it still sold very well in most countries. The album achieved no.2 in Austria, Finland and Switzerland, no.3 in Germany, Sweden and the USA, no.4 in the Netherlands and UK, no.5 in Italy and Norway, no.6 in Japan and Spain, no.7 in Zimbabwe, no.9 in Australia, no.12 in Canada, no.19 in New Zealand and no.21 in France.

Six singles were released from the album in various countries, but only the first four of them achieved Top 40 status anywhere:

- *I'm Your Baby Tonight*
- *All The Man That I Need*
- *Miracle*
- *My Name Is Not Susan*

I Belong To You rose to no.10 on Billboard's Hot R&B/Hip-Hop Songs chart, but failed to enter the Hot 100 in the United States. The single was also a minor no.54 and no.79 hit in the UK and the Netherlands, respectively.

We Didn't Know, a duet with Stevie Wonder, was the final single released from *I'M YOUR BABY TONIGHT* ~ it was only issued in North America. The single charted at no.20 on Billboard's Hot R&B/Hip-Hop Songs chart, but failed to enter the Hot 100.

Although it didn't win any Grammy Awards, singles from *I'M YOUR BABY TONIGHT* did pick up three nominations:

- Best Pop Vocal Performance, Female (1991): *I'm Your Baby Tonight*
- Best Pop Vocal Performance, Female (1992): *All The Man That I Need*
- Best R&B Vocal Performance, Female (1993): *I Belong To You*

5 ~ THE BODYGUARD

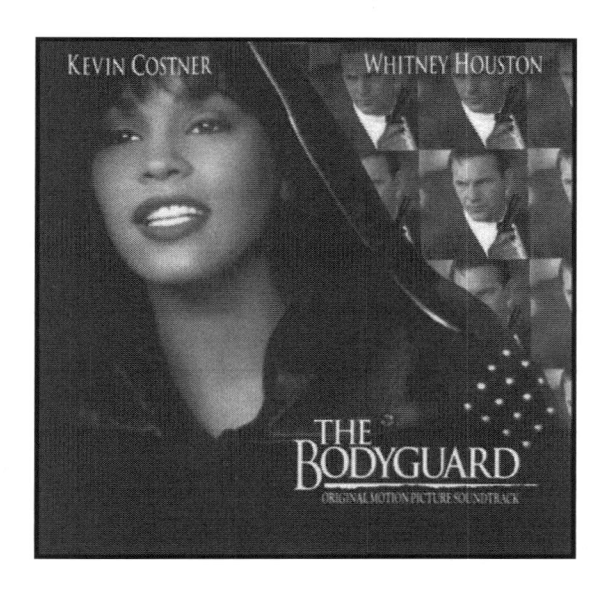

Whitney: *I Will Always Love You/I Have Nothing/I'm Every Woman/Run To You/Queen Of The Night/Jesus Loves Me*

Other Artists: *Even If My Heart Would Break* (Kenny G feat. Aaron Neville)/*Someday (I'm Coming Back)* (Lisa Stansfield)/*It's Gonna Be A Lovely Day* (S.O.U.L. S.Y.S.T.E.M.)/*(What's So Funny 'Bout) Peace, Love And Under-standing* (Curtis Stigers)/*Theme From The Bodyguard* (Alan Silvestri)/*Trust In Me* (Joe Cocker feat. Sass Jordan)

Whitney tracks produced by David Foster, except: *I'm Every Woman* produced by Narada Michael Walden, *Queen Of The Night* produced by L.A. Reid & Babyface, *Jesus Loves Me* produced by Whitney & BeBe Winans.

USA: Arista 18699 (1992).

5.12.92: 2-**1-1-1-1-1-1-1-1-1-1-1-1**-2-2-3-**1**-2-**1-1-1**-2-**1-1-1**-2-3-4-4-7-8-11-12-11-8-8-7-10-9-7-10-12-13-15-18-19-21-29-27-27-24-30-28-21-21-22-24-24-18-19-22-24-24-11-13-16- 6-11-18-25-25-32-34-36-42-35-47-54-70-51-55-52-62-74-75-78-71-73-79-87-88-93-x-x-x-x-x-x-x-x-x-90-85-91-91-89-86-86
25.02.12: 80-38-6-5-15-20-41-66-78

UK: Arista 18699 (1992).

28.11.92: 7-6-4-2-2-**1-1-1-1-1-1-1-1**-2-2-2-**1-1**-2-5-3-2-**1**-2-2-2-3-4-4-6-5-8-6-9-7-7-4-6-6-6-7-7-8-7-7-8-9-9-9-11-9-8-8-10-11-13-8-5-6-5-6-9-8-11-20-12-11-13-18-17-19-25-

DEC. 14, 1992/$1.25 64060 A JOHNSON PUBLICATION
JET
WHITNEY HOUSTON
And KEVIN COSTNER
Star In New Thriller,
'The Bodyguard'

19-17-22-23-21-21-19-19-21-18-22-21-20-19-21-27-27-29-47-x-x-42-25-25-22-28-29-28-36-40-40-45-44-x-49-48-49-39   (Compilations Chart)

Australia
14.12.92: peaked at no.**1** (5), charted for 80 weeks
26.02.12: 33-28-44-75

Austria
13.12.92: 34-9-9-7-3-2-**1-1-1-1-1-1-1-1-1**-2-2-5-6-3-4-6-7-10-10-12-20-14-17-30-26
24.02.12: 74-28-22-29-61

Belgium
16.09.95: 41-**20**-21-42

Canada
5.12.92: 19-4-**1-1-1-1-1-1-1-1-1-1-1-1-1**-2-2-2-3-4-4-4-4-5-5-5-5-6-7-6-12-10-19-28-31-27-29-26-23-23-21-19-19-20-21-29-28-36-35-62-62-68-67-75-81-82-80-80-75-48-31-32-37-33-29-27-25-21-22-35-35-35-34-58-73-86-91-91-90

Finland
12.92: peaked no.**1** (4 wks), charted for 22 weeks

France
22.06.96: 50
11.04.98: 69
21.04.01: 75-62-64
18.02.12: 22-**10**-25-39-55-78-89-95
25.11.17: 97

Germany
7.12.92: 98-58-24-24-18-12-**1-1-1-1-1-1-1-1-1-1-1**-2-2-2-2-2-3-6-8-11-17-20-21-23-23-28-25-17-15-14-15-14-17-16-17-19-29-24-34-34-43-46-53-61-63-59-62-57-57-64-53-59-59
2.03.12: 41-62

Italy
24.11.92: peaked at no.**1** (2), charted for 22 weeks
23.02.12: peaked at no.33, charted for 9 weeks

Japan
5.12.92: peaked at no.**1** (2 wks), charted for 78 weeks

Netherlands
28.11.92: 88-36-20-10-10-4-**1-1-1-1-1-1-1-1-1-1**-2-2-2-2-4-2-3-4-6-6-11-8-9-12-12-11-16-16-18-12-12-14-14-11-10-9-15-12-14-27-27-26-27-12-7-7-11-18-14-14-12-12-16-22-17-23-32-24-26-30-40-40-33-27-38-42-58-61-67-81-97
13.08.94: 95-80-78-74-73-84-97-97-100
16.09.95: 72-47-20-18-29-49-91

New Zealand
20.12.92: 38-38-38-38-4-**1-1-1-1-1-1-1**-2-1-2-2-3-5-6-7-8-6-10-13-13-15-26-24-39-35-49-45-48-x-46-46-x-42-35-31-45-52

Norway
26.12.92: 15-13-13-2-**1-1-1-1-1**-2-2-2-2-1-2-5-5-7-11-11-15-17-20

Spain
28.12.92: peaked at no.**1** (7 wks), charted for 50 weeks
20.02.05: 49-25-35-49-66-73-83

Sweden
9.12.92: 18-7-**1-1-1-1**-3-6-12-22-26 (bi-weekly)
27.10.93: 37 (bi-weekly)

Switzerland
6.12.92: 19-22-4-2-2-2-**1-1-1-1**-2-**1-1-1-1-1**-2-2-2-6-5-8-15-16-22-30-28-32-35-34
26.02.12: 43-88
26.06.16: 94

Zimbabwe
3.05.93: peaked at no.**1** (3)

Whitney was linked with several films, before she finally made a commitment to co-star in *The Bodyguard*.

Two films she passed on, principally because she didn't really want to play another artist who was still alive and active, were *Dreamgirls* and *What's Love Got To Do With It?*, a thinly veiled story of the Supremes and a Tina Turner biopic, respectively.

'Everybody thought of me doing it because it was so obvious,' said Whitney, referring to *Dreamgirls*. 'You want somebody who can sing and be a 'dreamgirl', get Whitney … whether I do it depends on how good the script is and what it says. If you're offering someone a specific part, I think the person who plays it should have some input.'

Whitney hesitated, too, when Kevin Costner approached her, to co-star with him in *The Bodyguard*.

'I wanted to do some acting,' she admitted, 'but I mean, I never thought I'd be co-starring with Kevin Costner! I thought, "I'll just get this little part somewhere, and I'll work my way up" ~ and all of a sudden I get this script, and I said, "I don't know. This is kind of ... big!" I was scared ... I wanted to do it. I made that clear at the very beginning. But I was stalling a little. I just wanted to be sure it was the right move for me.'

The Bodyguard was written by Lawrence 'Larry' Kasdan ~ originally, in 1976, it was proposed the two lead roles would be played by Steve McQueen and Diana Ross. McQueen, however, refused to accept second billing to Diana Ross and the project had to be shelved.

Three years later, another attempt to make the film also amounted to nothing, this time because of differences between the proposed co-stars, Diana Ross and Ryan O'Neal.

Kevin Costner, who played 'the bodyguard', learned about the script in 1985, when he was filming *Silverado*, with Larry Kasdan directing. Costner liked what he read, but both he and Kasdan were so busy, it was another five years before they finally got together, and agreed to produce the film together.

'Whitney Houston was the one person I saw in this role,' said Costner. 'She has the charm, grace and dignity to play Rachel ~ and she can sing! I really wanted her, and there was a moment in time where it was ~ could have maybe been somebody else. And I said, "No, I want to wait ~ I want to wait for Whitney".'

Whitney's initial reaction was lukewarm. 'I knew it was the right project,' she said, 'but Rachel (Marron)'s character had to be fleshed out a bit. In the first draft she was mean and bitchy all the time. I thought she should be a bit warmer.'

Other female leads were considered, including Madonna, but Larry Kasdan, producer Jim Wilson and Warner Brothers studio all agreed to wait for Whitney.

'We postponed the movie for a year to wait for Whitney,' said Costner. 'That's the game you play a lot of times with movies. Could somebody else play that role? Of course, somebody could have ~ but, nobody better.'

'It was something a friend of mine said to me that really helped me to decide on this,' said Whitney, 'and gave me the final impetus I needed to accept the role. She said, "Whitney, if you do this, do you realise what it will mean for other black actresses, for other black women, period?" Immediately I was encouraged. She was right. It's a very, very strong role for a black woman.'

'We had discussions with Larry Kasdan about directing his own script,' said Jim Wilson, 'but he had already committed to another film. Then we found Mick Jackson, who we felt had a superb sense of style that matched our feel for *The Bodyguard*, and suddenly we were on the right track.'

'You know, Kevin (Costner) is just the best,' said Whitney. 'He took me by the hand and showed me the ropes. He was so good to me and made me feel so comfortable. Movie making is a different thing ~ a long, drawn-out process.'

'When the first rush of *The Bodyguard* was sent to me,' said Clive Davis, 'there was little, if any, music at all. I mean, her acting was decent. It was good, but it was not bravura. I wrote a letter to the director and I said you've got to go back, you've got to shoot again.'

KEVIN COSTNER
WHITNEY HOUSTON
Never let her
out of your sight.
Never let
your guard down.
Never fall in love.
THE
BODYGUARD
15

'We'll come up with the music, we'll come up with great songs to show who Whitney is and what she is, and why she needs to be protected by a bodyguard. And the director at the time didn't get it ~ he fought it.'

Kevin Costner shared Davis's vision ~ and the original director was fired.

'Of course,' said Davis, 'the rest is history, because the songs are such a part of the film. The album has become the best-selling soundtrack album of all time.'

Originally, it was planned to include Jimmy Ruffin's *What Becomes Of The Brokenhearted* in the film, until it was discovered Paul Young had just covered the song, for another film, *Fried Green Tomatoes*.

'I didn't want to duplicate that,' said Costner, who suggested another song instead: Dolly Parton's *I Will Always Love You*. 'Dolly's song just was a song that I'd always really, really loved.'

But, concern was expressed how well radio would support a country song with an *a cappella* opening. Costner said, 'I don't really care ... but I wouldn't be too sure about that.'

There was also concern about how a mainstream audience might react to a mixed race romance. 'When Whitney was cast there was talk about, well ~ should we mention it, you know, in a scene?' said Costner. 'And all parties really looked at each other and we said, "No ~ let's not do that. This is a woman, this is not race".'

The Bodyguard had a budget of $25 million, and the storyline revolved around Whitney as Rachel Marron, an Oscar-nominated singer who is forced to hire a bodyguard, after she is stalked and receives death threats. The cast also included:

- Kevin Costner as Frank Farmer (*aka* 'The Bodyguard')
- Michele Lamar Richards as Nicki Marron (Rachel's sister)
- DeVaughan Nixon as Fletcher Marron (Rachel's young son)
- Gary Kemp as Sy Spector
- Bill Cobbs as Bill Devaney
- Ralph Waite as Herb Farmer
- Tomas Arana as Greg Portman
- Mike Starr as Tony Scipelli
- Christopher Birt as Henry

The film premiered on 25th November 1992 in North America, and opened to mixed reviews. However, commercially the film was a tremendous success, grossing $122 million in the States alone, and nearly $411 million globally.

Two songs featured in the film received Academy Award nominations, for Best Original Song: *I Have Nothing* and *Run To You*. Both songs lost out to Tim Rice & Alan Menken's *A Whole New World*, from *Aladdin*.

'I always knew I could sing,' said Whitney, 'but the acting came as a total surprise. The only person who said *The Bodyguard* would get that response was Kevin Costner.'

Asked if she felt Hollywood had accepted her as an actress, Whitney answered: 'I don't think they have a choice, I really don't. *The Bodyguard*, even if the critics didn't like it, the people did. People think the colour of Hollywood is black or white. The colour of Hollywood is green. It's called money ~ it's what they bank on.'

The accompanying soundtrack album is generally credited to Whitney, although she was responsible for only the first six of twelve tracks. Thanks to the mega-success of *I Will Always Love You*, the soundtrack's lead single, THE BODYGUARD hit no.1 around the world.

In the United States, the album topped the Billboard 200 for a mighty 20 weeks. The soundtrack went to no.1 in Australia, Austria, Canada, Finland, Germany, Italy, Japan, the Netherlands, New Zealand, Norway, Spain, Sweden, Switzerland and Zimbabwe.

In the UK, as it was a multi-artist soundtrack, the album was ineligible to enter the main album chart, but it did achieve 11 weeks at no.1 on the Top 50 Compilations chart.

Five of the six songs Whitney contributed to the album were released as singles, and all five were hits:

- *I Will Always Love You*
- *I'm Every Woman*
- *I Have Nothing*
- *Run To You*
- *Queen Of The Night*

It's Gonna Be A Lovely Day by S.O.U.L. S.Y.S.T.E.M., and Lisa Stansfield's *Someday (I'm Coming Back)*, were also hits.

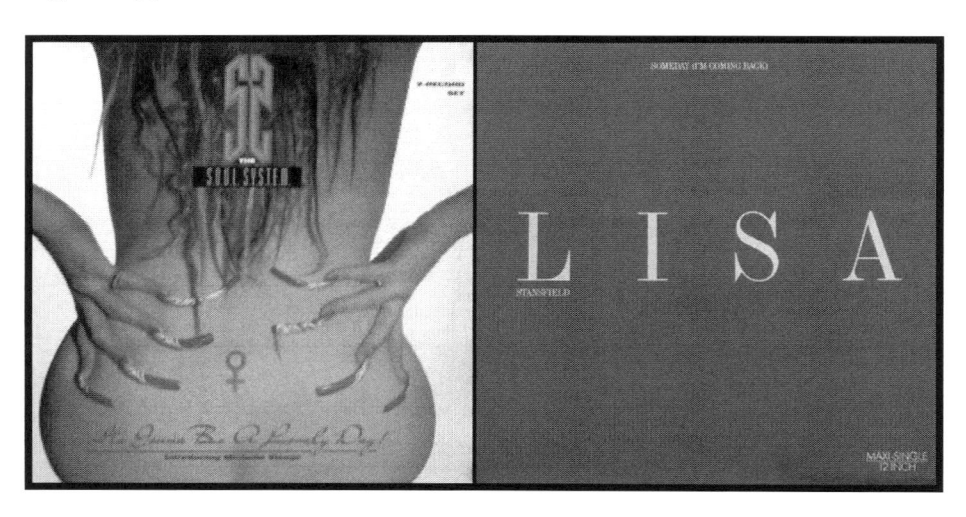

THE BODYGUARD won four Grammy Awards:

- Album Of The Year
- Record Of The Year: *I Will Always Love You*

- Best Pop Vocal performance, Female: *I Will Always Love You*
- Best R&B Vocal Performance, Female: *I'm Every Woman*

The soundtrack also picked up eight American Music Awards:

- Award Of Merit
- Favourite Pop/Rock Artist, Female
- Favourite Soul/R&B Artist, Female
- Favourite Pop/Rock Album
- Favourite Soul/R&B Album
- Favourite Adult Contemporary Album
- Favourite Pop/Rock Single: *I Will Always Love You*
- Favourite Soul/R&B Single: *I Will Always Love You*

The eight awards in a single evening was a record, for a woman, and equalled the all-time record set by Michael Jackson.

THE BODYGUARD re-entered the chart in several countries, following Whitney's passing in February 2012. The album rose to no.5 in the USA, no.10 in France, no.22 in Austria, no.28 in Australia, no.33 in Italy, no.41 in Germany and no.43 in Switzerland.

I WISH YOU LOVE: MORE FROM THE BODYGUARD

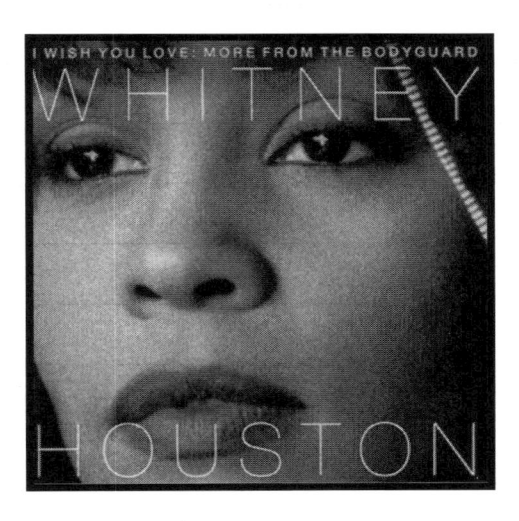

This album, released to mark the 25th anniversary of *The Bodyguard*, was released in 2017. It featured film versions, live performances and remixes of the six songs Whitney contributed to the soundtrack album:

I Will Always Love You (Alternate Mix)/I Have Nothing (Film Version)/I'm Every Woman (Clivilles & Cole House Mix I Edit)/Run To You (Film Version)/Queen Of The

Night (Film Version)/Jesus Loves Me (Film Version)/Jesus Loves Me (A Capella Version)/I Will Always Love You (Film Version)/I Have Nothing (Live From Brunei)/ Run To You (Live From The Bodyguard Tour)/Jesus Loves Me/ He's Got The Whole World In His Hands (Live From The Bodyguard Tour)/Queen Of The Night (Live From The Bodyguard Tour)/I Will Always Love You (Live From The Bodyguard Tour)/I'm Every Woman (Live From The Bodyguard Tour)

The release of the album was timed to coincide with a tribute to Whitney and *The Bodyguard*, performed by Christina Aguilera, at the American Music Awards on 19th November 2017. The album failed to chart in most countries, but it did achieve a lowly no.165 on the Billboard 200 in the United States.

6 ~ WAITING TO EXHALE

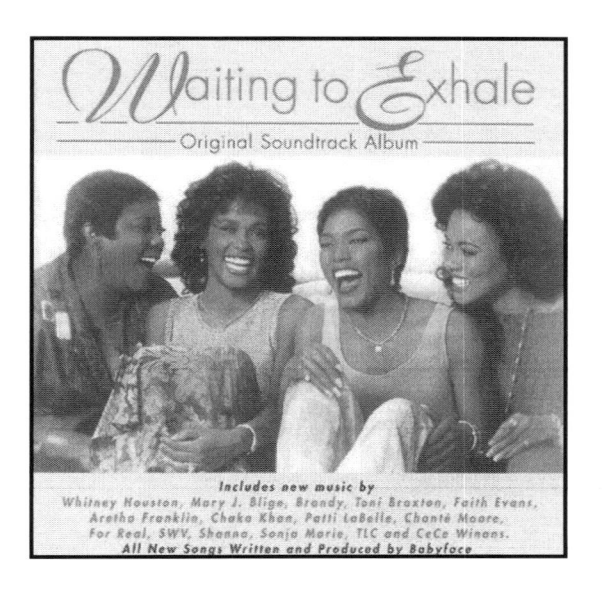

Whitney: *Exhale (Shoop Shoop)/Why Does It Hurt So Bad/Count On Me*

Other Artists: *Let It Flow* (Toni Braxton)/*It Hurts Like Hell* (Aretha Franklin)/*Sittin' Up In My Room* (Brandy)/*This Is How It Works* (TLC)/*Not Gon' Cry* (Mary J. Blige)/*My Funny Valentine* (Chaka Khan)/*And I Gave My Love To You* (Sonja Marie)/*All Night Long* (SWV)/*Wey U* (Chante Moore)/*My Love, Sweet Love* (Patti LaBelle)/*Kissing You* (Faith Evans)/*Love Will Be Waiting At Home* (For Real)/*How Could You Call Her Baby* (Shanna)

Whitney's tracks produced by Babyface.

USA: Arista 18796 (1995).

2.12.95: 3-5-5-5-4-2-2-**1-1-1-1-1**-2-3-3-4-5-7-7-10-10-11-12-15-13-13-17-25-27-33-43-50-58-69-72-69-73-81-82-95

UK: Arista 18796 (1995).

25.11.95: 21-25-37-40-42-42-38-37-27-27-10-**8**-12-14-15-22-26-28-31-38-34-38-41-46
17.08.96: 50   (Compilations Chart)

Australia
11.12.95: peaked at no.**7**, charted for 20 weeks

Austria
17.12.95: **14**-29-29-30-37-31-29-24-19-20-23-36-36-48-45

Belgium
2.12.95: 50-40-x-48-43
24.02.96: 44-42-50-34-**33**

Canada
4.12.95: 24-**3-3-3-3-3**-5-5-8-10-17-17-18-20-21-21-37-41-47-41-29-16-17-22-24-29-31-41-39-60-62-74-85-99-100

Germany
27.11.95: 83-x-37-44-55-62-47-40-41-**30**-33-32-39-50-55-62-75-81

Italy
9.01.96: peaked at no.**13**, charted for 7 weeks

Netherlands
25.11.95: 53-24-**16**-17-31-31-47-63-51-48-49-50-52-35-33-37-44-49-47-53-59-62-70-85-93

New Zealand
17.12.95: 27-39-39-39-x-20-17-**16**-24-21-19-20-28-33-50

Norway
16.03.96: **36-36**-x-38

Spain
13.11.95: peaked at no.**4**, charted for 24 weeks

Sweden
24.11.95: 31-26-25-32-37-36-**20**-34-31-37-36-35-34-32-28-34-x-48-53

Switzerland
12.12.95: 46-40-40-46-33-30-36-23-25-**20**-21-27-21-42-45

Zimbabwe
18.03.96: peaked at no.**1** (1)

Whitney's second film was based on the best-selling book of the same title by Terry McMillan. The story focused on four African-American women living in Phoenix, Arizona, and their relationships with each other and the men in their lives.

Echoing her *Saving All My Love For You* video, Whitney was cast in the role of Savannah Jackson, a television producer who believes ~ one day ~ her married lover will leave his wife for her.

Writer Terry McMillan wanted Whitney to play the character Savannah from the beginning. 'Whitney represents something wholesome and down-home,' she said. 'Little town girl makes it big. There's an innocence to Whitney, a vulnerability. Sometimes people think it's false, but it isn't. She takes a lot a criticism with grace and finesse ... everybody is trying to find out if Whitney was a bitch. She isn't. She's really down. She's blacker that most people think. I like her.'

'Her character is a lot like mine,' said Whitney. 'Savannah's very serious, a hard worker. Rachel, in *The Bodyguard* ~ now, her world and my world are a lot alike. I understand all that madness and craziness. But just Rachel herself, how she is ~ nothing like me at all. I was more of an actress in *Bodyguard* than I am in *Exhale*.'

'I believe in relationships,' said Whitney, 'and *Exhale* does that, too ... what your mama taught you, and what her mother may have taught her, is now different. Women are more independent. We had to be. It's not just about the men going out and being the greatest anymore.'

The film had an all-black cast, and 70% of the film crew were black as well. Shooting the film took sixty days, and Terry McMillan insisted on a black director: Forest Whitaker.

'Forest cares right down to the last detail,' said Whitney. 'He's very focused and always makes you feel very comfortable, like working with your brother ... the night before shooting, the entire cast and crew got together at a local bowling alley. I was first on the shooting schedule, and I remember telling Angela, Loretta and Lela how nervous I was. Angela said, "Just go in there and just do it". My sisters were most encouraging and I won't ever forget that.'

In addition to Whitney, the cast also included:

- Angela Bassett as Bernadine Harris
- Loretta Devine as Gloria Matthews
- Lela Rochon as Robin Stokes
- Gregory Hines as Marvin King
- Dennis Haysbert as Kenneth Dawkins
- Mykelti Williamson as Troy
- Michael Beach as John Harris, Sr.
- Brandon Hammond as John Harris, Jr.
- Wendell Pierce as Michael Davenport
- Donald Faison as Tarik Matthews
- Wesley Snipes as James Wheeler

The film's budget was $15 million, and *Waiting To Exhale* was released on 22nd December 1995 in the United States.

Whitney Houston
Angela Bassett
Waiting to Exhale
Read the Novel from POCKET BOOKS
Original Soundtrack Album Available on ARISTA RECORDS

'I'd like for people to leave the theatre knowing that they have been schooled,' said Whitney, 'let in on something that they maybe didn't know much about before. I hope they will have enjoyed watching the film as much as I enjoyed making it.'

As with *The Bodyguard*, the film opened to mixed reviews ~ however, it hit no.1 at the box office in North America, where it went on to gross over $67 million. Globally, the film grossed over $81 million.

'Babyface was chosen by (the film's director) Forest Whitaker to write a few songs, with Whitney's approval,' said Clive Davis. 'As 'Face kept writing more, he'd play them for me. I was awed by the magnitude of what he was accomplishing. My task was to use my position and credibility with 20th Century Fox to make sure the music made the film. L.A. (Reid), 'Face and I had already had the experience of *Boomerang* ~ a great soundtrack that's barely in the movie.'

Originally, the plan was for Whitney to record most, if not all the songs, for the accompanying soundtrack, but Whitney herself preferred other artists to record the majority of the songs, and she only recorded three ~ including a duet ~ herself. All three were issued as singles, and all three were hits:

- *Exhale (Shoop Shoop)*
- *Count On Me*
- *Why Does It Hurt So Bad*

A further four hit singles were released from *WAITING TO EXHALE*:

- *Sittin' Up In My Room*
- *Not Gon' Cry*
- *Let It Flow*
- *It Hurts Like Hell*

WAITING TO EXHALE hit no.1 in the States, spending five weeks at the top on the Billboard 200, but the soundtrack wasn't as successful in most other countries.

Elsewhere, the soundtrack achieved no.1 in Zimbabwe, no.3 in Canada, no.4 in Spain, no.7 in Australia, no.13 in Italy, no.14 in Austria, no.16 in the Netherlands and New Zealand, no.20 in Sweden and Switzerland, no.30 in Germany, no.33 in Belgium and no.36 in Norway.

Like *THE BODYGUARD* before it, as it was a multi-artist release, *WAITING TO EXHALE* was ineligible to enter the main album chart. It did, however, chart at no.8 on the Top 50 Compilations chart.

Terry McMillan's follow-up to *Waiting To Exhale*, titled *Getting To Happy*, was published in 2010.

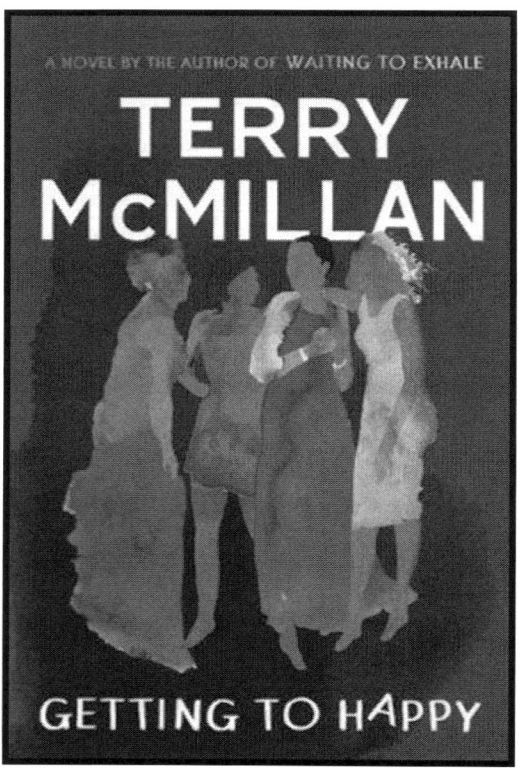

Set 15 years after *Waiting To Exhale*, *Getting To Happy* featured all the same lead characters as the first novel. There were plans to turn the sequel into a film, however, prior to her passing in February 2012 it hadn't been confirmed if Whitney was willing to reprise her role as Savannah Jackson or not.

7 ~ THE PREACHER'S WIFE

I Believe In You And Me/Step By Step/Joy/Hold On, Help Is On The Way/I Go To The Rock/I Love The Lord/Somebody Bigger Than You And I/You Were Loved/My Heart Is Calling/I Believe In You And Me (Single Version)/Step By Step (Teddy Riley Remix)/Who Would Imagine A King/He's All Over Me/The Lord Is My Shepherd/Joy To The World

All tracks performed by Whitney, except *The Lord Is My Shepherd* ~ performed by Cissy Houston with the Hezekiah Walker Choir.

Produced by Whitney & Mervyn Warren, except: *Step By Step* produced by Stephen Lipson, *Somebody Bigger Than You And I* produced by Whitney & Rickey Minor, *My Heart Is Calling* & *You Were Loved* produced by Babyface, *I Believe In You And Me (Single Version)* produced by David Foster.

USA: Arista 18951 (1996).

14.12.96: 12-4-**3-3**-5-4-6-7-8-12-18-25-28-33-38-38-39-43-44-60-76-95-91-59-71-97-95
3.03.12: 90-x-80

UK: Arista 44125 (1996).

14.12.96: 80-87-77-69-79-54-40-**35**-40-48-56

Australia
16.12.96: peaked at no.**27**, charted for 20 weeks

Austria
22.12.96: 22-22-24-23-12-11-**8**-11-11-14-22-20-21-30-29-36-35

Belgium
1.02.97: 42-41-37-35-x-x-x-**34**-38

Canada
9.12.96: 81-47-47-47-**29**-40-44-57-54-51-54-51-69-80-89-87-95

France
14.12.96: 45-46-46-**28**-**28**-33-35-38-46-45

Germany
9.12.96: 57-37-40-40-34-25-21-12-**9**-14-16-16-24-28-34-42-48-55-71-70-80

Italy
01.97: peaked at no.**22**, charted for 2 weeks

Netherlands
7.12.96: 95-86-77-77-74-73-66-71-62-51-46-49-24-**17**-27-42-68-77-99

Norway
18.01.97: **39**

Spain
2.12.96: peaked at no.**21**, charted for 19 weeks

Sweden
6.12.96: **16**-20-27-28-25-28-27-27-32-48-51

Switzerland
8.12.96: 19-16-15-15-18-36-19-18-15-12-15-**11**-**11**-16-25-28-38-36

Whitney's third film was a remake of the 1947 film, *The Bishop's Wife*, which starred Cary Grant and Loretta Young.

The film was re-titled *The Preacher's Wife*, and co-starred Denzel Washington. Whitney's mother Cissy appeared in the film as well, as a member of the church choir, and ex-Commodore Lionel Richie made his film debut as a nightclub owner. Whitney played the title role, Julia Biggs: the preacher's wife.

In the days leading up to Christmas, Julia's husband ~ the Reverend Henry Biggs ~ questions his ability to make a difference to his troubled home life and local community, when help arrives from a most unexpected source: a handsome angel called Dudley.

'The story appealed to me,' said Denzel Washington, 'because it's about the fundamental things we seem to have gotten away from in society: hope and faith in our fellow man, and in God, and the sense that family and church are the foundation of a community. I liked that about the story, as well as the idea of appearing in a film that would be saying positive, uplifting things.'

'Denzel started talking to me about this movie and how much he wanted me to do it,' said Whitney. 'I said I heard that Julia Roberts was slated to do it, but Denzel said no. I didn't think that would have worked, either. Denzel said you need someone who knows about church. He called me and we started talking about different things ~ working together, how good it would be because there is so much strife and stress and tribulation in the world, how spiritual it was, how the movie really hits home.

'I especially loved the idea that music would be part of the story. Music enhances a story. Singing a song, interpreting it, is like telling a story. People understand music sometimes when they don't understand words.'

'I'm usually acting in serious, heavy roles,' said Washington. 'This one is lighter, humorous and charming, and it was a nice change to be able to interact with the crew. Ordinarily, I'm off in a corner, brooding and preparing for a scene. The scenes here required an equal amount of concentration and preparation, but they were fun ... when Whitney agreed to come on board, everything began to fall into place naturally. And the fact that she would be able to sing Christmas songs in the movie, since music and church going are so much a part of the holiday, was a bonus.'

Whitney agreed. 'This was the most exciting thing for me,' she said. 'It gave me the opportunity to sing gospel, the music I love most. I've been waiting a long time to do something like this. Also, like Denzel, I believe in the theme of the film, that the church is the glue that holds the community together.'

'Julia and I clicked right away,' said Whitney, about her character, 'but she's more than just a loving mom and a wife. She cares about family values. She tries very, very hard to give back to the community. But she also gets angry. She gets ticked off. She's human. She has normal feelings, but she has to hold them back.'

The cast, in addition to Whitney as Julia Biggs, featured:

- Denzel Washington as Dudley
- Courtney B. Vance as the Rev. Henry Biggs (Julia's husband)
- Justin Pierre Edmund as Jeremiah Biggs (Julia & Henry's young son).
- Gregory Hines as Joe Hamilton
- Jenifer Lewis as Margueritte Coleman
- Darvel Davis, Jr. as Hakim
- Lionel Richie as Bristole
- Loretta Devine as Beverly
- Paul Bates as Saul Jefferys
- Lex Monson as Osbert

DENZEL
WASHINGTON
WHITNEY
HOUSTON
"Two Thumbs Up!"
-Siskel & Ebert
"Funny And Romantic!"
-Gannett Newspapers
The Preacher's Wife
ARISTA
TOUCHSTONE HOME VIDEO

- William James Stiggers, Jr. as Billy Eldridge.
- Marcella Lowery as Anna Eldridge
- Cissy Houston as Mrs Havergal

The film was directed by Penny Marshall and produced by Debra Martin Chase.

The Preacher's Wife opened on 13th December 1996 in North America, and went on to gross over $48 million. The film picked up an Academy Award nomination, for Best Music, Original Musical Or Comedy Score, but it didn't win.

Unlike *THE BODYGUARD* and *WAITING TO EXHALE*, the accompanying soundtrack album was all Whitney, with the exception of one song by her mom, Cissy. The album debuted on Billboard's Gospel albums chart in the States at no.1, a position it held for an amazing 26 consecutive weeks. The album also hit no.1 on the R&B chart, and peaked at no.3 on the Billboard 200.

The soundtrack didn't sell quite as well outside the United States, but it was a hit in most countries, charting at no.8 in Austria, no.9 in Germany, no.11 in Switzerland, no.16 in Sweden, no.17 in the Netherlands, no.21 in Spain, no.22 in Italy, no.27 in Australia, no.28 in France, no.29 in Canada, no.34 in Belgium, no.35 in the UK and no.39 in Norway.

Three singles were released from the album:

- *I Believe In You And Me*
- *Step By Step*
- *My Heart Is Calling*

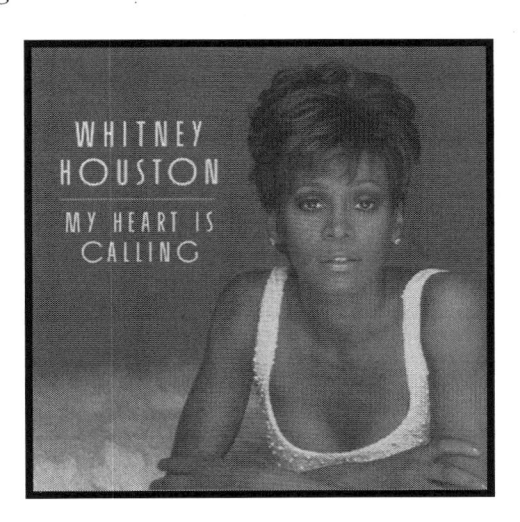

My Heart Is Calling was only released as a single in North America, and was only a minor hit, peaking at no.77 on the Hot 100 in the United States.

First The Bodyguard...
Then Waiting To Exhale... And Now

Whitney Houston
The Preacher's Wife

ORIGINAL SOUNDTRACK ALBUM

"A great pop album." The New York Times 11/21/96

"Whitney Houston is first and foremost a pop diva. No other female pop star quite rivals Houston in her exquisite vocal fluidity and purity of tone. An impeccably produced album." Los Angeles Times 11/24/96

"A bonanza for fans of pop music's paramount diva. 14 of its 15 tracks feature her glorious pipes." San Francisco Chronicle 12/1/96

★★★★! "Houston's heartfelt delivery is nothing short of breathtaking!" Chicago Sun Times 12/8/96

"The quintessential Whitney Houston album. There isn't a weak moment on this first-class effort." Richmond Times-Dispatch 12/5/96

"She cuts loose with those great pipes of hers. Her voice soars. There's 'I Believe In You And Me' and Annie Lennox's 'Step By Step,' and the Babyface-produced 'My Heart Is Calling.' They all give a thematic cohesiveness that soundtracks lack these days." USA Today 11/26/96

The Commitment Is Just Beginning!

Whitney picked up two Grammy nominations for *THE PREACHER'S WIFE*:

- Best R&B Album.
- Best R&B Vocal performance, Female: *I Believe In You And Me*

In both categories, Whitney lost out to Erykah Badu, for *BADUIZM* and *On & On*, respectively.

Whitney declined an invitation to attend the Grammy Awards ceremony, as she was disappointed her album hadn't been recognised as a gospel album, so hadn't been nominated in any gospel categories.

THE PREACHER'S WIFE is the no.1 best-selling gospel album of all time.

8 ~ MY LOVE IS YOUR LOVE

It's Not Right But It's Okay/Heartbreak Hotel/My Love Is Your Love/When You Believe/If I Told You That/In My Business/I Learned From The Best/Oh Yes/Get It Back/Until You Come Back/I Bow Out/You'll Never Stand Alone/I Was Made To Love Him

Produced by Babyface, except: *It's Not Right But It's Okay*, *If I Told You That* and *Get It Back* produced by Rodney Jerkins; Jerkins also produced *I Bow Out* with Babyface; *Heartbreak Hotel* produced by Soulshock & Karlin, *My Love Is Your Love* produced by Wyclef Jean & Jerry 'Wonder' Duplessis, *In My Business* and *Oh Yes* produced by Missy Elliott & Kelvin 'K.B.' Bradshaw; Lloyd 'Spec' Turner also produced *Oh Yes*; *I Learned From The Best* produced by David Foster, *I Was Made To Love Her* produced by Lauryn Hill.

USA: Arista 18699 (1998).

5.12.98: **13**-18-19-23-25-26-23-24-28-34-31-23-26-32-41-42-49-57-62-61-60-47-46-48-
   45-42-47-54-61-70-87-63-69-69-67-60-56-54-54-55-64-63-68-71-70-75-75-72-72-78-
   80-87-97-x-x-99-94-95-x-87-83-78-81-84-85-87-68-87-97
10.03.12: 30-31-52-69-95

UK: Arista 19037 (1998).

28.11.98: 27-36-51-56-55-54-71-62-57-51-60-56-58-37-22-10-5-13-17-16-22-30-30-31-
   29-27-18-10-13-10-9-6-5-5-**4**-**4**-5-6-6-10-12-15-14-18-25-8-30-25-34-39-57-57-55-62-
   48-32-28- 27-18-18-18-19-30-44-55-65-76-65-77-72

Australia
30.11.98: peaked at no.**24**, charted for 5 weeks

Austria
29.11.98: 43-22-15-18-21-21-16-13-20-24-33-33-37-36-13-26-21
23.05.99: 33-31-25-26-28-19-14-14-10-4-7-3-3-3-**1-1-1-1-1**-2-5-7-10-8-7-16-22-27-34-34-40-36

Belgium
28.11.98: 45-39-47
23.01.99: 39-36-44-x-43
22.03.99: 48-44-40-44-43-46-48
3.07.99: 43-32-23-13-9-4-4-4-3-3-3-4-**2-2**-3-4-10-15-20-30-36-49-x-x-38-x-50-44-48-43-38-49-x-50

Canada
7.12.98: 30-17-17-17-17-**13-13**-33-68-62-73-67-62-63-63-79-80-69-80-100-98-93-94-97-81-67-47-53-58-55-62-65-63-64-56-50-48-40-37-41-38-43-53-49-44-38-50-49-61-57-47-35-48-51-49-51-51-49-56-70-62-56-53-53-76-81-78-80-77-76-74

Finland
23.01.99: 38
10.07.99: 39-22-24-21-23-20-27-23-16-21-23-12-**5**-13-13-24-38

France
14.11.98: 14-6-12-16-15-18-17-26-32-37-47-40-49-44-49-46-31-22-18-22-18-21-21-31-33-42-46-45-62-55-52-57-62-47-42-29-28-15-7-3-4-3-**2-2**-7-8-10-11-14-15-17-20-23-22-24-23-21-22-19-22-18-20-31-38-41-53-54-65

Germany
30.11.98: 11-10-13-20-21-21-20-24-22-25-32-34-42-29-11-14-9-11-13-14-17-19-28-25-25-26-33-48-36-11-8-6-6-3-**2-2-2-2**-4-3-3-4-3-5-6-8-15-18-21-21-31-37-36-34-34-28-30-30-20-22-27-27-36-40-43-51-59-79-81-92-93

Italy
12.98: peaked at no.**4**, charted for 11 weeks

Japan
27.11.98: peaked at no.**12**, charted for 12 weeks

Netherlands
28.11.98: 51-52-63-72-72-41-39-31-35-36-38-52-63-58-60-40-26-27-33-35-40-39-37-40-34-33-50-53-44-30-25-21-20-17-15-5-**1-1-1**-3-5-7-10-14-17-25-27-33-39-43-55-67-65-52-52-5-47-47-47-44-41-46-48-37-19-19-26-42-54-53-64-74-64-65-72-77-81

Heartbreak Arrives & Love Soars!

Whitney Houston
my love is your love

Starring **Heartbreak Hotel**
(featuring Faith Evans and Kelly Price)
R&B: 7-1*-1* • Hot 100: 29-7*-4*
Explosive in the Whitney tradition!

"Singing with a bite in her voice like never before. Did you think she'd crumble? Did you think she'd lay down and die? Then check out My Love, pal, and hear Houston prove beyond a doubt that she will survive."
Rolling Stone

"With Love, Ms. Houston is the definitive pop-soul singer of her generation."
New York Times

"Houston's Love stands on its own. Soaring. Rollicking. The best of both worlds."
USA Today

my love is your love album: 34-31-23!
Already Past Double Platinum...
And Just Beginning.

ARISTA
www.arista.com

New Zealand
20.12.98: 41-47-47-43-29-19-**12**-14

28.03.99: 44-48
29.08.99: 48-50-40-x-40-45-30-35-40-47-29

Norway
27.12.97: 11
8.10.98: 5-7-9-11-12-7-7-**3-3**-5-7-13-8-18-31
14.08.99: 37-28-37-x-x-x-31-21-23

Spain
16.11.98: peaked at no.**12**, charted for 19 weeks

Sweden
26.11.98: 16-23-29-33-33-33-33-39-52-37-35-36-30-**7**-8-9-9-14-16-23-30-30-37-41-40-55-46-29-25-22-18-15-11-10-13-11-9-9-9-15-18-21-21-35-33-34-37
30.12.99: 47-53-56-44-53-56

Switzerland
29.11.98: 7-7-6-7-9-8-7-8-10-10-13-11-11-10-13-11-15-16-17-26-29-30-29-26-31-34-38-28-19-15-10-7-5-5-5-3-4-4-2-**1**-2-2-2-2-9-10-10-14-19-28-38-35-39-38-33-28-26-39-43-44-49-51-56-76-89-86

Whitney, when she went into the studio to record new songs, didn't know if her next project was going to be a greatest hits package with a few new tracks or a new album, but the sessions went so well the answer soon became clear.

'Clive (Davis) and I talked about this,' she said, 'and being that I haven't done a new album in over eight years, we felt it was time for a whole new album.'

'I wasn't into the syrupy kind of vibe,' said Whitney, explaining why she'd wanted a more 'street' sound. 'I just didn't feel like singing about *I Will Always Love You*. I'm a working mother, I'm a wife, I'm an artist. There are so many things that go into that, and it's not always like "everything is beautiful in its own way".'

Whitney readily admitted it wasn't an album she could have recorded five years earlier. 'I was much younger,' she said. 'I'm a lot more learned and a lot wiser about things. Being a wife and a mother kind of teaches you a little more about life and what you can endure ~ things you didn't think you could. I mean, I've endured a lot, in relationships and just in life, in the last ten years. I know more today that I did yesterday, so I can sing about it.'

'If anyone has underestimated the magnitude, the breadth of her incredible talent,' said Clive Davis, 'they're going to be surprised. You find when you get to the superstar level, the knives are always out, whether it's Madonna, Prince or Michael Jackson. They have to prove themselves, and they have to do it each time out. And Whitney's done that.'

'Today's music is basically youth-oriented,' said Whitney. 'It's lots of beats and rhythm. Sometimes in today's music, the lyric doesn't really play a major part. There are some great lyrics in these songs I've selected to do. That alone, I think, is going to be a surprise ~ just to hear the groove with somebody saying something, a storyline. That's very important to me.

'I've gone from singing too white to R&B diva, and now I'm hip hop. I guess it's flattering to know that I can sing it all. My mother always said if you can sing you can sing. Having a church background has allowed me to be able to sing every note, every lyric. I'm not a hip hop buyer. But I love Mary J. Blige – I love the best of hip hop. To me, Wyclef (Jean) is not hip hop, Faith (Evans) is not hip hop. Music is a wide range.

'Anyone who thinks all I have to do is sing has no idea. I don't just come in and they give me a song, and I sing it, and leave.'

Following the disappointing showing of the lead single, *When You Believe*, in the United States, *MY LOVE IS YOUR LOVE* debuted on the Billboard 200 at a relatively lowly no.13, and climbed no higher despite the success of later singles.

Globally, in terms of chart placings and chart longevity, the album was much more successful. *MY LOVE IS YOUR LOVE* went all the way to no.1 in Austria, the Netherlands and Switzerland, and achieved no.2 in Belgium, France and Germany, no.3 in Norway, no.4 in Italy and the UK, no.5 in Finland, no.7 in Sweden, no.12 in Japan, New Zealand and Spain, no.13 in Canada and no.24 in Australia.

The album produced five hit singles:

- *When You Believe*
- *Heartbreak Hotel*
- *It's Not Right But It's Okay*
- *My Love Is Your Love*
- *I Learned From The Best*

Whitney received seven Grammy Award nominations for *MY LOVE IS YOUR LOVE*, but came away with only one award:

- Best R&B Vocal Performance, Female: *It's Not Right But It's Okay*

She was also nominated for, but didn't win:

- Best Pop Collaboration with Vocals: *When You Believe*
- Best R&B Album
- Best R&B Song: *Heartbreak Hotel*
- Best R&B Song: *It's Not Right But It's Okay*
- Best R&B Performance by a Duo or Group with Vocal: *Heartbreak Hotel*
- Best Song Written for a Motion Picture, Television or Other Visual Media: *When You Believe*.

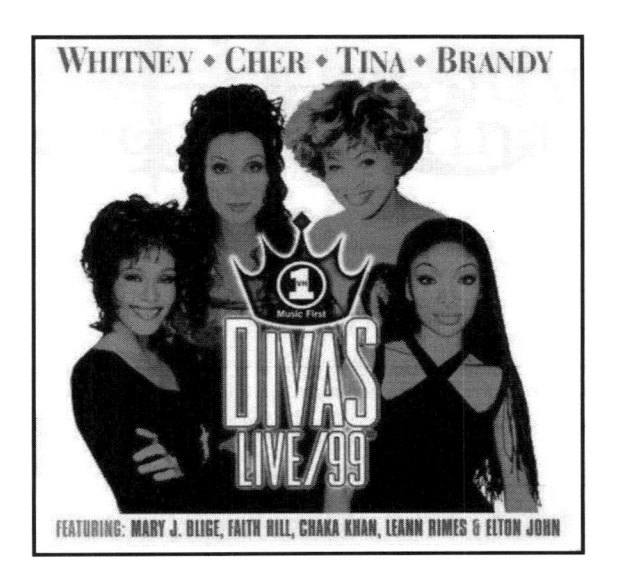

9 ~ VH-1 DIVAS LIVE/99

The Best ~ Tina Turner
The Bitch Is Back ~ Tina Turner & Elton John
Proud Mary ~ Tina Turner, Elton John & Cher
If I Could Turn Back Time ~ Cher
How Do I Live ~ LeAnn Rimes
I'm Still Standing ~ Elton John
Have You Ever?/Almost Doesn't Count ~ Brandy
(Everything I Do) I Do It For You ~ Brandy & Faith Hill
This Kiss ~ Faith Hill
Ain't No Way ~ Whitney & Mary J. Blige
I Will Always Love You ~ Whitney
I'm Every Woman ~ Whitney & Chaka Khan
I'm Every Woman (Reprise) ~ Whitney, Chaka Khan, Faith Hill, Brandy, LeAnn Rimes
    & Mary J. Blige

USA: Arista 07822 14604 2 (1999).

20.11.99: **90**

UK: Arista 07822 14604 2 (1999).

VH-1 DIVAS LIVE/99 wasn't a hit in the UK.

Austria
21.11.99: 45-**43**

France
15.01.00: 62-**42**-x-x-62-49-72

Germany
15.11.99: 85-**60**-80-100-66-88-89-89

Netherlands
6.11.99: 83-54-56-64-45-42-**41**-42-42-44-58-77-93

Switzerland
14.11.99: **14**-21-23-31-30-48-64-64-93

The VH-1 Divas Live 2: An Honors Concert For VH1's Save The Music concert was staged at New York's Beacon Theater on 13th April 1999, and was aired live on TV in the United States.

Among the show's presenters were Claudia Schiffer, Elizabeth Hurley and Sarah Michelle Gellar, while celebrity guests in attendance included Donald Trump and Hugh Grant.

During the concert Whitney performed:

- *It's Not Right But It's Okay*
- *Ain't No Way* (with Mary J. Blige)
- *My Love Is Your Love* (with Treach)
- *I Will Always Love You*
- *I'm Every Woman* (with Chaka Khan)
- *I'm Every Woman (Reprise)* (with Chaka Khan, Faith Hill, Brandy, LeAnn Rimes & Mary J. Blige)

It's Not Right But It's Okay and *My Love Is Your Love* were omitted from the *VH-1 DIVAS LIVE/99* album (and accompanying home video), but both were later made available via US iTunes.

Despite the impressive line-up, *VH-1 DIVAS LIVE/99* only spent one week on the Top 100 of the Billboard 200, at no.90, in the United States, and failed to chart in the UK. The album performed better in continental Europe, charting at no.14 in Switzerland, no.41 in the Netherlands, no.42 in France, no.43 in Austria and no.60 in Germany.

10 ~ THE GREATEST HITS

USA Disc 1 (Cool Down): *You Give Good Love/Saving All My Love For You/Greatest Love Of All/All At Once/If You Say My Eyes Are Beautiful/Didn't We Almost Have It All/Where Do Broken Hearts Go/All The Man That I Need/Run To You/I Have Nothing/I Will Always Love You/Exhale (Shoop Shoop)/Why Does It Hurt So Bad/I Believe In You And Me/Heartbreak Hotel/My Love Is Your Love/Same Script, Different Cast/Could I Have This Kiss Forever*

USA Disc 2 (Throw Down): *Fine/If I Told You That (Duet Version)/It's Not Right But It's Okay (Thunderpuss Mix)/My Love Is Your Love (Jonathan Peters Mix)/Heartbreak Hotel (Hex Hector Mix)/I Learned From The Best (HQ2 Mix)/Step By Step (Junior Vasquez Mix)/I'm Every Woman (Clivilles & Cole Mix)/ Queen Of The Night (CJ Mackintosh Mix)/I Will Always Love You (Hex Hector Mix)/Love Will Save The Day (Jellybean/David Morales Mix)/I'm Your Baby Tonight (Dronez Mix)/So Emotional (David Morales Mix)/I Wanna Dance With Somebody (Who Loves Me) (Junior Vasquez Mix)/How Will I Know (Junior Vasquez Mix)/Greatest Love Of All (Junior Vasquez Mix)/One Moment In Time/The Star-Spangled Banner (Live)*

This edition was also released in Canada and Mexico.

Circuit City Edition CD Bonus Tracks: *Greatest Love Of All (Club 69 Mix)/So Emotional (David Morales Emotional Club Mix)*

UK Disc 1 (Cool Down): *Saving All My Love For You/Greatest Love Of All/One Moment In Time/I Have Nothing/I Will Always Love You/Run To You/You Give Good Love/All At Once/Where Do Broken Hearts Go/If You Say My Eyes Are Beautiful/Didn't We Almost Have It All/All The Man That I Need/Exhale (Shoop Shoop)/Count On Me/I Believe In You*

And Me/I Learned From The Best/ Same Script, Different Cast/Could I Have This Kiss Forever

UK Disc 2 (Throw Down): *If I Told You That (Duet Version)/Fine/My Love Is Your Love/It's Not Right But It's Okay/Heartbreak Hotel/Step By Step/Queen Of The Night (CJ Mackintosh Mix)/I'm Every Woman/Love Will Save The Day/I'm Your Baby Tonight/So Emotional/I Wanna Dance With Somebody (Who Loves Me)/How Will I Know/I Will Always Love You (Hex Hector Mix)/Greatest Love Of All (Club 69 Mix)/It's Not Right But It's Okay (Thunderpuss Mix)/I'm Your Baby Tonight (Dronez Mix)*

This edition was released internationally.

USA: Arista 14626 (2000).

3.06.00: 5-9-11-14-20-23-27-30-36-41-43-52-55-64-68-82-90
25.02.12: 6-**2-2-2**-6-6-9-12-24-30-35-28-41-33-52-56-68-79

UK: Arista 75739 (2000).

27.05.00: **1-1**-2-3-5-6-7-5-5-6-6-7-11-5-8-9-10-13-16-16-16-17-20-16-16-18-22-9-13-15-12-15-14-14-20-25-35-37-37-38-43-58-65-72-52-64-78-76-88-95-x-x-x-x-x-x-37-39-41-54
7.08.04: 94-87-x-x-82-x-x-x-x-54-60-99-77-60-57-75-72-86-x-96-91-91
9.04.05: 83-95
22.10.05: 96
4.02.06: 96-x-97-x-91-58-59-72-61-61-65-63-77-x-x-x-x-89-84-92
16.09.06: 96
25.02.12: 7-36-99
25.10.18: 100
24.01.19: 98

Australia
15.05.00: peaked at no.6, charted for 18 weeks
26.02.12: **3**-10-15-28-37-57-85-x-x-x-87-84

Austria
28.05.00: **3-3**-5-7-7-10-12-20-15-21-22-21-21-27-25-27-32-35-48
24.02.12: 42-66

Belgium
20.05.00: 15-**2-2-2**-3-4-5-5-7-9-12-13-15-16-19-21-19-20-23-24-29-30-37-31-43
23.12.00: 42-34-34-30-32-42-42-44

218

Canada
29.05.00: **4**-11-10-13-13-26-18-25-45-43-38-47-52-74-76-80-80-84-85

Finland
13.05.00: 15-14-14-16-19-15-11-**7**-11-15-13-8-16-14-25-30-38-39-x-x-17-20-15-20-23-28-x-32-30-30-31-35-39

France
11.02.12: 99-27-9-18-33-44-66-82-92
18.02.12: **5**-26 (*THE DIVAS*)

Germany
29.05.00: **2**-4-4-7-8-10-13-12-19-23-25-30-30-29-31-32-35-33-33-45-51-52-58-65-75-76-87-81-95-57-45-45-40-56-61-71-85-95
2.03.12: 37-85

Italy
25.05.00: peaked at no.**4**, charted for 37 weeks

Japan
20.05.00: peaked at no.**4**, charted for 16 weeks

Netherlands
20.05.00: 15-**2**-3-5-5-10-10-9-6-5-8-14-23-27-28-29-18-13-11-16-31-29-30-35-49-62-59-59-77-74-81-90-90-87-89-93

New Zealand
25.06.00: **9**-19-26-34-39-45-x-48-50-48-41-46-41-43-44
20.02.12: 18

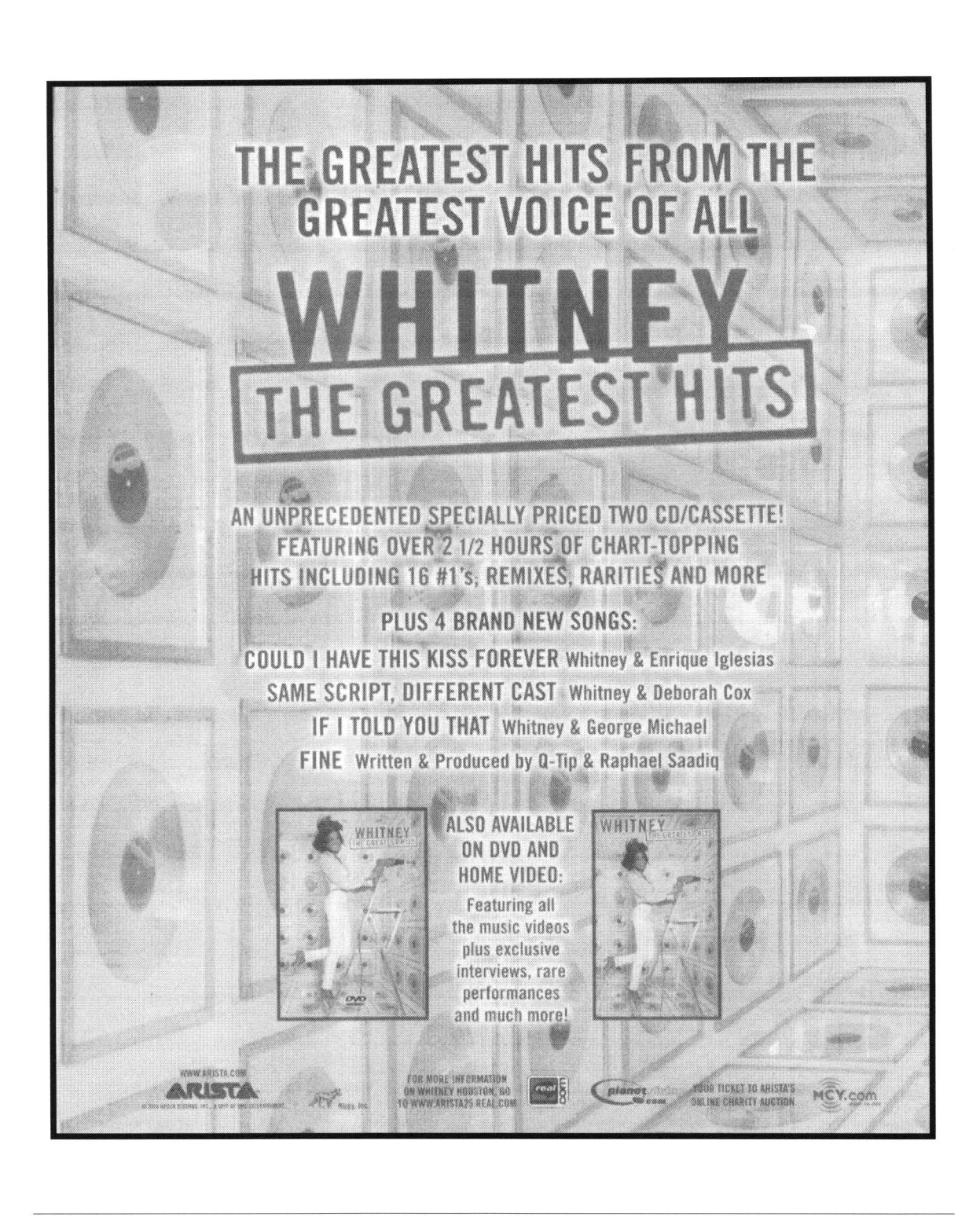

THE GREATEST HITS FROM THE GREATEST VOICE OF ALL

WHITNEY
THE GREATEST HITS

**AN UNPRECEDENTED SPECIALLY PRICED TWO CD/CASSETTE!
FEATURING OVER 2 1/2 HOURS OF CHART-TOPPING
HITS INCLUDING 16 #1's, REMIXES, RARITIES AND MORE**

PLUS 4 BRAND NEW SONGS:

COULD I HAVE THIS KISS FOREVER Whitney & Enrique Iglesias
SAME SCRIPT, DIFFERENT CAST Whitney & Deborah Cox
IF I TOLD YOU THAT Whitney & George Michael
FINE Written & Produced by Q-Tip & Raphael Saadiq

ALSO AVAILABLE ON DVD AND HOME VIDEO:
Featuring all the music videos plus exclusive interviews, rare performances and much more!

WWW.ARISTA.COM
ARISTA

FOR MORE INFORMATION ON WHITNEY HOUSTON, GO TO WWW.ARISTA25.REAL.COM

YOUR TICKET TO ARISTA'S ONLINE CHARITY AUCTION
MCY.com

Norway
20.05.00: 11-15-10-7-**6**-8-11-13-15-16-11-14-15-16-22-32
25.02.12: 11-38

Spain
30.04.06: **90**

Sweden
25.05.00: **4-4**-6-8-9-9-7-10-7-8-10-12-14-16-11-10-9-12-19-18-17-22-33-23-33-32-42-x-x-49-49-43-38-48-42-50

Switzerland
21.05.00: 29-3-**2**-4-3-5-5-7-8-11-15-18-18-18-17-20-30-32-36-33-39-42-41-58-63-75-86-x-x-x-x-95-79-82-x-85
26.02.12: 14-14-16-19-28-53-70-87-98
9.09.18: 26-86
21.04.19: 60

Whitney's first international compilation included seven tracks that hadn't appeared on one of her albums before, including three previously unreleased duets:

- *If You Say My Eyes Are Beautiful* ~ with Jermaine Jackson.
- *Same Script, Different Cast* ~ with Deborah Cox.
- *Could I Have This Kiss Forever* ~ with Enrique Iglasias.
- *Fine.*
- *If I Told You That* ~ with George Michael.
- *One Moment In Time.*
- *The Star-Spangled Banner (Live)* ~ USA edition only

A promotional 'preview' five track CD-ROM was given away free with *The Mail On Sunday* newspaper dated 10th December 2000 in the UK. It featured the following tracks:

- *Heartbreak Hotel* (video)
- *My Love Is Your Love (Wyclef Remix)*
- *I Learned From The Best* (video)
- *Greatest Mega-Mix*
- *Greatest Hits CD Commercial* (video)

THE GREATEST HITS debuted at no.1 in the UK, and charted at no.2 in Belgium, Germany, the Netherlands and Switzerland, no.3 in Austria, no.4 in Canada, Italy, Japan and Sweden, no.5 in the USA, no.6 in Australia and Norway, no.7 in Finland and no.9 in New Zealand.

Four of the previously unreleased tracks on the compilation were released or promoted as singles, with three of them achieving Top 40 status in one or more countries:

- *Same Script, Different Cast*
- *If I Told You That*
- *Could I Have This Kiss Forever*

The one exception was *Fine*, which spent a solitary week at no.50 in Sweden, but wasn't a hit anywhere else.

Following Whitney's passing in February 2012, THE GREATEST HITS re-entered the charts in many countries, peaking at no.2 in the USA, no.3 in Australia, no.5 in France, no.7 in the UK, no.11 in Norway, no.14 in Switzerland, no.18 in New Zealand, no.37 in Germany and no.42 in Austria.

11 ~ LOVE, WHITNEY

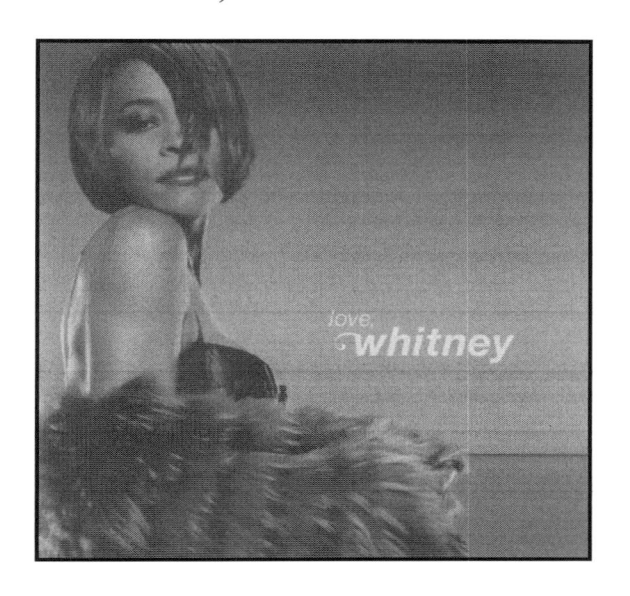

Until You Come Back/I Have Nothing/Why Does It Hurt So Bad/You Give Good Love/All The Man That I Need/Where Do Broken Hearts Go/Just The Lonely Talking Again/Exhale (Shoop Shoop)/Miracle/For The Love Of You/Saving All My Love For You/Run To You/I Believe In You And Me/Didn't We Almost Have It All/All At Once/I Will Always Love You

USA: Not Released.

UK: Arista 14725 (2001).

16.02.02: 33-**22**-56-89

Austria
9.12.01: **42**-58-57-59-72-73

Italy
6.12.01: peaked at no.**10**, charted for 12 weeks

Japan
5.12.01: peaked at no.**34**, charted for 5 weeks

Netherlands
9.02.02: 35-36-**24**-24-33-46-60

Sweden
29.03.02: 18-**12**-19-36-39-45

Switzerland
9.12.01: 39-44-**37-37**-38-41-40-64-51-65-74-74-78

This compilation of ballads ~ a mix of hits and album tracks ~ was released in Europe and the Far East, but wasn't issued in the United States.

Although *LOVE, WHITNEY* was released towards the end of 2001, the compilation didn't chart until early 2002 in the UK when, boosted by the Valentine's Day market, it rose to no.22.

LOVE, WHITNEY also achieved no.10 in Italy, no.12 in Sweden, no.24 in the Netherlands, no.34 in Japan, no.37 in Switzerland and no.42 in Austria.

12 ~ JUST WHITNEY...

USA: *One Of Those Days/Tell Me No/Things You Say/My Love/Love That Man/Try It On My Own/Dear John Letter/Unashamed/You Light Up My Life/Whatchulookinat*

UK: *Whatchulookinat/Tell Me No/One Of Those Days/Things You Say/My Love/Love That Man/Try It On My Own/Dear John Letter/Unashamed/You Light Up My Life/Whatchulookinat (P. Diddy Remix)*

The UK edition was released internationally.

Two Disc Edition with Bonus DVD featured: *Whatchulookinat* (Video)/*Love To Infinity Megamix* (Video)/*Whatchulookinat* (Behind the Scenes).

Produced by Babyface, except: *One Of Those Days* and *Dear John Letter* produced by Kevin Briggs, *Whatchulookinat* produced by Bobby Brown & Balewa Muhammad, *Things You Say* produced by Missy Elliott, Charlie & Kenny Bereal, *My Love* produced by Teddy Bishop & Gordon Chambers, *Unashamed* produced by Troy Taylor & The Formula, *Love That Man* co-produced by Rob Fusari, *You Light Up My Life* co-produced by Rickey Minor.

USA: Arista 14747 (2002).

28.12.02: **9**-30-36-41-41-48-51-50-68-97-100
17.03.12: 50-65-79

UK: Arista 19037 (2002).

7.12.02: **76**-99

Austria
8.12.02: **33**-37-56-58-69-69-71

Canada
12.02: peaked at no.**85**

France
30.11.02: **25**-41-55-65-57-63-70-85-88

Germany
9.12.02: **16**-39-48-48-53-52-55-84-88

Italy
28.11.02: peaked at no.**20**, charted for 8 weeks

Japan
27.11.02: peaked at no.**41**, charted for 9 weeks

Netherlands
7.12.02: **70**-92-x-x-90-91

Switzerland
8.12.02: **10**-12-23-23-39-49-45-40-57-71-74-80-92

For her fifth studio album, Whitney aimed to create 'a positive, feel good, very soul-oriented album, something I felt was missing. I hear lots of things on the radio, but I don't hear any R&B songs with bold, new flavour ~ songs you can sing along to and love the melody. That's what I was looking for.'

Whitney's vision was shared by L.A. Reid.

'We really wanted to re-establish a core urban base for Whitney,' he said. 'It was important to do that, because for an artist of her calibre, it's easy to get lost and start to not pay attention or understand the value in our core urban market. That's so key for her. It's not like it once was ... if you look at black artists with success, you find they're making music for their core, and not necessarily for the masses.

'Whitney's core following of loyal fans have rallied behind her in a way that underscores a profound love affair with their favourite singer. Their support of Whitney has resulted in another crowning achievement in a career already filled with amazing accomplishments. I am just thrilled that *JUST WHITNEY*... is an album that has more than fulfilled expectations of fans all over the world.'

'This album for me is about surviving,' said Whitney, 'raising a family, being a wife or girlfriend and all the challenges that go along with those things. These songs are more about creating a mood, than about anything in particular.'

JUST WHITNEY... debuted on the Billboard 200 at no.9, but tumbled to no.30 the following week, and could only manage three weeks in the Top 40.

In many countries, *JUST WHITNEY...* proved to be Whitney's least successful studio album to date. The album achieved no.10 in Switzerland, no.16 in Germany, no.20 in Italy, no.25 in France, no.33 in Austria and no.41 in Japan, but it was only a minor hit in Canada, the Netherlands and the UK.

Three singles were released from *JUST WHITNEY...*:

- *Whatchulookinat*
- *One Of Those Days*
- *Try It On My Own*

The lead single, *Whatchulookinat*, was reasonably successful, but *One Of Those Days* and *Try It On My Own* both struggled. The latter did achieve Top 40 status in Canada, but the former was only a minor hit in the Netherlands, Switzerland and the USA.

In Australia, *Whatchulookinat* and *One Of Those Days* were released as a double A-side, but the single narrowly failed to enter the Top 40.

13 ~ THE ULTIMATE COLLECTION

I Will Always Love You/Saving All My Love For You/Greatest Love Of All/One Moment In Time/I Wanna Dance With Somebody (Who Loves Me)/How Will I Know/So Emotional/When You Believe/ Where Do Broken Hearts Go/I'm Your Baby Tonight (Remix)/Didn't We Almost Have It All/Run To You/Exhale (Shoop Shoop)/If I Told You That (Duet Version)/I Have Nothing/I'm Every Woman/It's Not Right But It's Okay/My Love Is Your Love

Japan bonus DVD: *Greatest Love Of All/Saving All My Love For You/Didn't We Almost Have It All/I Wanna Dance With Somebody (Who Loves Me)/I'm Your Baby Tonight/I Will Always Love You/I'm Every Woman/ Exhale (Shoop Shoop)*

USA: Not Released.

UK: Arista 717701 (2007).

10.11.07: 5-**3**-12-13-10-7-10-11-12-28-29-42-51-56-55-29-54-42-58-83
16.08.08: 48-50-47-48-60-83
24.10.09: 62-22-22-28-34-48-58-58-56-57-46-39-39-39-47-47-42-44-46-52-56-46-39-35-37-37-38-49-53-64-71-92-98-94-93-96-67-53-67-67-73-66-68-63-58-80-97-93
15.10.11: 100
11.08.12: 79-70-98-98
12.01.13: 86-65-62-71-69
14.09.13: 78
3.05.14: 11-14-32-39-38-47-47-77-86-76-63-84-68-82-36-22-28-27-45-85
27.09.14: 79-89

22.11.14: 33-56-86   (with *LIVE – HER GREATEST PERFORMANCES*)
21.02.15: 67-71-62-69-59-73-88-83-80-77-86-74-60-84-76-75-98-x-x-x-x-98-45-79-87-
   82-74-31-50-59-64-73-67-75-73-59-49-56-60-73-54-67-77-85-83-68-69-46-40-32-41-
   32-26-22-23-25-25-27-28-34-56-58-59-63-50-53-48-61
8.09.16: 34-34-35-39-50
23.02.17: 18-26-25-25-27-20-30-48-57-54-85-88-84-68-77-76-91-x-97-87-84-79-79-68-
   76-72-66-81-75-52-56-45-58-62-64-64-62-67-55-67-73-86-100-100-99-96-86-81-83-
   73-66-52-47-47-51-43-37-43-32-38-46-51-57-52-64-59-58-70-74-94-86-82-79-57-67-
   68-73-60-62-65-57-72-66
7.02.19: 79-68-60-51-65-70-67-74-75-74-73-87-77-86-80-73-75-83-80-89-71-72-76-69-
   62-52-46-45-41-43-38-48-50-48-46-53-58-58-57-72-79-78-84-90-x-x-x-80-72-67-65-
   65-57-31-44-52-52-57-67-64-53-50-42-   (still charting)

Australia
2.12.07: 85-39-44-54-59-48-36-31-34-56-54-73-66-66-72-68-95-x-92-98
25.10.09: 83-77-77
20.12.09: 81-68-83-60-76-80-70-53-48-64-55-34-29-24-27-45-53-59-68-73-77-80-60-74-
   82
26.02.12: 12-**3-3**-5-13-22-33-46-52-71-63-54-65-70-99-57-32-29-30-40-47-76-97-78-93-
   85-80-81-94

Austria
16.11.07: 38-43-59-72-75
11.09.09: 16-12-18-32-55-75-71
24.02.12: 7-**1-1**-2-2-7-11-13-11-13-29-48-46-50-65-61-x-56-x-x-75-x-68-x-64-x-53
8.08.14: 61-75

Canada
02.12: peaked at no.**15**

Finland
1.03.08: 19-22-29-40
24.01.09: **16**-22-29-33
18.02.12: 25

France
18.02.12: **52**-x-82-79-95

Germany
11.09.09: 39-39-52-75-91-78-96
24.02.12: 11-**3**-9-15-20-28-45-42-49-62-73-87-80-90-98

Italy
1.11.07: peaked at no.**5**, charted for 55 weeks

Norway
5.01.08: 8-5-5-**4**-**4**-6-9-16-18-25-30-24-25-28
18.02.12: 28-**4**-6-11-11-18-22-20-39-25-36-31-39
11.08.12: 31

New Zealand
5.11.07: 9-9-11-13-22-14-16-18-21-28-35-x-38
20.02.12: **2**-3-4-6-7-11-12-10-12-13-16-15-11-6-13-17-19-16-26-39-37-31-32

Spain
10.02.08: 38-**28**-33-38-46-47-66
11.03.12: 71-77

Sweden
13.12.07: 20-14-12-**10**-17-30-28-44-58-60

Switzerland
18.11.07: 98
13.09.09: 70
26.02.12: **5**-**5**-14-23-33-40-77-80-72-84-x-99
20.01.13: 79-61-49-90-97
3.08.14: 51-53-65-62
4.01.15: 77

Whitney's first major single disc compilation of hits, surprisingly, wasn't released in her homeland. It was released in most other countries, and in Japan a CD/DVD set was released, with eight music videos featured on the DVD:

Greatest Love Of All/Saving All My Love For You/Didn't We Almost Have It All/
I Wanna Dance With Somebody (Who Loves Me)/I'm Your Baby Tonight/I Will
Always Love You/I'm Every Woman/Exhale (Shoop Shoop)

The compilation was titled *THE BEST SO FAR* in Brazil.
   THE ULTIMATE COLLECTION charted at no.3 in the UK, no.4 in Norway, no.5 in Italy, no.9 in New Zealand, no.10 in Sweden, no.12 in Austria, no.16 in Finland, no.28 in Spain, no.31 in Australia and no. 39 in Germany.
   In several countries, *THE ULTIMATE COLLECTION* returned to the charts, following Whitney's passing in February 2012. The compilation hit no.1 in Austria, and rose to no.2 in New Zealand, no.3 in Australia and Germany, no.4 in Norway, no.15 in Canada and no.25 in Finland.

14 ~ I LOOK TO YOU

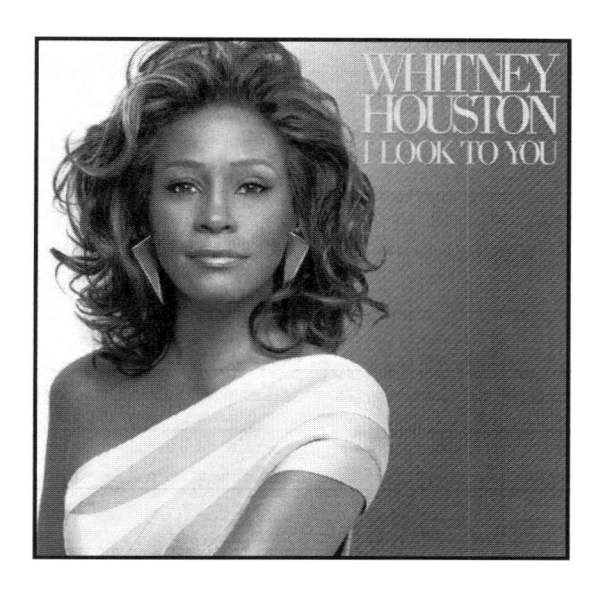

Million Dollar Bill/Nothin' But Love/Call You Tonight/I Look To You/Like I Never Left/A Song For You/I Didn't Know My Own Strength/Worth It/For Lovers/I Got You/Salute

US iTunes Pre-order Bonus Track: *I Didn't Know My Own Strength (Club Remix).*

Japan Bonus Track: *I Didn't Know My Own Strength (Daddy's Groove Magic Island Radio Mix).*

Million Dollar Bill produced by Swizz Beatz, *Nothin' But Love* & *For The Lovers* produced by Danja, *Call You Tonight* & *A Song For You* produced by Stargate, *I Look To You* produced by Harvey Mason, Jr., Emanuel Kiriakou & Tricky Stewart, *Like I Never Left* & *I Got You* produced by Akon, *I Didn't Know My Own Strength* produced by David Foster, *Worth It* produced by Eric Hudson, *Salute* produced by R. Kelly.

USA: Arista 10033 (2009).

19.09.09: **1**-4-2-4-13-14-15-21-33-49-71-62-59-99-x-63-58
3.03.12: 65-16-13-19-17-44-79-89

UK: RCA 710033 (2009).

31.10.09: **3**-7-13-24-36-46-44-52-51-48-64-62-80-98

Australia
20.09.09: **16**-21-19-33-60-33-47-64-93

Austria
11.09.09: **3**-5-9-10-17-13-18-27-45-48-x-x-x-63-71-x-x-75

Belgium
12.09.09: 10-**7**-9-9-13-19-26-32-44-42-68-97-80-88-88-x-99-99-96

Canada
09.09: peaked at no.**1**

Finland
12.09.09: **17**-x-36

France
5.09.09: **3**-10-18-22-29-33-46-39-41-56-72-88

Germany
11.09.09: **1**-5-7-12-14-17-15-28-43-64-75-89-90-92-96
1.01.10: 79-88

Italy
3.09.09: peaked at no.**1** (2), charted for 27 weeks

Netherlands
12.09.09: **1**-6-10-20-27-40-44-46-72-76-80-x-42-53-47-48-51-52-33-27-58-67-78-79-77-x-x-x-x-76

New Zealand
14.09.09: **10**-18-25

Norway
12.09.09: **2**-4-5-9-20-27-27

Spain
20.09.09: **3**-6-8-13-16-20-24-37-46-50-66-82-91-92-87-x-85

Sweden
4.09.09: **2**-2-3-4-11-14-15-20-21-33-47
15.01.10: 56

Switzerland
13.09.09: **1**-4-8-12-12-18-17-20-28-32-45-62-80
26.02.12: 42

After all the troubles and difficulties in her personal life, Whitney had to be talked into returning to a recording studio.

'I kind of got comfortable with being left alone,' she admitted, 'just being a mom who would take her daughter off to school, and who would pick her up from school. I liked that vibe, I liked that feeling, because I never really had the opportunity. I was always travelling with her all the time.

'At one point in time, I almost decided that I didn't want to be in it anymore. The music had changed, the industry had changed, the quality had changed ~ and I didn't like it ... Christina Aguilera, Jennifer Hudson and Beyoncé Knowles ~ they stirred my curiosity about coming back and making a record. But that's only part of the industry. To actually sing, perform and have people come to hear a real voice, a God given gift, is really important to me. It's almost like we are dealing with an industry that had turned to soft porn. Instead of listening to a voice, an instrument, a gift from God, we had to watch people take off their clothes constantly. It left nothing to the imagination, nothing you could long for. You couldn't say, "Oh, that song, that melody, that voice".'

Her mentor, Clive Davis, played an important role in pushing Whitney to change her mind.

'He called me one day and said, "It's time", and I said, "Time for what?" And he says, "Time for you to come back and sing for us again" ... when Clive called me, I was pretty ready to buy my island home (and retire), but he said, "No, you're going to sing again, people want to hear you". It's very special, and I feel humbled to be asked to do it again and want to be heard.'

Whitney felt less confident about returning to the spotlight.

'I am not geared for it,' she admitted. 'It goes along with the territory. I'm still going to remain the very quiet, private person I've been for the last ten years. I just want to be recognised for my music, and for what it does and how it inspires people, and how it makes people feel, as opposed to talking about Whitney all the time kind of thing. That's done, it's passed, and I would just like to be recognised for my music.'

Once she had decided to go ahead, and record a new album, Whitney knew what she wanted.

'I wanted the record like *My Love Is Your Love*, with an island feel,' she said. 'I wanted an island record because *My Love Is Your Love* is so huge ~ it has its own fashion with Wyclef ... I wanted that feeling, but I didn't know who. And Clive came and said, "Akon is the guy that we're going to work with", and I was like, "OK, Akon. OK, I can deal with that".'

'To be reunited with Whitney is so fulfilling,' said Clive Davis. 'The album provides the most exciting challenge I've ever had and whatever happens, I know it's very special. It's music and her voice will once again impact millions all over the world for many years to come.'

Originally, Whitney's new album was rumoured to be titled 'Undefeated', but this proved to be incorrect.

I LOOK TO YOU was officially launched with a listening party at the Mandarin Oriental Hotel, London, on 14th July 2009. Nine songs were premiered, with *Call You Tonight* cited as the most likely lead single.

A second listening party was staged a week later, hosted by Whitney and Clive Davis, in New York, with a third listening party taking place at the Beverley Hilton Hotel in Beverley Hills, California, on 23rd July.

I LOOK TO YOU debuted at no.1 in the States, on both the Billboard 200 and R&B chart, but spent only one week at the top on both charts. The album also hit no.1 in Canada, Germany, Italy, the Netherlands and Switzerland, and achieved no.2 in Norway and Sweden, no.3 in Austria, France, Spain and the UK, no.7 in Belgium, no.10 in New Zealand, no.16 in Australia and no.17 in Finland.

Two singles were released from the album:

- *I Look To You*
- *Million Dollar Bill*

Promos were also released for a further three tracks:

- *I Didn't Know My Own Strength*
- *Worth It*
- *Nothin' But Love*

15 ~ THE COLLECTION

Box-Set of 5 Albums: *WHITNEY HOUSTON, WHITNEY, I'M YOUR BABY TONIGHT, THE BODYGUARD & MY LOVE IS YOUR LOVE.*

USA: Not Released.

UK: Arista/Sony Music 88697 65766 2 (2010).

THE COLLECTION wasn't a hit in the UK.

Spain
19.02.12: **70**-92

Sweden
24.02.12: **32**-36-51

Tragically, Whitney was found dead in her Beverly Hilton Hotel suite on 11th February 2012.
    THE COLLECTION, a box-set of five of Whitney's albums, including *THE BODYGUARD*, was originally issued in 2010. It was the first of a number of releases to chart for the first time, following her passing ~ it achieved no.32 in Sweden and no.70 in Spain.

16 ~ THE ESSENTIAL

CD1: *Saving All My Love For You/Greatest Love Of All/One Moment In Time/I Have Nothing/I Will Always Love You/Run To You/You Give Good Love/All At Once/Where Do Broken Hearts Go/If You Say My Eyes Are Beautiful/Didn't We Almost Have It All/All The Man That I Need/Exhale (Shoop Shoop)/Count On Me/I Believe In You And Me/I Learned From The Best/Same Script, Different Cast/Could I Have This Kiss Forever (Metro Mix)*

CD2: *If I Told You That (& George Michael)/Fine/My Love Is Your Love/It's Not Right But It's Okay/Heartbreak Hotel/Step By Step/Queen Of The Night (CJ McKintosh Mix)/I'm Every Woman (Clivilles & Cole Mix)/Love Will Save The Day/I'm Your Baby Tonight/So Emotional/I Wanna Dance With Somebody (Who Loves Me)/How Will I Know/I Will Always Love You (Hex Hector Mix)/Greatest Love Of all (Club 69 Mix)/It's Not Right But It's Okay (Thunderpuss Mix)/I'm Your Baby Tonight (Dronez Mix)*

USA: Not Released.

UK: Arista 88697829802 (2010).

25.02.12: 40-17-**7**-22-20-32-50-72-89

Australia
26.02.12: 20-**7**-8-11-16-25-27-26-31-39-46-44-66-77

Austria
24.02.12: 61-29-**26**-35-70-59-67

Canada
02.12: peaked at no.**3**

France
18.02.12: 56-**51**-80-89

Germany
24.02.12: 51-**20**-29-39-61-81-87

Italy
23.02.12: peaked at no.**21**, charted for 13 weeks

Switzerland
26.02.12: 70-**15-15**-37-60
13.05.12: 97

This 2CD compilation, which wasn't released in the United States, failed to chart anywhere when it was originally released in 2010.

Two years on, following Whitney's passing, *THE ESSENTIAL* rose to no.3 in Canada, no.7 in Australia and the UK, no.15 in Switzerland, no.20 in Germany, no.21 in Italy, no.26 in Austria and no.51 in France.

Rolling Stone

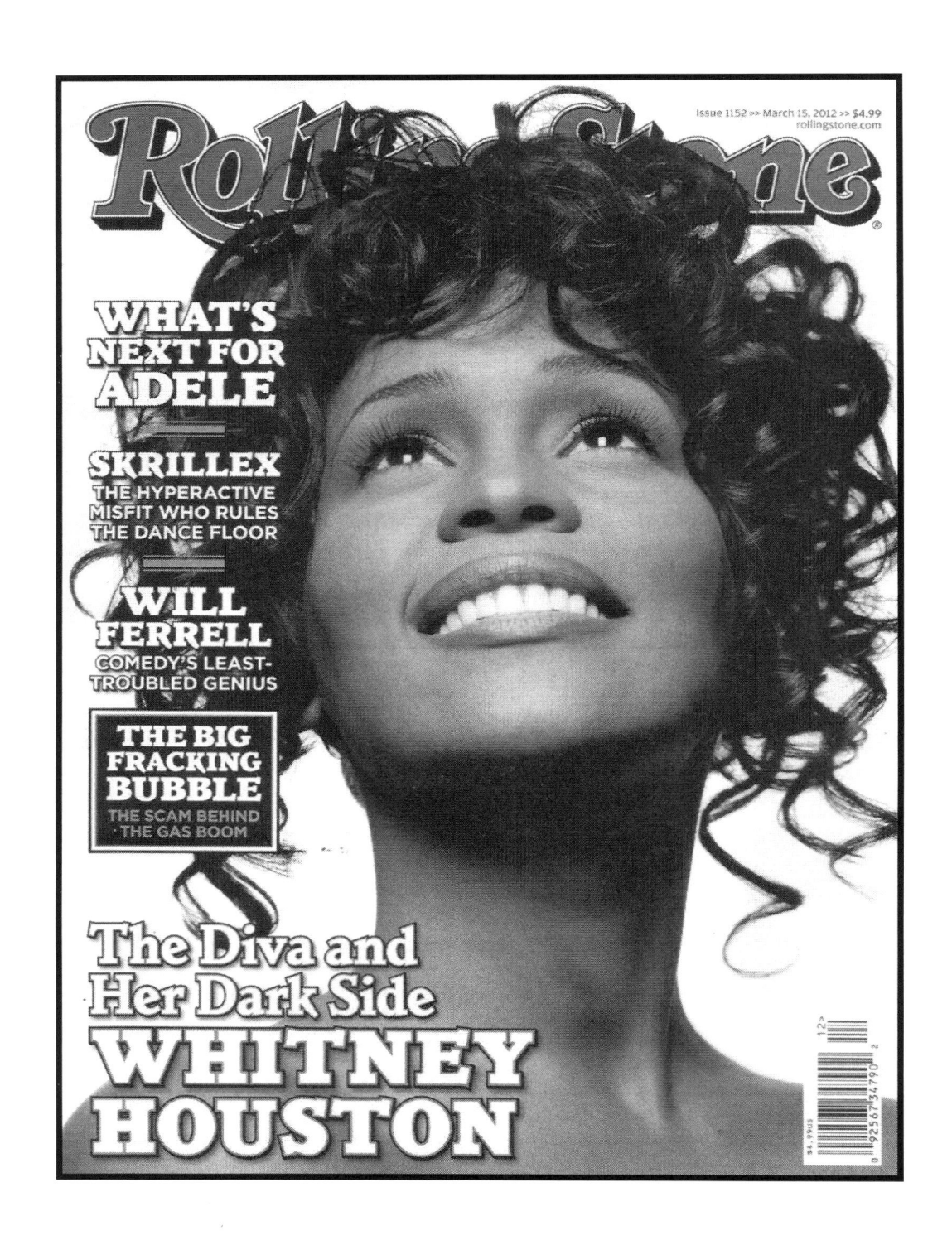

Issue 1152 >> March 15, 2012 >> $4.99
rollingstone.com

WHAT'S NEXT FOR ADELE

SKRILLEX
THE HYPERACTIVE MISFIT WHO RULES THE DANCE FLOOR

WILL FERRELL
COMEDY'S LEAST-TROUBLED GENIUS

THE BIG FRACKING BUBBLE
THE SCAM BEHIND THE GAS BOOM

The Diva and Her Dark Side
WHITNEY HOUSTON

17 ~ TRIPLE FEATURE

Box-Set of 3 Albums: *I'M YOUR BABY TONIGHT, MY LOVE IS YOUR LOVE & JUST WHITNEY ....*

USA: Arista A775919 (2010).

10.03.12: 73-**21**-38-61

UK: Not Released.

This collection of three of Whitney's albums was originally released in the United States in 2010, but it didn't enter the Billboard 200 until after her passing in February 2012, when it peaked at no.21.

JORDIN SPARKS
WHITNEY HOUSTON
DEREK LUKE
MIKE EPPS
CARMEN EJOGO
TIKA SUMPTER
OMARI HARDWICK
AND
CEELO GREEN AS BLACK
SPARKLE

18 ~ SPARKLE

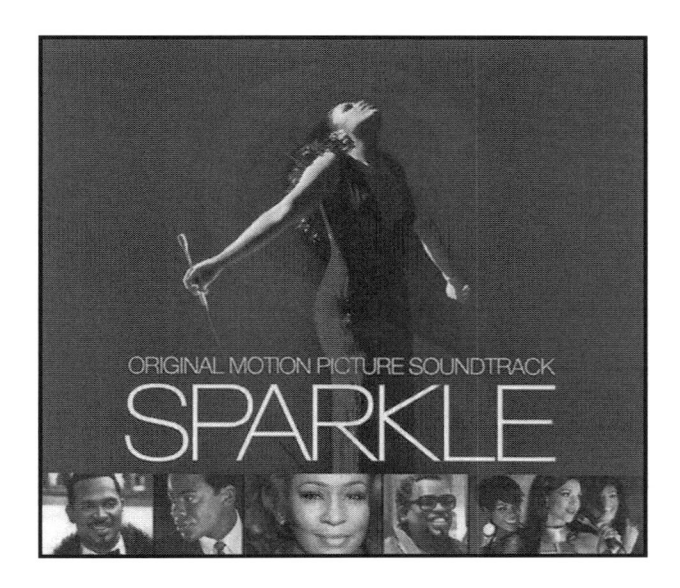

Whitney: *His Eye Is One The Sparrow/Celebrate* (with Jordin Sparks)

Other Artists: *I'm A Man* (Cee-Lo Green)/*Yes I Do* (Carmen Ejogo)/*Running* (Goapele)/ *Jump* (Jordin Sparks, Carmen Ejogo & Tika Sumpter)/*Hooked On Your Love* (Jordin Sparks, Carmen Ejogo & Tika Sumpter)/*Something He Can Feel* (Jordin Sparks, Carmen Ejogo & Tika Sumpter)/*Look Into Your Heart* (Jordin Sparks)/*One Wing* (Jordin Sparks)/ *Love Will* (Jordin Sparks)

Produced by R. Kelly.

USA: RCA 88725420462 (2012).

18.08.12: **26**-42

UK: RCA 88725452732 (2012).

SPARKLE wasn't a hit in the UK.

Inspired by the Supremes, *Sparkle* was a musical originally released in 1976 ~ it starred Irene Cara in the title role, and featured music composed and produced by Curtis Mayfield.
    The musical was re-made in 2011, and filming was wrapped up just three months before Whitney's passing. In what would be her final film role, Whitney played Emma Anderson, a retired professional singer who is over-protective of her three daughters, and forbids them following in her footsteps, to pursue a career in music.

This time around, Sparkle Anderson was played by *American Idol* winner Jordin Sparks, in what was her movie debut. The cast also included:

- Carmen Ejogo as Tammy 'Sister' Anderson
- Tika Sumpter as Delores 'Dee' Anderson
- Derek Luke as Stix
- Mike Epps as Satin Struthers
- Omari Hardwick as Levison 'Levi' Robinson
- CeeLo Green as Black
- Terrence J. as Red
- Michael Beach as Reverend Bryce

Sparkle was directed by Salim Akil and, as well as songs composed for the original film by Curtis Mayfield, featured new songs written by R. Kelly.

The film, by TriStar Productions, premiered on 17th August 2012 in the United States, and was dedicated to Whitney's memory.

Sparkle made its box-office debut at no.5, and went on to gross nearly $25 million in North America.

The *SPARKLE* soundtrack featured two tracks by Whitney, a cover of *His Eye Is On The Sparrow* and a duet with Jordin Sparks, *Celebrate*. The album made its debut in the United States at no.26 on the Billboard 200, which proved to be its peak position. The album failed to enter the chart anywhere else.

Celebrate, the last song Whitney recorded before she died, was released as the lead single from *SPARKLE* in the United States. The accompanying music video, which would have featured Whitney, was previewed on Entertainment Tonight on 4th June 2012, and premiered on BET's 106 & Park on the 27th June.

'When we did the song,' said Jordin Sparks, 'we planned on it (the video) being Whitney and me. But she's not here, so we wanted to make it a tribute to her, so it's fun, upbeat and exciting. There are clips from the movie and the main cast is in the video, too ... they all come over to my house singing along to Whitney's music, and we're missing her and celebrating her as well. It's actually pretty simple, but when you watch it and hear her voice along with it, it makes it so much more.'

Celebrate rose to no.39 on Billboard's R&B chart in the USA, but it failed to enter the Hot 100, and it wasn't a hit anywhere else.

Whitney's version of *His Eye Is On The Sparrow*, a gospel hymn written by Charles H. Gabriel and Civilla D. Martin in 1905, was also promoted as a single in the United States, but it wasn't a hit.

19 ~ I WILL ALWAYS LOVE YOU – THE BEST OF

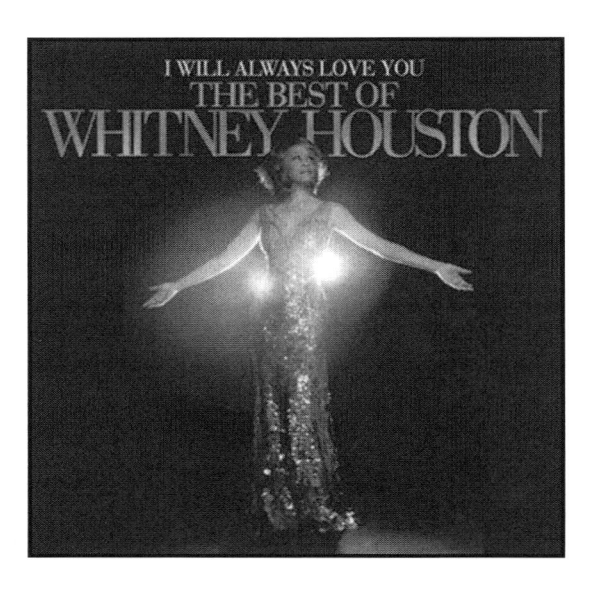

You Give Good Love/Saving All My Love For You/How Will I Know/Greatest Love Of All/I Wanna Dance With Somebody (Who Loves Me)/Didn't We Almost Have It All/So Emotional/Where Do Broken Hearts Go/I'm Your Baby Tonight/All The Man That I Need/I Will Always Love You/I'm Every Woman/I Have Nothing/Exhale (Shoop Shoop)/I Believe In You And Me (Single Version)/My Love Is Your Love (Radio Edit)/I Look To You (& R. Kelly)/Never Give Up

CD2 (Deluxe Edition): *Love Will Save The Day/One Moment In Time/It Isn't, It Wasn't, It Ain't Never Gonna Be/My Name Is Not Susan/I Belong To You/Run To You/Queen Of The Night/Count On Me/Step By Step/It's Not Right But It's Okay/I Learned From The Best (Radio Edit)/If I Told You That/Heartbreak Hotel/Million Dollar Bill*

Japan Bonus Track: *All At Once*

USA: Arista/RCA 88725472232, Arista/RCA 88765413932 (Deluxe Edition) (2012).

1.12.12: **14**-58-53-66-88-99-x-99-98-x-x-x-x-99

UK: Arista/RCA 88725472232, Arista/RCA 88765413932 (Deluxe Edition) (2012).

1.12.12: **29**-46-57-62-58-74-81-94

Belgium
19.01.13: **99**

Italy
22.11.12: peaked at no.**37**, charted for 9 weeks

Netherlands
17.11.12: **61**

New Zealand
10.12.12: 37-**29**

Spain
18.11.12: **44**-46-55-61-69-77-71-65-56-72-80-83-85-75

Switzerland
25.11.12: **87**

Released nine months after her passing, *I WILL ALWAYS LOVE YOU – THE BEST OF* was Whitney's first international posthumous release, and it came in a one CD standard edition and a 2CD deluxe edition.

The compilation included two previously unreleased tracks, *Never Give Up* and a re-worked version of *I Look To You*, which was turned into a duet with composer R. Kelly. The duet was promoted as a digital single, but it wasn't a hit.

I WILL ALWAYS LOVE YOU – THE BEST OF generally disappointed sales-wise, charting at no.14 in the USA, no.29 in New Zealand and the UK, no.37 in Italy and no.44 in Spain. The compilation was a minor hit in Belgium, the Netherlands and Switzerland, but it failed to chart in many countries.

20 ~ LIVE – HER GREATEST PERFORMANCES

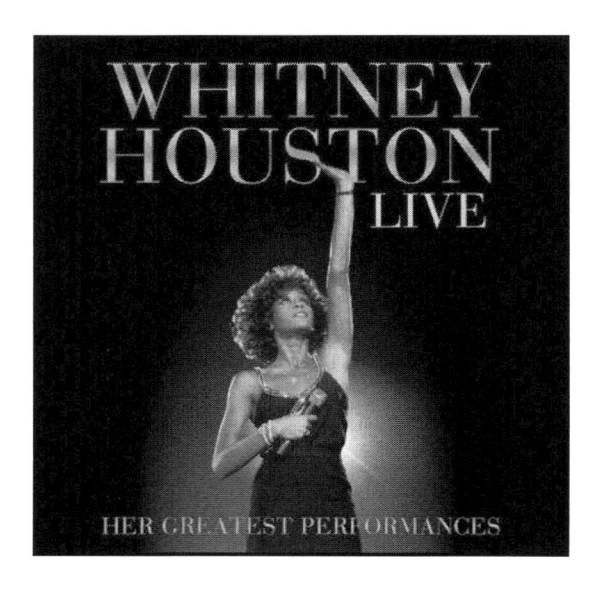

CD: *Home* (The Merv Griffin Show, 1983)
    You Give Good Love (The Tonight Show Starring Johnny Carson, 1985)
    How Will I Know (The BRIT Awards, 1987)
    One Moment In Time (31st Grammy Awards, 1989)
    Greatest Love Of All (That's What Friends Are For: Arista Records 15th Anniversary Concert, 1990)
    I Wanna Dance With Somebody (Who Loves Me) (That's What Friends Are For: Arista Records 15th Anniversary Concert, 1990)
    The Star Spangled Banner (Super Bowl XXV, 1991)
    All The Man That I Need (Welcome Home Heroes, 1991)
    I'm Your Baby Tonight (Welcome Home Heroes, 1991)
    A Song For You (Welcome Home Heroes, 1991)
    Medley: I Loves You Porgy/And I'm Telling You I'm Not Going/I Have Nothing (21st Annual American Music Awards, 1994)
    I'm Every Woman (Concert for a New South Africa, 1994)
    I Will Always Love You (Concert for a New South Africa, 1994)
    My Love Is Your Love (Late Show with David Letterman, 1998)
    I Believe In You And Me (16th Annual World Music Awards, 2004)
    I Didn't Know My Own Strength (Oprah Winfrey Show, 2009)

DVD: as CD, with two bonus tracks:
    My Love Is Your Love (music video, after *I Will Always Love You*)
    When You Believe (71st Annual Academy Awards, 1999), after *My Love Is Your Love* (The Late Show with David Letterman)

USA: Arista/RCA 88843083512 (2014).

29.11.14: **19**-45-83

UK: Arista/RCA 88843083512 (CD/DVD), Arista/RCA 88875042232 (CD + *THE ULTIMATE COLLECTION*) (2014).

22.11.14: **33**-56-86   (with *THE ULTIMATE COLLECTION*)
22.11.14: 66

France
24.11.14: **99**

Italy
20.11.14: peaked at no.**34**, charted for 2 weeks

Japan
11.14: peaked at no.**43**

Netherlands
15.11.14: **63**

Spain
16.11.14: **43**-73-79-98

Surprisingly, given she was known as 'The Voice', Whitney never released a live solo album while she was alive, although she was one of several artists featured on *VH-1 DIVAS LIVE/99*.

This album and DVD, as the title suggests, featured some of Whitney's greatest live performances spanning two and a half decades, starting with *Home* from 1983 and cumulating with *I Didn't Know My Own Strength* in 2009.

'Whitney's live CD/DVD will stun everyone,' Clive Davis predicted. 'It definitely shows why she was totally unique, absolutely in the first rank of all-time. For me, it's been very emotional. The set vividly confirms that there really was no one like her ... her amazing vocals and the songs that have stood the test of time combine to truly hypnotise over and over.'

However, as with *I WILL ALWAYS LOVE YOU – THE BEST OF*, sales of *LIVE – HER GREATEST PERFORMANCES* were generally disappointing. The album made its bow at no.19 on the Billboard 200 in the United States, but climbed no higher and dropped out of the Top 100 after just three weeks.

Elsewhere, the album charted at no.34 in Italy, no.43 in Japan and Spain, and was a minor hit in France, the Netherlands and the UK.

In countries where *THE ULTIMATE COLLECTION* had been released, *LIVE – HER GREATEST PERFORMANCES* was also released as a 2CD set, comprising the CD from the *LIVE* release, plus *THE ULTIMATE COLLECTION*. This release proved more popular than the CD/DVD edition in the UK, where it made it chart debut at no.33 ~ 33 places higher than the CD/DVD edition of *LIVE*.

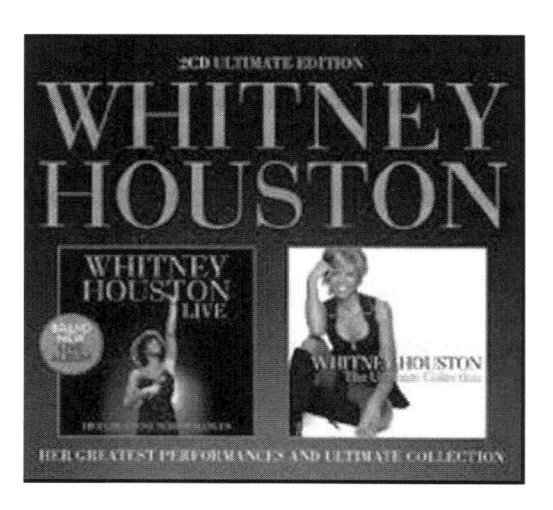

THE ALMOST TOP 40 ALBUMS

Two of Whitney's albums have made the Top 50 in one or more countries, but failed to enter the Top 40 in any.

ALL THE BEST

This compilation, released in several continental European countries in 2011, shared the same track listing as *THE ULTIMATE COLLECTION*. Following Whitney's passing in February 2012, the album charted at no.44 in Switzerland, and was a minor no.76 hit in Germany.

ONE WISH ~ THE HOLIDAY ALBUM

Released in November 2003, Whitney's album of Christmas songs included *Joy To The World* and *Who Would Imagine A King*, which she originally recorded for *THE PREACHER'S WIFE*, and featured a version of *The Little Drummer Boy*, which she recorded as a duet with her daughter, Bobbi Kristina.

ONE WISH ~ THE HOLIDAY ALBUM spent four weeks on the Top 100 of the Billboard 200, peaking at no.49, but surprisingly it wasn't a hit anywhere outside the United States.

WHITNEY'S TOP 15 ALBUMS

This Top 15 has been compiled using the same points system as for the Top 30 Whitney Singles listing.

Rank/Album/Points

1 *THE BODYGUARD* – 3791 points

2 *WHITNEY* – 3218 points

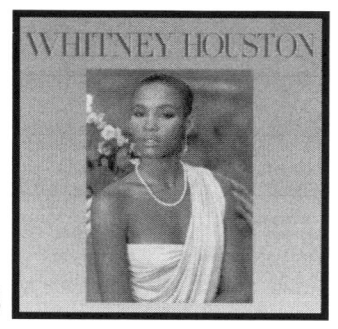

3 *WHITNEY HOUSTON* – 3016 points

Rank/Album/Points

4 *MY LOVE IS YOUR LOVE* – 2331 points

5 *THE GREATEST HITS* – 1923 points

6. *THE ULTIMATE COLLECTION* – 1869+ points
7. *I'M YOUR BABY TONIGHT* – 1746 points
8. *I LOOK TO YOU* – 1643 points
9. *WAITING TO EXHALE* – 1315 points
10. *THE PREACHER'S WIFE* – 1099 points

11. *THE ESSENTIAL* – 581 points
12. *JUST WHITNEY...* – 560 points
13. *LOVE, WHITNEY* – 458 points
14. *I WILL ALWAYS LOVE YOU – THE BEST OF* – 355 points
15. *LIVE – HER GREATEST PERFORMANCES* – 285 points

A comfortable win for *THE BODYGUARD*, ahead of Whitney's first two albums, with *WHITNEY* taking second place ahead of *WHITNEY HOUSTON*. *MY LOVE IS YOUR LOVE* comes in at no.4, ahead of her most successful compilation, *THE GREATEST HITS*.

Whitney's most recent release to make the Top 15 in her posthumous live album, *LIVE – HER GREATEST PERFORMANCES*, which sneaks in at no.15, just ahead of *VH-1 DIVAS LIVE*.

ALBUMS TRIVIA

To date, Whitney has achieved twenty Top 40 albums in one or more of the countries featured in this book. There follows a country-by-country look at her most successful albums, starting with her homeland.

Note: in this trivia section, the soundtrack albums *THE BODYGUARD*, *WAITING TO EXHALE* and *SPARKLE*, plus *VH-1 DIVA's LIVE/99* are counted among Whitney's albums, although strictly speaking all four are multi-artist releases.

WHITNEY IN THE USA

Whitney has achieved 16 hit albums in the USA, which spent 597 weeks on the Top 100 of the Billboard 200 chart.

No.1 Albums

1986	*WHITNEY HOUSTON*
1987	*WHITNEY*
1992	*THE BODYGUARD*
1996	*WAITING TO EXHALE*
2009	*I LOOK TO YOU*

Most Weeks at No.1

20 weeks	*THE BODYGUARD*
14 weeks	*WHITNEY HOUSTON*
11 weeks	*WHITNEY*

Albums with the most weeks

137 weeks	*WHITNEY HOUSTON*
109 weeks	*THE BODYGUARD*
71 weeks	*MY LOVE IS YOUR LOVE*
69 weeks	*WHITNEY*
46 weeks	*I'M YOUR BABY TONIGHT*
40 weeks	*WAITING TO EXHALE*
35 weeks	*THE GREATEST HITS*
29 weeks	*THE PREACHER'S WIFE*
24 weeks	*I LOOK TO YOU*
14 weeks	*JUST WHITNEY...*

RIAA (Recording Industry Association of America) Awards

The RIAA began certifying Gold albums in 1958, Platinum albums in 1976, and multi-Platinum albums in 1984. Gold = 500,000, Platinum = 1 million. Awards are based on shipments, not sales, and each disc is counted individually (so, for example, a double album has to ship 500,000 to be eligible for Platinum).

18 x Platinum	*THE BODYGUARD* (November 2017)	= 18 million
13 x Platinum	*WHITNEY HOUSTON* (July 1999)	= 13 million
9 x Platinum	*WHITNEY* (November 1995)	= 9 million
7 x Platinum	*WAITING TO EXHALE* (September 1996)	= 7 million
4 x Platinum	*I'M YOUR BABY TONIGHT* (April 1995)	= 4 million
4 x Platinum	*MY LOVE IS YOUR LOVE* (May 2000)	= 4 million
3 x Platinum	*THE PREACHER'S WIFE* (June 1998)	= 3 million
5 x Platinum	*THE GREATEST HITS* (July 2012)	= 2.5 million
Platinum	*JUST WHITNEY* (January 2003)	= 1 million
Platinum	*I LOOK TO YOU* (December 2009)	= 1 million
Gold	*ONE WISH: THE HOLIDAY ALBUM* (January 2018)	= 500,000
Gold	*I WILL ALWAYS LOVE YOU – THE BEST OF* (March 2020)	= 500,000

WHITNEY IN AUSTRALIA

Whitney has achieved 11 hit albums in Australia, which spent 437 weeks on the chart.

No.1 Albums

1985	*WHITNEY HOUSTON*
1987	*WHITNEY*
1993	*THE BODYGUARD*

Most weeks at No.1

11 weeks	*WHITNEY HOUSTON*
5 weeks	*THE BODYGUARD*
3 weeks	*WHITNEY*

Albums with the most weeks

126 weeks	*WHITNEY HOUSTON*
84 weeks	*THE BODYGUARD*
76 weeks	*THE ULTIMATE COLLECTION*
62 weeks	*WHITNEY*
27 weeks	*THE GREATEST HITS*

23 weeks	*I'M YOUR BABY TONIGHT*
20 weeks	*WAITING TO EXHALE*
20 weeks	*THE PREACHER'S WIFE*
14 weeks	*THE ESSENTIAL*
9 weeks	*I LOOK TO YOU*

ARIA (Australian Recording Industry Association) Accreditations

The current ARIA accreditations are: Gold = 35,000, Platinum = 70,000.

5 x Platinum	*THE BODYGUARD* = 350,000
4 x Platinum	*WHITNEY HOUSTON* = 280,000
3 x Platinum	*WHITNEY* = 210,000
2 x Platinum	*THE GREATEST HITS* = 140,000
2 x Platinum	*THE ULTIMATE COLLECTION* = 140,000
Platinum	*I'M YOUR BABY TONIGHT* = 70,000
Gold	*THE PREACHER'S WIFE* = 35,000
Gold	*MY LOVE IS YOUR LOVE* = 35,000

WHITNEY IN AUSTRIA

Whitney has achieved 14 hit albums in Austria, which spent 310 weeks on the chart.

No.1 Albums

1987	*WHITNEY*
1993	*THE BODYGUARD*
1999	*MY LOVE IS YOUR LOVE*
2012	*THE ULTIMATE COLLECTION*

Most weeks at No.1

9 weeks	*THE BODYGUARD*
5 weeks	*MY LOVE IS YOUR LOVE*
4 weeks	*WHITNEY*

Albums with the most weeks

49 weeks	*MY LOVE IS YOUR LOVE*
48 weeks	*WHITNEY*
36 weeks	*THE BODYGUARD*
35 weeks	*THE ULTIMATE COLLECTION*
33 weeks	*WHITNEY HOUSTON*

21 weeks	*THE GREATEST HITS*
20 weeks	*I'M YOUR BABY TONIGHT*
17 weeks	*THE PREACHER'S WIFE*
15 weeks	*WAITING TO EXHALE*
13 weeks	*I LOOK TO YOU*

WHITNEY IN BELGIUM (Flanders)

Since 1995, Whitney has achieved seven hit albums in Belgium (Flanders), which spent 115 weeks on the chart.

Her most successful albums are *MY LOVE IS YOUR LOVE* and *THE GREATEST HITS*, which both peaked at no.2.

Albums with the most weeks

44 weeks	*MY LOVE IS YOUR LOVE*
33 weeks	*THE GREATEST HITS*
18 weeks	*I LOOK TO YOU*

WHITNEY IN CANADA

Whitney has achieved eight hit albums on Canada's RPM chart, which spent 441 weeks on the chart. A further four albums have charted since 2000, when RPM folded, but the number of weeks each spent on the chart is not known.

No.1 Albums

1986	*WHITNEY HOUSTON*
1987	*WHITNEY*
1992	*THE BODYGUARD*
2009	*I LOOK TO YOU*

Most weeks at No.1

18 weeks	*WHITNEY HOUSTON*
12 weeks	*THE BODYGUARD*
11 weeks	*WHITNEY*

Albums with the most weeks

129 weeks	*WHITNEY HOUSTON*

78 weeks	*THE BODYGUARD*
71 weeks	*MY LOVE IS YOUR LOVE*
59 weeks	*WHITNEY*
35 weeks	*WAITING TO EXHALE*
33 weeks	*I'M YOUR BABY TONIGHT*
19 weeks	*THE GREATEST HITS*
17 weeks	*THE PREACHER'S WIFE*

WHITNEY IN FINLAND

Whitney has achieved eight hit albums in Finland, which spent 165 weeks on the chart.

No.1 Albums

1987	*WHITNEY HOUSTON*
1993	*THE BODYGUARD*

Most weeks at No.1

8 weeks	*WHITNEY*
4 weeks	*THE BODYGUARD*

Albums with the most weeks

41 weeks	*WHITNEY HOUSTON*
30 weeks	*THE GREATEST HITS*
22 weeks	*I'M YOUR BABY TONIGHT*
22 weeks	*THE BODYGUARD*
21 weeks	*WHITNEY*
18 weeks	*MY LOVE IS YOUR LOVE*

WHITNEY IN FRANCE

Whitney has achieved 14 hit albums in France, which spent 166 weeks on the chart.

Her most successful album is *MY LOVE IS YOUR LOVE*, which peaked at no.2.

Albums with the most weeks

68 weeks	*MY LOVE IS YOUR LOVE*
18 weeks	*WHITNEY*
14 weeks	*THE BODYGUARD*

12 weeks	*I LOOK TO YOU*
10 weeks	*THE PREACHER'S WIFE*

WHITNEY IN GERMANY

Whitney has achieved 14 hit albums in Germany, which spent 405 weeks on the chart.

No.1 Albums

1987	*WHITNEY*
1993	*THE BODYGUARD*
2009	*I LOOK TO YOU*

Most weeks at No.1

11 weeks	*WHITNEY*
11 weeks	*THE BODYGUARD*

Albums with the most weeks

71 weeks	*MY LOVE IS YOUR LOVE*
68 weeks	*WHITNEY HOUSTON*
62 weeks	*THE BODYGUARD*
40 weeks	*THE GREATEST HITS*
34 weeks	*WHITNEY*
27 weeks	*I'M YOUR BABY TONIGHT*
22 weeks	*THE ULTIMATE COLLECTION*
21 weeks	*THE PREACHER'S WIFE*
17 weeks	*WAITING TO EXHALE*
17 weeks	*I LOOK TO YOU*

WHITNEY IN ITALY

Whitney has achieved 15 hit albums in Italy, which spent 283 weeks on the chart.

No.1 Albums

1986	*WHITNEY HOUSTON*
1987	*WHITNEY*
1993	*THE BODYGUARD*
2009	*I LOOK TO YOU*

Most weeks at No.1

5 weeks	*WHITNEY*
4 weeks	*WHITNEY HOUSTON*
2 weeks	*THE BODYGUARD*
2 weeks	*I LOOK TO YOU*

Albums with the most weeks

55 weeks	*THE ULTIMATE COLLECTION*
37 weeks ·	*THE GREATEST HITS*
36 weeks	*WHITNEY HOUSTON*
31 weeks	*THE BODYGUARD*
27 weeks	*I LOOK TO YOU*
21 weeks	*WHITNEY*
17 weeks	*I'M YOUR BABY TONIGHT*
13 weeks	*THE ESSENTIAL*
12 weeks	*LOVE, WHITNEY*
11 weeks	*MY LOVE IS YOUR LOVE*

WHITNEY IN JAPAN

Whitney has achieved ten hit albums in Japan, which spent 254+ weeks on the chart.

No.1 Albums

1993	*THE BODYGUARD*

THE BODYGUARD spent two weeks at no.1.

Albums with the most weeks

78 weeks	*THE BODYGUARD*
76 weeks	*WHITNEY HOUSTON*
26 weeks	*WHITNEY*
19 weeks	*I'M YOUR BABY TONIGHT*
16 weeks	*THE GREATEST HITS*
12 weeks	*DANCIN' SPECIAL*
12 weeks	*MY LOVE IS YOUR LOVE*

WHITNEY IN THE NETHERLANDS

Whitney has achieved 14 hit albums in the Netherlands, which spent 510 weeks on the chart.

No.1 Albums

1987	*WHITNEY*
1993	*THE BODYGUARD*
1999	*MY LOVE IS YOUR LOVE*
2009	*I LOOK TO YOU*

Most weeks at No.1

10 weeks	*THE BODYGUARD*
5 weeks	*WHITNEY*
3 weeks	*MY LOVE IS YOUR LOVE*

Albums with the most weeks

106 weeks	*WHITNEY HOUSTON*
93 weeks	*THE BODYGUARD*
77 weeks	*MY LOVE IS YOUR LOVE*
75 weeks	*WHITNEY*
36 weeks	*THE GREATEST HITS*
28 weeks	*I'M YOUR BABY TONIGHT*
25 weeks	*WAITING TO EXHALE*
25 weeks	*I LOOK TO YOU*
19 weeks	*THE PREACHER'S WIFE*
13 weeks	*VH-1 DIVAS LIVE/99*

WHITNEY IN NEW ZEALAND

Whitney has achieved 10 hit albums in New Zealand, which spent 305 weeks on the chart.

No.1 Albums

1986	*WHITNEY HOUSTON*
1987	*WHITNEY*
1993	*THE BODYGUARD*

Most weeks at No.1

8 weeks	*THE BODYGUARD*
2 weeks	*WHITNEY*

Albums with the most weeks

112 weeks	*WHITNEY HOUSTON*
43 weeks	*WHITNEY*
40 weeks	*THE BODYGUARD*
35 weeks	*THE ULTIMATE COLLECTION*
21 weeks	*I'M YOUR BABY TONIGHT*
20 weeks	*MY LOVE IS YOUR LOVE*
15 weeks	*THE GREATEST HITS*
14 weeks	*WAITING TO EXHALE*

WHITNEY IN NORWAY

Whitney has achieved 10 hit albums in Norway, which spent 161 weeks on the chart.

No.1 Albums

1986	*WHITNEY HOUSTON*
1987	*WHITNEY*
1993	*THE BODYGUARD*

Most weeks at No.1

11 weeks	*WHITNEY*
10 weeks	*WHITNEY HOUSTON*
6 weeks	*THE BODYGUARD*

Albums with the most weeks

28 weeks	*WHITNEY HOUSTON*
28 weeks	*THE ULTIMATE COLLECTION*
23 weeks	*THE BODYGUARD*
22 weeks	*MY LOVE IS YOUR LOVE*
18 weeks	*THE GREATEST HITS*
16 weeks	*WHITNEY*
15 weeks	*I'M YOUR BABY TONIGHT*

WHITNEY IN SPAIN

Whitney has achieved 12 hit albums in Spain, which spent 243 weeks on the chart.

No.1 Albums

1993   *THE BODYGUARD*

THE BODYGUARD spent seven weeks at no.1.

Albums with the most weeks

57 weeks	*THE BODYGUARD*
51 weeks	*WHITNEY*
27 weeks	*I'M YOUR BABY TONIGHT*
24 weeks	*WAITING TO EXHALE*
19 weeks	*THE PREACEHR'S WIFE*
19 weeks	*MY LOVE IS YOUR LOVE*
16 weeks	*I LOOK TO YOU*
14 weeks	*I WILL ALWAYS LOVE YOU – THE BEST OF*

WHITNEY IN SWEDEN

Whitney has achieved 12 hit albums in Sweden, which spent 243 weeks on the chart.

No.1 Albums

1986	*WHITNEY HOUSTON*
1987	*WHITNEY*
1993	*THE BODYGUARD*

Most weeks at No.1

12 weeks	*WHITNEY HOUSTON*
8 weeks	*WHITNEY*
8 weeks	*THE BODYGUARD*

Albums with the most weeks

53 weeks	*MY LOVE IS YOUR LOVE*
34 weeks	*THE GREATEST HITS*
32 weeks	*WHITNEY HOUSTON*
24 weeks	*WHITNEY*

24 weeks	*THE BDYGUARD*
18 weeks	*WAITING TO EXHALE*
16 weeks	*I'M YOUR BABY TONIGHT*
12 weeks	*I LOOK TO YOU*
11 weeks	*THE PREACHER'S WIFE*
10 weeks	*THE ULTIMATE COLLECTION*

WHITNEY IN SWITZERLAND

Whitney has achieved 16 hit albums in Switzerland, which spent 337 weeks on the chart.

No.1 Albums

1987	*WHITNEY*
1993	*THE BODYGUARD*
1999	*MY LOVE IS YOUR LOVE*
2009	*I LOOK TO YOU*

Most weeks at No.1

11 weeks	*WHITNEY*
9 weeks	*THE BODYGUARD*

Albums with the most weeks

69 weeks	*MY LOVE IS YOUR LOVE*
44 weeks	*THE GREATEST HITS*
34 weeks	*WHITNEY HOUSTON*
33 weeks	*THE BODYGUARD*
23 weeks	*I'M YOUR BABY TONIGHT*
23 weeks	*THE ULTIMATE COLLECTION*
20 weeks	*WHITNEY*
18 weeks	*THE PREACHER'S WIFE*
15 weeks	*WAITING TO EXHALE*
14 weeks	*I LOOK TO YOU*

WHITNEY IN THE UK

Whitney has achieved 15 hit albums in the UK, which have spent 710 weeks on the Top 100 albums chart.

No.1 Albums

1987	*WHITNEY*
1992	*THE BODYGUARD*
2000	*THE GREATEST HITS*

Most Weeks at No.1

11 weeks	*THE BODYGUARD* (Compilations Chart)
6 weeks	*WHITNEY*
2 weeks	*THE GREATEST HITS*

Albums with the most Top 100 weeks

320+ weeks	*THE ULTIMATE COLLECTION*
119 weeks	*WHITNEY HOUSTON*
107 weeks	*THE BODYGUARD* (Compilations Chart)
102 weeks	*WHITNEY*
92 weeks	*THE GREATEST HITS*
70 weeks	*MY LOVE IS YOUR LOVE*
29 weeks	*I'M YOUR BABY TONIGHT*
25 weeks	*WAITING TO EXHALE* (Compilations Chart)
14 weeks	*I LOOK TO YOU*
11 weeks	*THE PREACHER'S WIFE*

The BRIT Certified/BPI (British Phonographic Industry) Awards

The BPI began certifying albums in 1973, and between April 1973 and December 1978, awards related to a monetary value and not a unit value. Thanks to inflation, this changed several times over the years:

- April 1973 – August 1974: Silver = £75,000, Gold = £150,000, Platinum = £1 million.
- September 1974 – December 1975: Gold raised to £250,000, others unchanged.
- January 1976 – December 1976: Silver raised to £100,000, others unchanged.
- January 1977 – December 1978: Silver raised to £150,000, Gold raised to £300,000, Platinum unchanged.

When this system was abolished, the awards that were set remain in place today: Silver = 60,000, Gold = 100,000, Platinum = 300,000. Multi-Platinum awards were introduced in February 1987.

In July 2013 the BPI automated awards, and awards from this date are based on actual sales since February 1994, not shipments.

7 x Platinum	*THE BODYGUARD* (January 1994)	= 2.1 million
7 x Platinum	*WHITNEY* (February 2016)	= 2.1 million
5 x Platinum	*THE GREATEST HITS* (July 2013)	= 1.5 million
5 x Platinum	*THE ULTIMATE COLLECTION* (April 2017)	= 1.5 million
4 x Platinum	*WHITNEY HOUSTON* (January 1989)	= 1.2 million
3 x Platinum	*MY LOVE IS YOUR LOVE* (January 2000)	= 900,000
Platinum	*I'M YOUR BABY TONIGHT* (November 1990)	= 300,000
Gold	*I LOOK TO YOU* (November 2009)	= 100,000
Silver	*THE PREACHER'S WIFE* (July 2013)	= 60,000
Silver	*THE ESSENTIAL* (July 2013)	= 60,000
Silver	*I WILL ALWAYS LOVE YOU – THE BEST OF* (July 2013)	= 60,000

WHITNEY IN ZIMBABWE

Whitney has achieved four hit albums in Zimbabwe.

No.1 Albums

1987	*WHITNEY*
1993	*THE BODYGUARD*
1996	*WAITING TO EXHALE*

Most weeks at No.1

4 weeks	*WHITNEY*
3 weeks	*THE BODYGUARD*

Note: the number of weeks each album spent on the chart is unknown.

Printed in Great Britain
by Amazon